Judy Garton-Sprenger • Philip Prowse

Inspired
Student's Book 4

CONTENTS

		COMMUNICATIVE AIMS	VOCABULARY	GRAMMAR	PRONUNCIATION
Welcome!	6–7	Talking about studying	Studying Classroom activities		
Preview Units 1–2	8–9				

Unit 1 — BODY AND MIND

		COMMUNICATIVE AIMS	VOCABULARY	GRAMMAR	PRONUNCIATION
1 It doesn't matter	10–11	Talking about food and drink Writing about junk food	Food and drink	Verbs not usually used in progressive forms	Syllable stress
2 What's it for?	12–13	Describing objects and saying what they're for Describing a sequence of events Listening to and writing a recipe	Kitchen equipment Recipe	Gerund as subject *by/for* + gerund *after/before* + participle clause	Linking consonant sounds
3 When people expect to get better …	14–15	Talking about illness and medicine Reading an article about alternative medicine Writing a paragraph giving arguments for and against	Health Illness and treatment	Verb + gerund or infinitive	Weak forms
4 Integrated Skills Discussing and correcting information	16–17	Reading Matching statements and paragraphs: *Reality Check* Listening Noting details about beliefs Speaking Correcting information Writing A paragraph discussing the truth of a statement Learner Independence Thinking skills; Word creation: noun and adjective suffixes	Popular beliefs Natural events Useful expressions	Review	
Inspired Extra!	18–19	Language Links Skit *The Expert* Consolidation & Extension Your Choice!			
Culture	20–21	**Happiness and success**			

Unit 2 — CREATIVITY

		COMMUNICATIVE AIMS	VOCABULARY	GRAMMAR	PRONUNCIATION
1 I don't think it's art!	22–23	Talking about activities that continue up to now Matching texts with pictures Listening for details in a conversation Role-play: a celebrity interview Writing about recent activities	Materials Art	Present perfect progressive with *for* and *since*	/b/ bear /p/ pair
2 I've been hoping …	24–25	Talking about recent events Reading Web forum postings Writing a paragraph comparing achievements and ambitions	Acting Movie making	Present perfect: simple and progressive	Syllable stress
3 She had been reading a book	26–27	Talking about a sequence of past events Listening for details: biography Writing a description of an author's life	Story telling	Past perfect: simple and progressive	Syllable stress
4 Integrated Skills Telling a folk tale	28–29	Reading Connecting ideas: *The Professor and the Wise Ferryman* Listening Checking predictions Speaking Discussion Writing A folk tale Learner Independence Thinking skills; Word creation: noun suffix *-ment*	School subjects Folk tales Useful expressions	Linking words: *neither … nor*	
Inspired Extra!	30–31	Project Group magazine Consolidation & Extension Your Choice!			
Review Units 1–2	32–33	**Self Assessment**			

CONTENTS

		COMMUNICATIVE AIMS	VOCABULARY	GRAMMAR	PRONUNCIATION
Preview Units 3–4	34–35				

Unit 3 — SCIENCE AND DISCOVERY

		COMMUNICATIVE AIMS	VOCABULARY	GRAMMAR	PRONUNCIATION
1 **Light travels incredibly fast**	36–37	Describing and comparing the way things happen Listening for details Writing comparisons of achievements	Science	Comparison of adverbs Adverbs of degree Position and order of adverbial phrases	Numbers
2 **What a fantastic sight!**	38–39	Making exclamations Expressing result Reading a blog Writing descriptions of exciting events	The world under the ocean Adjectives	*What (a/an) …!* *so/such (a/an) …* Result clauses: *so/such … that* Order of adjectives	Exclamations
3 **It won't be cheap**	40–41	Talking about future events, schedules, arrangements, and plans Listening to a tour schedule Discussing predictions Writing about future plans and making predictions	Space flight and tourism Phrasal verbs with *down*, *on*, and *off*	Future review: simple future, simple present, present progressive, and *going to*	Exclamations
4 **Integrated Skills** **Describing events and consequences**	42–43	Reading Connecting ideas: *People who changed the world* Listening Correcting mistakes Speaking Giving reasons for an opinion Writing Profile of a significant person Learner Independence Thinking skills; Word creation: noun suffixes *-sion* and *-tion*	Medicine Environment Radio Navigation Useful expressions	Linking words: expressing cause and result	
Inspired Extra!	44–45	**Language Links** **Skit** *Space Talk* **Consolidation & Extension** **Your Choice!**			
Culture	46–47	**Young Scientists**			

Unit 4 — GETTING IT RIGHT

		COMMUNICATIVE AIMS	VOCABULARY	GRAMMAR	PRONUNCIATION
1 **Some things won't have changed**	48–49	Discussing possible future lifestyles Making predictions Reading an article about life in the future Writing personal predictions	Technology Phrasal verbs with *out*	Future progressive Future perfect	List intonation
2 **We won't halt global warming until …**	50–51	Talking about future possibility Listening to opinions about global warming Role-play: a conversation about traveling Writing: sentence completion	Global warming	First conditional with *if* and *unless* Future time clauses with *when*, *as soon as*, and *until*	Two-syllable words stressed differently as nouns and verbs
3 **If you could choose …**	52–53	Talking about imaginary or unlikely situations Expressing wishes about the present Listening to a radio call-in show Writing about wishes	Tourism and travel	Second conditional *wish/if only* + simple past	Sentence stress and intonation
4 **Integrated Skills** **Debating an issue**	54–55	Reading For and against: *Direct Action* article Listening Completing notes on a debate Speaking Debate Writing A balanced account of a controversial issue Learner Independence Thinking skills; Word creation: prefixes *anti-* and *non-*	Politics Formal debate Useful expressions	Linking words: adding information and giving examples	
Inspired Extra!	56–57	**Project** *Future predictions* **Consolidation & Extension** **Your Choice!**			
Review Units 3–4	58–59	**Self Assessment**			

CONTENTS

		COMMUNICATIVE AIMS	VOCABULARY	GRAMMAR	PRONUNCIATION
Preview Units 5–6	60–61				

Unit 5 — EXTRAORDINARY PEOPLE

		COMMUNICATIVE AIMS	VOCABULARY	GRAMMAR	PRONUNCIATION
1 If the ship hadn't hit an iceberg …	62–63	Talking about unreal or imaginary past events Expressing regret about the past Writing about a significant past event	Ocean voyages Historical events	Third conditional *wish/if only* + past perfect	Sentence stress and weak forms
2 You have to be careful	64–65	Expressing obligation and lack of obligation Listening to a radio show and checking details Writing about qualifications for jobs	Routines Qualifications	*must, can't, have to,* and *need to* *don't have to* and *don't need to*	Contrastive stress
3 What could have happened to them?	66–67	Making deductions and speculating about the past Writing about an unexplained mystery	Aviation Phrasal verbs with *up*	*must have* and *can't have* *could/may/might have*	Sentence stress and weak forms
4 Integrated Skills **Contrasting facts and ideas**	68–69	Reading Connecting ideas: Magazine article about women's soccer Listening Completing a text Speaking Discussing male/female equality Writing Paragraphs contrasting male and female situations Learner Independence Thinking skills; Word creation: adjective suffix *-ous*	Sports Useful expressions	Linking words: *whereas* and *while*	
Inspired Extra!	70–71	Language Links Skit *The Break-in* Consolidation & Extension Your Choice!			
Culture	72–73	**Saying the right thing**			

Unit 6 — ON THE MOVE

		COMMUNICATIVE AIMS	VOCABULARY	GRAMMAR	PRONUNCIATION
1 I promised I wouldn't forget!	74–75	Reporting what people said Interviewing Writing a report of interviews	Travel Reporting verbs	Reported speech with various reporting verbs	Stress in two-syllable verbs
2 The waitress wanted to know if …	76–77	Reporting what people asked Listening to an interview and checking details Writing a report of a conversation	Restaurant Food	Reported questions	Sentence stress and intonation
3 You'd like to stay there, wouldn't you?	78–79	Asking for agreement and checking information Taking a quiz Writing descriptions of places	Buildings	Tag questions	Intonation in tag questions
4 Integrated Skills **Reporting and summarizing what people said**	80–81	Reading Topics: *Family Vacations* interview Listening Note taking Speaking Interviewing and reporting an interview Writing A report summarizing an interview Learner Independence Thinking skills; Word creation: adjectives formed with *well*	Vacations Useful expressions	Review	
Inspired Extra!	82–83	Project *Ideal vacation* Consolidation & Extension Your Choice!			
Review Units 5–6	84–85	**Self Assessment**			

CONTENTS

		COMMUNICATIVE AIMS	VOCABULARY	GRAMMAR	PRONUNCIATION
Preview Units 7–8	86–87				

Unit 7 — GETTING THE MESSAGE ACROSS

			COMMUNICATIVE AIMS	VOCABULARY	GRAMMAR	PRONUNCIATION
1	Good job— keep it up!	88–89	Describing changes and experiences Reading an article about English idioms Listening to a conversation about a kitchen makeover Answering a questionnaire	Idioms Furniture, fixtures, and fittings	Passive tenses	*been* and *being*
2	She deserves to be awarded a prize	90–91	Talking about what's right Reading an article about the discovery of DNA Writing about teenage attitudes	Science	Passive infinitive *either … or* *both … and*	Syllable stress
3	They couldn't call up a doctor	92–93	Using the phone Role-play: phone conversation Writing messages	Cell phones Telephone language Phrasal verbs	Phrasal verbs	Stress and intonation
4	Integrated Skills Discussing languages	94–95	Reading Connecting ideas: *Language Death or Language Murder?* article Listening Completing notes on a debate Speaking Debate Writing Arguments for and against Learner Independence Thinking skills; Word creation: verb prefix *re-*	Languages Useful expressions	Linking words: *not only … but also* Non-defining relative clauses	
Inspired Extra!		96–97	Language Links Skit *Find a Friend* Consolidation & Extension Your Choice!			
Culture		98–99	Your Culture			

Unit 8 — MAKING THE GRADE

			COMMUNICATIVE AIMS	VOCABULARY	GRAMMAR	PRONUNCIATION
1	He wasn't able to get a job	100–101	Talking about past ability Expressing purpose Reading an article about success stories Reading and writing a poem	Achievements	*could(n't)*, *was(n't) able to*, *managed to* *in order to* *so that*	Syllable stress
2	They had to pay	102–103	Expressing obligation and ability Reading an article about school in the past and in the future Listening to interviews Completing a questionnaire	Education	Modal expressions in the past and future	Intonation
3	It made me feel great	104–105	Talking about obligation, permission, and prohibition Reading an article about a singer/songwriter Listening to an interview about rules	Music Family rules	*make* and *let* *be allowed to*	/ŋ/ lo**ng** /ŋg/ lo**ng**er
4	Integrated Skills Making an application	106–107	Reading Topics: letter of application Listening Telephone interviews: matching information and checking predictions Speaking Role-play: telephone interview Writing Application form and letter of application Learner Independence Thinking skills; Word creation: noun suffix *-ness*	Volunteering Useful expressions	Review	
Inspired Extra!		108–109	Project *Ideal school* Consolidation & Extension Your Choice!			
Review Units 7–8		110–111	Self Assessment			

Language File 112   **Word List** 121   **Pronunciation Guide** 127   **Irregular Verbs** 127

Welcome! Thinking Skills

MAXIMIZE YOUR BRAIN POWER!

LEARNING POWER

Thinking about how you learn is an important skill. Answer the questionnaire by writing U (Usually), S (Sometimes), or R (Rarely) for each statement.

Learning questionnaire

1. I find it easy to concentrate.
2. I keep trying even when a task is difficult.
3. My head is full of questions.
4. When I learn, I try to make links with what I know.
5. I see things in my mind's eye.
6. I work slowly and carefully.
7. I make good use of the resources around me.
8. I plan my learning carefully.
9. I keep a record of my learning.
10. I reflect on my learning to see what I could do better.
11. I work well as part of a team.
12. I can easily see other people's points of view.

Compare your answers with other students.

MEMORY BUILDING

Here's an activity that you can use to improve your memory. Try it and see what you think.

Look at these 20 words for one minute and try to remember as many as possible.

happy	reggae	banana	crime	painter	
blues	doctor	lonely	rice	kick	engine
rock	teacher	spaghetti	sad		
worried	rap	cousin	pilot	salad	

How did you do? Did you notice that the words (except *crime*, *kick*, *engine,* and *cousin*) are in groups: feelings, music, food, and jobs? You can use the Word List to make similar activities.

You'll find more memory building activities in the *Learner Independence* and *Your Choice!* sections.

DEVELOPING LOGIC

Solving puzzles helps develop your thinking skills. Try this one!

What can run but never walks,
has a mouth but never talks,
and has a bed but never sleeps?

There are brainteasers and crossword puzzles in every unit of the Workbook.

LEARNING STYLES

Read about four learning styles and decide which is most like you. The *Your Choice!* sections at the end of every unit have activities for each learning style. Try different activities—it's good to know your own learning style, but it's also good to experiment with other ways of learning.

CONSTRUCTION
You …
- enjoy grammar practice exercises.
- like working with the teacher.
- are good at homework and tests.
- enjoy writing more than discussion.
- don't like games or group work.

REFLECTION
You …
- always want to know why and find rules for things.
- like working hard on your own and getting things right.
- prefer listening, reading, and writing to speaking.
- sometimes don't finish work and are unhappy if it isn't perfect.

ACTION
You …
- like listening and speaking more than reading and writing.
- enjoy fun activities and moving around more than exercises and homework.
- like doing lots of different things and working with other people.
- like games more than writing and grammar.

INTERACTION
You …
- really enjoy learning languages.
- love group and pair work and prefer speaking to writing.
- don't like exercises or rules.
- like working with others and discussing personal things.

BODY AND MIND

Brain power is about your body as well as your mind. Try these two techniques.

Take a break!
When you're studying at home, stop every 20–30 minutes, stand up, stretch, and move around for two or three minutes. This will give you fresh energy.

Walk and breathe in time!
This simple technique helps you relax, gives you energy, and improves your breathing and therefore your voice. "Walking meditation" is something that you can do every day on your way to or from school. Start walking with your left foot and breathe in through your nose for four steps (left, right, left, right). Then breathe out through your mouth for three steps (left, right, left). Don't breathe for one step (right), then breathe in again. Try it—you'll be amazed!

Answer to brainteaser: A river.

PREVIEW
UNITS 1-2

COMMUNICATIVE AIMS
LEARNING HOW TO ...

1. Talk about food and drink
2. Describe objects and say what they're for
3. Describe a sequence of events
4. Talk about illness and medicine
5. Talk about activities that continue up to now
6. Talk about recent events
7. Talk about a sequence of past events

Antony Gormley has been working with iron to make unique sculptures since the 1980s.

TOPICS AND VOCABULARY

Food and drink
Kitchen equipment
Health
Popular beliefs
Natural events
Materials
Art
Acting
Movie making
Story telling
School subjects
Folk tales

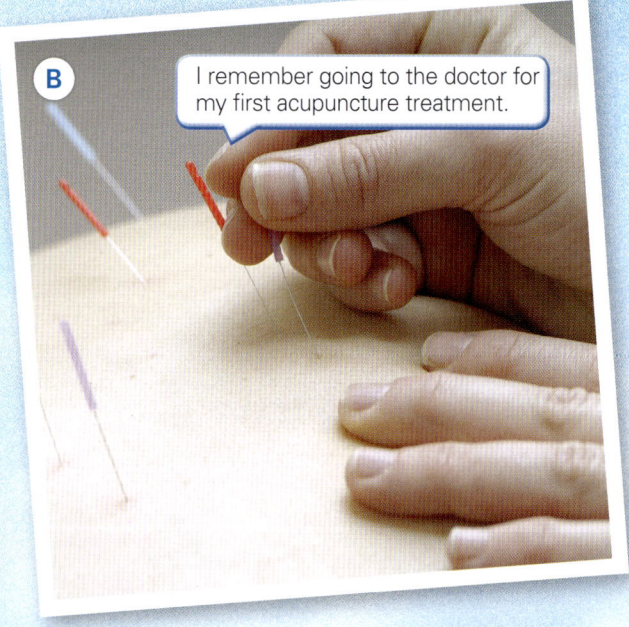

I remember going to the doctor for my first acupuncture treatment.

1 Match five of the communicative aims (1–7) with the pictures (A–E).

2 Complete the words on the right and put them into categories.

- Food and drink
- Materials
- Health and illness

br_nze   br_ad   b_tter
c_rdboard   c_ncrete   dr_g
fru_t   head_che   ir_n
j_ice   on_on   op_ration
p_in   p_tient   pl_stic
r_bber   s_rgery   v_getable

8

C

It's for opening cans.

D

She had been thinking about her horror story for some time, when she had an extraordinary dream.

E

We need to eat at least five portions of different fruits and vegetables a day.

4 Do the *Healthy Living Survey* with three other students.

Healthy Living Survey
How healthy is your lifestyle?

Food and drink	Do you eat five different kinds of fruits and vegetables a day? How often do you eat candy and potato chips? Which do you drink more of: water and milk, or soda and coffee?
Exercise	How often do you play team sports a week? Do you go running or swimming? Do you ever go to the gym?
Getting around	Do you … walk or ride a bike? go by bus or car? use the elevator or take the stairs?
Being good to yourself	Do you … get enough sleep? go to the doctor if you feel sick? talk to someone if you have a problem?

Tell another group about the results of your survey.

Believe it or not!
Your brain uses less power than the light in your refrigerator. It uses 12 watts of power. During a day, your brain uses about 300 calories, the amount of energy contained in a medium hot dog or two large bananas.

3 🔘 1.02 Listen to extracts 1–3 from Units 1 and 2. Match them with three of the text types A–D.

A A description of an object
B A post on a Web forum for actors
C The beginning of a story
D An extract from a biography

PREVIEW

9

1 BODY AND MIND

1 It doesn't matter

Talking about food and drink
Verbs not usually used in progressive forms

1 OPENER

Read *Food and Drink: Fact or Fiction?* and decide: true or false? Discuss your answers with another student.

Food and Drink: Fact or Fiction?

1. Bottled water is purer than tap water.
2. A vegetarian diet is the healthiest.
3. Eating cheese gives you nightmares.
4. Dried fruit is not as healthy as fresh fruit.
5. Margarine contains less fat than butter.
6. A food label that includes the words "low fat" indicates a healthy choice.
7. Neither fruit juice nor diet drinks are bad for your teeth.
8. Experts disagree with each other about what healthy eating is.

2 READING

🔊 1.03 Match statements 1–8 in exercise 1 with paragraphs A–H. Then listen and check.

3 AFTER READING

Answer the questions.

1. Which of the statements 1–8 in exercise 1 are true, which are false, and which could be true or false?
2. Why do experts appear to disagree about healthy eating?
3. What were experts saying 20 years ago?
4. What does advertising make us believe?
5. Why is it a bad idea to eat late in the evening?
6. What is an example of an unhealthy vegetarian diet?
7. Why do people think that "low fat" products are OK? Are they right?
8. Why do some people prefer bottled water?

Your response What are your favorite things to eat and drink? Are they good or bad for you? How do you know?

4 PRONUNCIATION

Write the words in the correct column.

bottled   contain   decay   depend   digest   expert
fiction   label   nightmare   portion   prefer
product   protein   reduce   relax   suppose

■ ▪	▪ ■
bottled	contain

🔊 1.04 Now listen and check. Repeat the words.

A In fact, the main messages about healthy eating have stayed the same for some time. For example, 20 years ago experts were saying that we should reduce the amount of fat that we eat. And, over 50 years ago they were emphasizing the importance of fruit and vegetables. They appear to disagree because the media often exaggerate when reporting scientific research.

B In fact, both are. Fruit juice contains sugar, which can damage your teeth. Diet drinks are often acidic, which means that they can cause tooth decay. The best drinks for your teeth are water or milk.

C As part of a balanced diet, we need to eat at least five portions of different fruits and vegetables a day. It doesn't matter whether they are fresh, frozen, canned, or dried (but fruit juice only counts as one portion a day). The only thing that dried fruit lacks, and fresh fruit has, is vitamin C, but both are equally healthy.

D It often seems from advertising that this is true. However, while butter and margarine contain different kinds of fat, they both contain a similar amount of fat.

5 SPEAKING

Discuss these statements with another student using verbs from the Word Bank.

- The best way to lose weight is to skip a meal.
- Healthy food is boring and expensive.
- I like junk food—what's wrong with that?
- I take vitamins, so I don't have to worry about what I eat.
- It's not a good idea to go swimming right after a meal.
- Eating lots of carrots helps you see better in the dark.

> Some people believe in skipping meals, but they soon feel hungry and eat lots of snacks.

> I prefer to eat normally and get exercise.

Word Bank Verbs not usually used in progressive forms

agree/disagree appear believe consist
contain depend feel hear include know
lack like/dislike love matter mean
need prefer promise realize recognize
remember see seem smell sound
suppose taste think understand want

Extension Which of the verbs in the Word Bank can you find in the texts in exercise 2? Choose five of the verbs and write sentences.

Hamburgers contain a lot of fat.

6 WRITING

Read the texts in exercise 2 again and write two paragraphs about junk food.

Paragraph 1: Why do some people choose to eat junk food?
Paragraph 2: Why is too much junk food bad for you?

E It's not *what* you eat, but *when* you eat, that matters. Scientists agree that it's not a good idea to eat just before you go to bed. You can't relax properly while you're digesting food.

F It depends. Vegetarian diets can be very healthy. But if your vegetarian diet consists of French fries and cookies, then that's a different matter. Make sure that your diet includes food with the protein, vitamins, and minerals you normally get from meat.

G Not at all. "Low" products must contain 25% less fat than usual, so people suppose that they are OK. But these types of foods are often very high in fat to start with. So a "low fat" product can still have a high amount of fat.

H This is a popular myth. Although some people think that bottled water tastes or smells better, there's nothing to prove that it's always purer than tap water. In fact, in the U.S., it's believed that 25–30% of bottled water comes from tap water. And do you realize that bottled water can cost up to 10,000 times more than tap water?

LANGUAGE WORKOUT

Complete.

Verbs not usually used in progressive forms
Fruit juice _____ (contain) sugar.
It often _____ (seem) that this is true.
It _____ (not matter) whether they are fresh, frozen, ...
People _____ (suppose) that they are OK.
They _____ (think) that bottled water _____ (taste) better.

Many of these verbs refer to states (including mental states, e.g., *think*) rather than actions, or to the senses (e.g., *taste*). Modal verbs (e.g., *can*) do not have progressive forms.

▶ Answers and Practice
Language File page 112

1 BODY AND MIND

2 What's it for?

Describing objects and saying what they're for
Describing a sequence of events
Gerund as subject
by/for + gerund
after/before + participle clause

A B C D E

1 OPENER

Look at these photos of gadgets. What do you think each item is for?

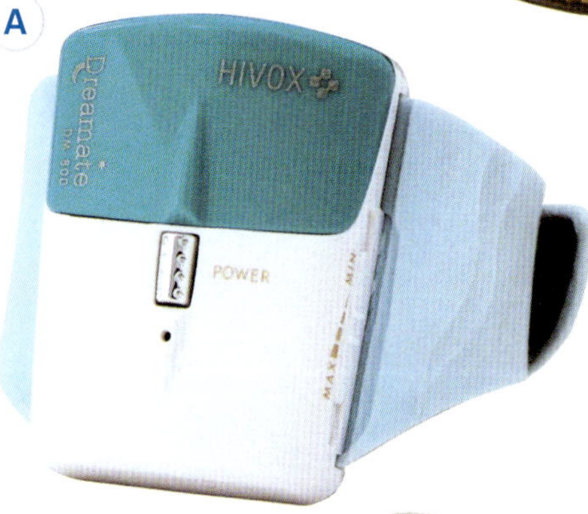

2 READING

🔊 1.05 Read *Gadget Mania!* and match the photos with the descriptions. Then listen and check.

3 AFTER READING

True or false? Correct the false sentences.

1. The key looks like a bottle opener.
2. You can't unlock your front door with the key.
3. You can get to sleep easily by wearing the "sleep inducer."
4. Experts recommend wearing the "sleep inducer" for three hours a night.
5. The sandwich toaster is for roasting sandwiches.
6. By hiding somewhere in the room, Clocky makes you get out of bed.
7. The soccer ball is for making music.
8. You can make a light work by plugging it into the ball.

Your response Which two of the gadgets would you like to have and why?

Gadget Mania!

1. This looks like a door key, but in fact, it's a clever gadget for opening bottles. Keep this bottle opener on your key ring, and you'll never be thirsty again when you're out and about. But when you come home, don't try to open your front door with it!

2. Going to sleep is easy with this "sleep inducer." If you suffer from insomnia, you can get to sleep by wearing this watch-like gadget on your wrist. It relaxes your muscles, and experts say using it for 30 minutes before bedtime will soon show effects. Keep one by your bed and never worry about sleepless nights again.

3. Do you like making toasted sandwiches? Then this sandwich toaster is the answer. It produces perfect toasted sandwiches and it's small enough to fit in a kitchen drawer. It comes with lots of delicious recipes and you can use it at home, on the barbecue, or when you go camping.

4. An ordinary alarm clock wakes you up, but Clocky® is an alarm clock on wheels that also makes sure you get out of bed. When the alarm goes off and you press the snooze button, the clock rolls off the night table onto the floor and finds a place to hide. When the alarm clock sounds again, you have to get out of bed and look for it, so you are fully awake before turning it off. Clocky's inventor, Ms. Gauri Nanda, was a student when she came up with the idea, after struggling to get up in the morning.

5. Playing soccer is great fun and now there is a soccer ball called sOccket, which generates and stores electricity. Four female students at Harvard University in the U.S. thought of it after learning that 95% of people in Africa live without electricity. sOccket's electricity can be used to charge a cell phone or power an LED light. Fifteen minutes of soccer can produce three hours of LED light. In the picture, you can see the soccer ball with a light plugged in.

4 VOCABULARY

Match the words for kitchen equipment with pictures 1–8.

> **Word Bank** Kitchen equipment
>
> bread knife   can opener   cheese grater   coffee maker
> corkscrew   frying pan   teakettle   toaster

🔊 1.06 Listen and check. Then ask and answer questions using these phrases.

> boil water   fry food   grate cheese   make coffee
> make toast   open bottles   open cans   slice bread

A What's number 1?
B It's a can opener. It's for opening cans.

> **Extension** Think of other gadgets and write sentences beginning *It's for ...ing ...* Read your sentences to other students. Can they identify the gadgets?

5 PRONUNCIATION

🔊 1.07 Listen and repeat.

> Linking consonant sounds
> front_door   bed_time   sand_wich
> night_table   great_fun
> bread_knife   cork_screw

6 LISTENING

🔊 1.08 Look at this recipe for Spaghetti Carbonara. The instructions A–H are in the wrong order. Try to put them in the right order. Then listen and see if you are right.

Spaghetti Carbonara
Serves 4

Ingredients: 350 g spaghetti, 175 g bacon, 2 medium onions, 50 ml olive oil, 4 eggs, 100 ml cream, 100 g grated Parmesan cheese, salt

A Meanwhile, boil 3–4 liters of water in a saucepan.
B Then stir in the egg, cream, and cheese mixture.
C Chop the onions and bacon into small pieces.
D Sprinkle with the rest of the Parmesan cheese and serve immediately.
E When the pasta is cooked, drain it, and add the onions and bacon.
F Put the spaghetti in the boiling water, add salt, and stir for a few seconds.
G Heat the oil in a frying pan, and fry the onions and bacon slowly, until the onions are almost clear.
H While the pasta is cooking, use a fork to beat the eggs and cream together in a bowl, and then add half the Parmesan cheese.

7 SPEAKING

Check your answers to exercise 6 using *after/before ...ing*.

A First, chop the onions and bacon into small pieces.
B After chopping the onions and bacon, fry them slowly.
A Before frying the onions and bacon, heat the oil in a frying pan.

8 WRITING

Look up how to make a dish that you like in a cookbook or on the Web, and write down the ingredients. Then write a recipe explaining how to make the dish, using the recipe in exercise 6 to help you.

> **LANGUAGE WORKOUT**
>
> Complete.
>
> **Gerund as subject**
> _____ (go) to sleep is easy.
> _____ (play) soccer is great fun.
>
> **by/for + gerund**
> You can get to sleep **by** _____ (wear) this watch-like gadget.
> It's a clever gadget **for** _____ (open) bottles.
>
> **after/before + participle clause**
> She came up with the idea **after** _____ (struggle) to get up in the morning.
> You are fully awake **before** _____ (turn) it off.
>
> ▶ Answers and Practice
> Language File page 112

1 BODY AND MIND

3 When people expect to get better ...

Talking about illness and medicine
Verb + gerund or infinitive

> Much so-called alternative medicine is at best harmless and at worst dangerous.

> My father took herbal medicine when he tried to quit smoking last year. It didn't work. But that's probably his fault, because he didn't remember to take it every day.

> I remember going to the doctor for my first acupuncture treatment for back pain. I pretended to be calm, although I couldn't help feeling nervous! I didn't exactly enjoy having acupuncture, but it didn't hurt, and the next day my back was much better.

> Research shows that patients who tried having acupuncture for bad headaches had fewer headaches, and saw the doctor less often, than those who didn't try it.

Alternative Medicine
Is it all in the mind?

More and more people are choosing to use alternative medicine each year.

Alternative medicine may be news, but it's not new. It's modern medicine that is new—for example, the first synthetic drug, aspirin, dates only from 1899. But alternative medicine goes back thousands of years. Acupuncture, inserting fine needles at selected points in the body, was used in China over 2,000 years ago and keeps growing in popularity. A TV show on alternative medicine showed a young Chinese woman having open-heart surgery without a general anesthetic—but with acupuncture. There seemed to be no doubt that acupuncture stopped the woman from feeling pain. The needles appeared to change the brain's reaction to pain.

Herbal medicine, treating illness and pain with natural remedies, is the oldest system of medicine in the world. Herbalists are prepared to spend more time than modern doctors with patients so they can treat them as individuals.

But there are two sides to the issue. Independent scientists question whether there is proper research evidence for the claims for alternative medicine. They expect to see scientific proof from tests and trials. Supporters of alternative medicine say its critics are influenced by pharmaceutical companies who want to avoid losing sales of their very profitable drugs.

And then there's the "placebo" effect. In a major trial in the U.S., a group of patients had a normal operation for bad knee pain. Another group of patients with knee pain also believed they had operations. But, in fact, all the surgeon did was cut the knee open and close it again. Both groups had the same positive results from their "operations." In other words, the effect of real and fake operations was the same.

So what does this experiment tell us about medicine? Simply this: when people expect to get better, they often do.

1 OPENER

Can people who are sick get better without the help of modern medicine? Do you know anyone who uses alternative medicine?

2 READING

🔘 1.09 Read *Alternative Medicine*. What is the most surprising information in the text?

14

3 AFTER READING

True or false? Correct the false sentences.

1. Patients who had acupuncture for headaches saw the doctor more often.
2. Acupuncture can often help people with back pain.
3. More and more people are trying acupuncture.
4. A Chinese woman had a major operation without a general anesthetic.
5. Acupuncture needles seem to change the way the brain reacts to pain.
6. Herbalists treat each patient as being different.
7. Independent scientists want to see proof of the claims for alternative medicine.
8. The effects on those patients who had a real knee operation and those who didn't were different.

Your response If you had a bad pain or serious illness, would you try acupuncture? Why/Why not?

4 PRONUNCIATION

🔊 1.10 Listen and repeat.

Weak forms: /ət/, /əv/, /tə/

at best … at worst	a group of patients
at selected points	remember to take it
thousands of years	two sides to the issue
system of medicine	appeared to change

5 SPEAKING

What would you do in these situations? Complete the sentences for each situation and then tell another student.

Situations
You want to go on vacation on your own.
You want to pass your final exams.
You want to go to an all-night party.

1. I'd try to …
2. I wouldn't risk …
3. I'd promise to …
4. I'd avoid …
5. I'd remember to …

> I'd try to save up some money.

> I wouldn't risk going without telling my parents.

> I'd promise to call home regularly.

Extension Write three more situations beginning *You want to …* . Ask your partner to say what he/she would do in each situation.

6 VOCABULARY

Make a word map for medicine. Use words from this lesson, and add other words you know.

7 SPEAKING

Interview three other students about their views on alternative and modern medicine and write down their answers.

> What are the differences between modern medicine and alternative medicine?

> Modern medicine is scientific.

> Alternative medicine sometimes works, but we don't know how.

> I wouldn't risk trying alternative medicine.

8 WRITING

Read the text in exercise 2 again and make a list of the advantages and disadvantages of alternative medicine. Write a paragraph giving your views on alternative medicine using the list and your notes from exercise 7.

LANGUAGE WORKOUT

Complete.

Verb + gerund or infinitive
Some verbs are followed by the gerund, e.g., *avoid, can't help, dislike, enjoy, keep, quit, stop*.
Some verbs are followed by the infinitive, e.g., *appear, choose, decide, expect, pretend, seem, want*.
And some verbs can be followed by **either** the gerund **or** the infinitive, e.g., *try, remember, forget*.

Patients who tried _____ (have) acupuncture …
He tried _____ (quit) smoking last year.
try + gerund = do something to see what happens
try + infinitive = attempt something difficult

I remember _____ (go) to the doctor.
He didn't remember _____ (take) it every day.
remember/forget + gerund refers to an action in the past.
remember/forget + infinitive refers to a necessary action and looks ahead.

▶**Answers and Practice**
Language File pages 112–113

1 BODY AND MIND

4 Integrated Skills
Discussing and correcting information

1 OPENER

Match these statements with photos A–F.

- Lightning never strikes the same place twice.
- Spinach is a great source of iron.
- It takes seven years to digest chewing gum.
- You get less wet by running in the rain than by walking.
- Flying is the safest way to travel.
- The Great Wall of China is the only man-made structure visible from the Moon.

Reality Check

1 This idea was probably made up to stop children from swallowing the stuff, but it's nonsense. It may be a little more difficult to break down than other things we eat, but actually it doesn't take very long to digest.

2 This is a common belief, but it's false. Astronauts in space can see the Great Wall before leaving the Earth's orbit, as well as several other things like airports, highways, and even bridges. But the truth is that the famous landmark is not visible from the Moon.

3 This is probably true. Many people are afraid of flying because they believe it's risky, but statistics show that it's safer than crossing the street, and there is a greater chance of accidents with other forms of transportation. However, the chances of surviving a plane crash are low.

4 Popeye claimed his strength came from this vegetable, but it isn't a particularly good source of iron. In fact, it contains an acid that stops the body from absorbing most of the iron. However, it is a rich source of healthy things, such as vitamins A, C, and E.

5 This is a myth. People believe that fewer raindrops land on them if they run because they spend less time in the rain. But in reality you can get wetter by running, because more rain hits your chest when you run than when you walk. On the other hand, if you run to the nearest shelter, you will get less wet. Of course, carrying an umbrella is the best way to avoid getting wet!

6 This is a famous saying, but is it a fact? On the contrary, lightning frequently hits the same place more than once. This is particularly true of high places—the Empire State Building in New York is struck 100 times every year on average, and in one storm it was struck 15 times in 15 minutes. The building is even designed as a lightning conductor to stop lightning from hitting other buildings.

READING

2 Read *Reality Check* and match the statements in exercise 1 with paragraphs 1–6. Which statements are actually true?

3 What do the words in *italics* refer to?

Paragraph
1 … actually *it* doesn't take very long to digest.
2 … *the famous landmark* is not visible from the Moon.
3 … they believe *it's* risky …
4 … *it* isn't a particularly good source of iron.
5 People believe that fewer raindrops land on *them* …
6 *The building* is even designed as a lightning conductor …

LISTENING

4 Here are three more statements. Discuss whether each one is true or false.

1 The number of people alive today is greater than the number who have ever died.
2 It's essential to drink at least eight glasses of water a day.
3 We use only ten percent of our brains.

🔊 1.11 Now listen to an expert discussing the statements and check.

5 🔊 1.11 Listen again and complete the notes below.

1
The estimated number of people who have died in the last …
Modern humans appeared …
Experts believe the number of dead in human history is …

2
A lot of the water we need is provided by …
We can take in water by drinking …
The sensible thing is to …

3
Brain scans and other tests show …
We use different parts of our brain for different activities …
We don't use all our muscles at the same time, so …

6 SPEAKING

Look at your notes in exercise 5, and tell each other the facts about the three statements in exercise 4. You can use the phrases in the box.

Correcting information
actually   in fact
It isn't true.   It's false/nonsense/a myth.
More formal
in reality   the truth is that   on the contrary

7 GUIDED WRITING

Choose one of the statements in exercise 4, and write a paragraph discussing it. Use your notes from exercise 5, phrases from the box in exercise 6, and the *Reality Check* article to help you.

LEARNER INDEPENDENCE

8 Thinking skills: Use your brain to think about words! For each of these words from Unit 1, try to answer the questions below.

decay   delicious   frozen
nightmare   saucepan   snooze

- What does it mean? Is it a noun and/or a verb, or an adjective?
- Can you remember its context in the unit?
- What other words do you associate with it?
- What other words can you use with it?
- What does it sound like?

Now compare your answers with another student.

Which word do you think is the most useful? Why?
Which word do you like best? Why?

9 Word creation: Complete the chart with words from Unit 1.

Noun	Adjective
_____	acidic
danger	_____
harm	_____
health	_____
herb	_____
_____	ill
_____	important
_____	real
risk	_____
sense	_____
_____	strong
thirst	_____
_____	true

10 🔊 1.12 **Phrasebook:** Find these useful expressions in Unit 1. Then listen and repeat.

It's not a good idea to …
That's a different matter.
Not at all.
Do you realize that …?
What's wrong with that?
It didn't work.
It's nonsense.
On the other hand …
The sensible thing is to …

Now write sentences that could come before five of the expressions.

1 BODY AND MIND
Inspired EXTRA!

LANGUAGE LINKS

Match these international words with the descriptions of their origins.

> banana chocolate coffee curry hamburger
> pizza salad sushi tea yogurt

International words for food and drink

1. The name of this food comes from an Italian word meaning "pie."
2. This word came to England through Dutch *thee* and Malay *teh*, and is originally from southeast China.
3. The word for this dish comes from the southern Indian language, Tamil: *kari*, which means "sauce."
4. Spanish and Portuguese explorers discovered this yellow fruit, and its name is a West African word.
5. This became an English word in the 17th century, probably from the Italian word *caffé*. However, Turkish *kahveh* and Arabic *qahwah* are earlier versions. The Arabic word may come from Kaffa, a place in Ethopia where the plant was first grown.
6. The Romans liked dishes with raw vegetables and a salty dressing, and our word comes from Latin *salare*, which means "put salt on."
7. This word came from Turkey (with the same spelling) in the 1620s and has had lots of different spellings in English, including *yaourt*.
8. This word comes from the Aztec language of South America and was brought to Europe by the Spanish. It was first used to describe a drink known in Aztec as *xocolatl*.
9. This is a Japanese dish of rice with raw fish or vegetables.
10. This word for meat in a bread roll came to the U.S. in the 1870s from the German city of Hamburg.

Find out the origin of these international words for food.

> chop suey fondue kebab omelette paella
> salami spaghetti sauerkraut tandoori tortilla

SKIT *The Expert*

🔊 1.13 Read and listen.

MAN Yes, can I help you?
WOMAN I want to dye.
MAN Excuse me? What did you say? You want to die?
WOMAN I want to dye it. It's my shirt.
MAN Diet! Ah, yes, you've come to the right man. I'm a diet expert. Now, why do you want to diet? Is your shirt too small?
WOMAN It's not the size—it's the color. I don't like it. It's white and I want it to be brown.
MAN There's nothing wrong with your color—you look fine. And anyway, a diet won't change your color. Try lying in the sun.
WOMAN Listen! I want to dye it brown.
MAN Sorry. I don't have any brown diets. I have high-energy diets, all-meat diets, fruit diets, lots of diets, but no color diets.
WOMAN I don't want to dye the collar! I want to dye the whole shirt. And these jeans. They're the right size, but the wrong color.
MAN You can't change your genes—you're born with them.
WOMAN No, I wasn't! I bought them last week. In a new jeans store on Main Street.
MAN A genes store!
WOMAN Yes. But if you won't help me, I'll take them back to the store and change them.
MAN How interesting! I've always wanted to change my genes. I could be tall and have lots of hair. I think I'll come with you!

Now act out the skit in pairs.

Game Acrosswords

- Choose a long word from this unit. Write the word across the top of a piece of paper, and down the left-hand side. Then write the same word backward down the right-hand side of the paper.
- Make a copy and give it to another student. Both of you try to find words that begin with the letter on the left and end with the letter on the right. You can use a dictionary to help you. It doesn't matter if you can't find words for all the lines.
- Score one point for each letter. The student with the most points wins.

S	Y	N	T	H	E	T	I	C
Y								I
N	E	X						T
T	A	K						E
H	I	G						H
E	X	T	I	N	C			T
T	R	A	I					N
I	D	E	N	T	I	F		Y
C	H	A	N	G	E			S

UNIT 1

CONSOLIDATION

LESSON 1 Look at exercise 5 on page 11. Write sentences responding to the statements.

Some people believe in skipping meals, but they soon feel hungry and eat lots of snacks.

LESSON 2 Look at exercise 4 on page 13. Write sentences about the kitchen equipment.

A bread knife is for slicing bread.

LESSON 3 Look at the Language Workout on page 15. Write five sentences about things that happened last week using five of the verbs + gerund or infinitive.

I couldn't help being late for school because the bus broke down.

EXTENSION

LESSON 1 Write notes for a food diary, describing what you have eaten and drunk in the last 24 hours. Then show your notes to another student and discuss them.

A You had cereal and fruit for breakfast. What did you have to drink?
B Tea—I dislike coffee. In fact, I like hot chocolate best. How about you?
A I didn't have breakfast—it doesn't matter. I can get some potato chips during break.

LESSON 2 Look at exercise 7 on page 13 and the recipe you wrote in exercise 8. Write sentences about the recipe using *after/before ...ing*.

LESSON 3 Look at exercise 5 on page 15. Then complete sentences 1–5 below for these situations:

- You want to ask another student for a date.
- You want to ask your parents for money to buy an MP3 player.

1 I'd expect to …
2 I'd keep …
3 I wouldn't dare to …
4 I'd suggest …
5 I'd ask to …

YOUR CHOICE!

CONSTRUCTION Gerund or infinitive?

Complete with the correct form of the verb.

1 She enjoys _____ (go) to see the herbalist because he seems _____ (understand) her.
2 Acupuncture appears _____ (help) my pain so I'm going to keep _____ (have) it.
3 He decided _____ (take) aspirin because he didn't want _____ (risk) _____ (have) a headache all day.
4 Always late? Try _____ (set) your watch five minutes fast.
5 Did you remember _____ (lock) the door?
6 He'll never forget _____ (meet) Nelson Mandela.
7 She tried _____ (explain) what to do, but he didn't understand.
8 I remember _____ (take) my glasses off but now I can't find them.
9 Don't forget _____ (give) me a call when you arrive.

REFLECTION Gerund and infinitive

Complete.

- *avoid*, *enjoy*, and *suggest* are examples of verbs that are followed by the _____.
  appear, *expect*, and *refuse* are examples of verbs that are followed by the _____.
- Some verbs like *remember*, _____ , and _____ can be followed by either gerund or infinitive, but with different meanings. For example, *remember* + _____ refers to something it is important to do in the future, while *remember* + _____ refers to something that happened in the past.
- Other verbs, for example, *hate*, *like*, *love*, and *prefer*, can be followed by _____ gerund or infinitive with the _____ meaning.

ACTION Topics

- Work in a small group.
- Choose six topics from this list:
  animals clothes countries environment feelings food health home leisure sports television travel
- Choose a letter for the group by opening a book, closing your eyes, and pointing with your finger.
- Work on your own in the group. For each topic, write down as many words as you can beginning with the chosen letter. You have ten minutes.
- Then read aloud your lists, scoring one point for each word and two points for any words the others haven't thought of.

INTERACTION Special events and feelings

- Work in a small group.
- Tell each other about:
  Something special that happened to you recently.
  A place that is special for you.
  A number that is special for you.
- Answer the other students' questions.

1 Culture

Natalia (Costa Rica)

Takumi (Japan)

Happiness and success

We asked four teenagers about their views on happiness and success.

What do you think is the key to happiness?

Natalia Did you know that Costa Rica is supposed to be one of the happiest countries in the world? But it's certainly not one of the richest countries, so what's our secret? I think a major factor is that family, friendship, and community networks are very important in our society. Also, we really care about our environment and we try to live in tune with nature.

Takumi Happiness is essentially peace of mind. It's not about material goods, getting the latest gadget, or designer clothes. The trouble is that it's hard not to be materialistic here in Japan when there's so much pressure to buy things. But you can't be happy if you always want more—money can't buy happiness.

Lucy I know money isn't the answer, although it's obviously important to have enough to live on. But in the end, people can't be happy if they think about themselves all the time. Happiness isn't about doing what you want, but about doing what you can for others. One of the best ways to make yourself happy is to make someone else happy—kind and generous people are happier people.

Alex For me, the key to happiness is a healthy lifestyle, with plenty of exercise. I go to a sports club after school and we do all kinds of activities, like swimming, basketball, and ice hockey. It makes me feel better, I have more energy—and it keeps me out of trouble!

What does "success" mean to you?

Lucy I think it's a question of priorities. In this age of capitalism and globalization, people often measure success in terms of their personal wealth. In other words, the more money you have, the more successful you are. So lots of young people in the U.S. want to be rich and famous. That's not my priority, although I'd like to be rich and famous—who wouldn't?!

Natalia The truth is that success means different things to different people. For me, if someone is successful, it's because they have achieved their own goals. That may mean having lots of money and possessions, or it may mean climbing a mountain, or overcoming a disability. But I think the key to success is education, because it gives you the opportunity to make the most of your life.

Alex That's a more difficult question than it seems. "Success" sounds very positive, but take sports, for example. I love sports—both as a participant and as a spectator. However, in any sport, there can only be one winner and lots of losers. We shouldn't forget that it is taking part in a competition that's important—not winning it.

Takumi I believe that the key to success is to think positively and keep trying. Don't be discouraged by failure—learn from your mistakes and do your best. As the great basketball player Michael Jordan once said: "I can accept failure, everyone fails at something. But I can't accept not trying."

Culture

Alex (Canada)

Lucy (U.S.)

1 READING

Read the text and complete the sentences with Alex, Lucy, Natalia, or Takumi.

1 _____ thinks physical activity is important for happiness.
2 _____ suggests that it's better to give than to receive.
3 _____ and _____ think that society places a high value on material goods.
4 _____ doesn't think that winning is the most important thing.
5 _____ thinks that friends and family are the key to happiness.
6 _____ believes that it's important not to give up.
7 _____ says that it's important to help others.
8 _____ and _____ don't believe that money guarantees happiness.
9 _____ thinks that education enables you to be the best you can be.
10 _____ believes that there are many different ways of being successful.

2 VOCABULARY

Match the words 1–10 with their definitions a–j.

1 essentially *adv*
2 materialistic *adj*
3 generous *adj*
4 capitalism *n*
5 globalization *n*
6 wealth *n*
7 priority *n*
8 overcome *v*
9 participant *n*
10 discouraged *adj*

a something that is put first
b the idea that the world is developing a single economy and culture
c someone who takes part in something
d basically
e succeed in dealing with a problem
f believing that money and possessions are the most important aspect of life
g economic system controlled by individuals and private companies, not by government
h feeling that it is useless to try to do something
i large amount of money and valuable things
j happy to give money or time

3 SPEAKING

Discuss these questions.

1 What makes you happy?
2 "It's better to give than to receive." Do you agree? Why/Why not?
3 The Olympic® motto is: "The most important thing is not winning but taking part." Do you agree? Why/Why not?
4 Would you like to be rich and famous? Why/Why not?
5 Which of the four teenagers' answers do you agree and disagree with most? Why?

4 MINI-PROJECT
Happiness and success

Work with another student and think about your answers to these questions.
- What do you think is the key to happiness?
- What does "success" mean to you?

Write two paragraphs answering each question, giving reasons for your points of view.

Read your work carefully and correct any mistakes. Then show your answers to other students.

21

2 CREATIVITY

1 I don't think it's art!

Talking about activities that continue up to now
Present perfect progressive with *for* and *since*

1 OPENER

Look at the photos of works of art. What do they show?

What materials were used to create these works? Choose from these words.

Word Bank Materials

bronze cardboard concrete
dung gold iron plaster plastic
rubber sandstone wood

2 READING

Read the information about four famous modern artists. Match them with their work in photos A–D. Which artist uses the most unusual material(s)?

1 Antony Gormley has been working with iron to make unique sculptures since the 1980s. He's a sculptor who is interested in the human body, and many of his works are based on his own body— "the only part of the material world that I live inside." His work is often displayed outside: in the countryside, on the roofs of buildings, and by rivers or the ocean. A striking example of his work is *Horizon Field*, which is made up of 100 life-size human figures placed high up in the Austrian Alps, including some in cable cars and chairlifts.

2 Tracey Emin's first piece of public art is *Roman Standard*. It's a bronze sculpture of a bird on top of a four-meter-high pole. Emin said: "Since 1992, I've been making a series of drawings and prints of birds. I've always had the idea that birds are the angels of this earth and that they represent freedom." Reactions to the sculpture are not all positive: "I don't think it's art—it's a complete waste of money!" The bird is certainly small—in fact, it disappears if you stand directly in front of it and only reappears if you move to the left or right.

3 Since the late 1980s, Rachel Whiteread has been creating unusual sculptures of everyday domestic items—the empty spaces under chairs and staircases, around bathtubs, and inside cupboards and rooms. One of the most famous of these was her first public sculpture, the award-winning *House*—a concrete cast of the inside of a townhouse. Her huge work called *Embankment* consisted of 14,000 white plastic boxes cast from ten different cardboard boxes. Whiteread also uses materials like plaster, rubber, and styrofoam™ to define the space around or inside objects and buildings.

4 For many years, prize-winning artist Chris Ofili has been using elephant dung in his paintings as a symbol of his African heritage. He also stands his paintings on elephant dung, which he gets free of charge from the London Zoo. One of his best-known works is *No Woman No Cry*, the title of a Bob Marley song. The painting is a tribute to the family of Stephen Lawrence, a London teenager who was murdered by a racist gang. The boy's face can be seen in each of the crying woman's tears.

A

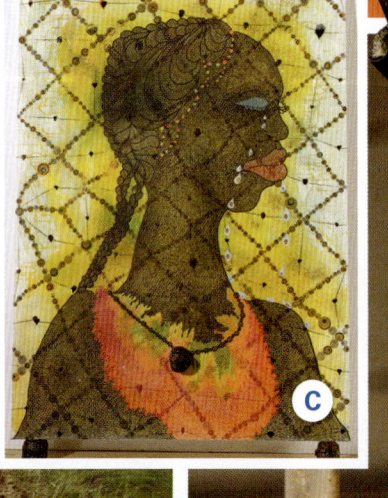
B

C

D

3 AFTER READING

Answer the questions.

1. How long has Antony Gormley been creating sculptures?
2. What kind of material does he often use?
3. How long has Tracey Emin been making drawings and prints of birds?
4. What's her *Roman Standard* bird made of?
5. How long has Rachel Whiteread been making sculptures of everyday items?
6. What was *House* made of?
7. What other materials does Whiteread use?
8. What's unusual about Chris Ofili's work?

Your response What do you think of the works of art in the photos?

4 LISTENING

🔘 1.14 Look at the photo of the statue. Is there anything unusual about it?

Now listen and find the answers to these questions.

1. How long has the man been taking pictures?
2. Has the woman been standing completely still?
3. How long has she been standing there?
4. Why is she wet?
5. How long has she been performing as a living statue?
6. What has she been studying?
7. What has she been trying to do?

5 PRONUNCIATION

🔘 1.15 Listen and repeat.

/b/ bear	/p/ pair
back	pack
bowl	pole
bulb	pulp
cab	cap
symbol	simple

Now listen and write the words you hear.

Extension Think of five other words for each sound and write two lists. Read words from each list to another student, who writes them under *bear* or *pair*.

6 ROLE-PLAY

Act out an interview between a journalist and a celebrity (real or imaginary). At each stage of the interview, the journalist asks follow-up questions using the present perfect progressive and writes down the celebrity's answers.

Journalist
- Ask what the celebrity has been doing recently.
- Ask what else he/she has been doing.
- Ask about his/her home and family.
- Ask about his/her relationships.
- Thank the celebrity for talking to you.

Celebrity
- Talk about your recent work.
- Talk about leisure activities.
- Reply.
- Reply.

— What have you been doing recently?
— I've been working on a new movie.

Now change roles.

7 WRITING

Write an article about the celebrity you interviewed using the present perfect progressive.

The famous actor Carol Charisma has been working hard recently. She's been making a movie for six months, and she's been rehearsing a new play since last week.

LANGUAGE WORKOUT

Complete.

Present perfect progressive
Since 1992, I've _____ _____ a series of drawings and prints of birds.
For many years, Chris Ofili _____ _____ _____ elephant dung in his paintings.
How long _____ Antony Gormley _____ _____ sculptures?

We can use the present perfect progressive with *for* and *since* to talk about a continuous or repeated activity that started in the past and continues up to now.
We can also use this tense to talk about recently completed continuous actions that have present results:
I can tell she's been crying. (Her eyes are red.)

▶ Answers and Practice
Language File page 113

2 CREATIVITY

2 I've been hoping ...

Talking about recent events
Present perfect: simple and progressive

An EXTRAordinary job!

Believe it or not, a very popular temporary job is being a movie extra. So what's it like, and how do you find work? You start at 6 or 7 a.m. and work a nine- or ten-hour day. But most of the time is spent waiting for things to happen, so be prepared to feel cold, hungry, and bored! Listen carefully to any instructions about how to move or look because there may be several "takes" for each scene, and you will have to do exactly the same thing each time. You may catch sight of some stars—but no autographs or photographs! To get work, you need to join a casting agency, which will charge about 15% of the $150 or so a day you are paid. And there are more extras than jobs—many extras only work a few days a month or even a year. But in what other job can you work with a big Hollywood star and see yourself on screen in a feature film a year later?

The Extras Web Forum

Topic: How much work have you had this year?

I've only had two jobs so far and they were both commercials. There doesn't seem to be much work right now. Last year, my first job was in February—a movie about soccer. Freezing! What's it been like for others?

Dan   17:44

I've been working on the new Bond movie this week. It's good money, but there's a lot of hanging around, as usual. We're on location today, and we've been waiting for them to start for almost six hours. They've been trying to get the lighting right, but every time they do, it starts raining!

Frank   19:15

It does seem quiet. I've been calling the agency first thing every morning, but haven't had any work. Last year was very different—my best job was doubling for Penelope Cruz, so I had to kiss Daniel Craig, which was rather nice. 😊😊😊

Anastasia   20:11

I've been hoping to get something since I joined the agency four months ago. But no luck yet.

Jon   23:50

That's odd! My phone's been ringing nonstop all week (not when I'm on set, of course!) and I've had plenty of job offers. But some of the work has been rather badly paid.

Brooke   04:18

1 OPENER

Have you ever wanted to be in a movie or on TV? One way is to become an "extra"—someone you see in the background in a movie. What do you think life is like as an extra?

2 READING

🔊 1.16 Read the texts. What are the two most interesting facts in them?

UNIT 2

5 PRONUNCIATION

🔴 1.17 Listen and check your answers to exercise 4. Repeat the words and mark the stress.

6 SPEAKING

Make lists of five things you've always wanted to do and have done this year, and of five things you've been looking forward to doing but haven't done yet. Think about:

> activities to do   books to read
> movies to see   places to visit   food to try
> things to get   people to meet
> skills to learn   things to do better

Compare your lists with another student and discuss them.

> I've always wanted to get up early and watch the sun rise, and I did it last Sunday.

> I've been meaning to do that too—what time did you get up?

3 AFTER READING

Complete the questions with *How*, *What*, *When*, *Where*, or *Who*. Then answer the questions.

1 _____ do extras usually begin work?
2 _____ has Anastasia been doing every morning?
3 _____ hasn't had a job yet this year?
4 _____ enjoyed a screen kiss?
5 _____ was Dan's first job last year?
6 _____ is surprised that others haven't had much work?
7 _____ is Frank working today?
8 _____ has had lots of offers of work?
9 _____ has been working on a spy movie?
10 _____ much are extras paid?
11 _____ have people been calling a lot this week?
12 _____ do you get a job as an extra?

Your response What do you think is the most interesting/boring part of being an extra? Why?

7 WRITING

Look at the lists you made in exercise 6. Write a paragraph comparing your lists with another student's, using some of these words and phrases.

> We have both …   We both want to …
> So have/do I.   on the other hand
> but   however

LANGUAGE WORKOUT

Complete.

Present perfect: simple and progressive
Some of the work _____ _____ rather badly paid.
I _____ only _____ two jobs so far.
The simple present perfect is used to describe a completed action or series of actions.

I _____ _____ _____ on the new Bond movie.
I _____ _____ _____ the agency every morning.
The present perfect progressive is used to describe an action that continues up to now. It is also used for a repeated series of actions.

We use the simple present perfect to focus on *how many*.
I _____ _____ plenty of job offers.
We use the present perfect progressive to focus on *how long* when talking about continuous temporary activities.
My phone _____ _____ _____ all week.

▶ Answers and Practice
Language File page 113

4 VOCABULARY

Find these words and phrases in the lesson, and match them with their definitions.

Word Bank Movie making

agency   commercial *n*   double *v*   feature film
on location   on screen   on set   take *n*

1 section of a movie that is recorded without stopping
2 in a movie or on TV
3 act in the place of another actor in a movie
4 business that helps people find work
5 where a movie is shot, often in a studio
6 advertisement on film
7 where a movie is shot, not in a studio
8 full-length movie

Extension Use words and phrases from the Word Bank to write five sentences giving your own opinions.

The funniest TV commercial is …

25

2.3 CREATIVITY
She had been reading a book

Talking about a sequence of past events
Past perfect: simple and progressive

FRANKENSTEIN

Everyone has heard of *Frankenstein*, the story of the scientist who created a monster. But did you know that the author Mary Shelley wrote this bestselling story when she was a teenager?

In 1816, when Mary was 18, she and the poet Percy Bysshe Shelley spent the summer with friends near Lake Geneva in Switzerland. But there had been a massive volcanic eruption in Indonesia the previous year, and the summer of 1816 was extremely gray, cold, and wet. The friends were trapped inside the house, and, one day in June, they each agreed to make up a horror story to entertain themselves.

Mary had enjoyed writing stories as a child. She had been thinking about her horror story for some time, when she had an extraordinary dream. It was about a scientist who created a human being, but then he realized that he hadn't made a man, he had produced a monster. And so the idea for *Frankenstein* was born. Mary said later that in the summer of 1816 she had "stepped out from childhood into life." She completed *Frankenstein* in 1817, and it was published the following year.

Just before Mary started writing *Frankenstein*, she had been reading a book about chemistry. She and her friends had also been discussing the work of the scientist Luigi Galvani, who had investigated the effect of electricity on dead animals.

In Mary's story, a Swiss scientist named Victor Frankenstein used parts of dead bodies to construct a giant man. The man came to life, but he was incredibly ugly. Frankenstein was horrified by the creature that he had made, and he abandoned him. The monster tried to interact with people, but everyone was terrified of him and he was very lonely. He blamed his creator for making him so ugly, and he killed Frankenstein's brother, his best friend, and his wife. So Frankenstein decided he must destroy his creation, and he followed the monster to the ice and snow of the Arctic, where they both died.

Frankenstein warns of the dangers of creating artificial life, and it's often described as the first science-fiction novel. And Mary Shelley's famous story, written 200 years ago, has inspired over 50 movies, as well as plays, TV shows, and comics.

1 OPENER
Which of these words do you expect to find in the text?

author   bestselling   cardboard
horror story   monster
novel   plastic   poet
science-fiction   vitamin

2 READING
1.18 Read the text. What was the inspiration for *Frankenstein*?

3 AFTER READING
True, false, or no information? Correct the false sentences.

1 Mary Shelley was in Switzerland in the summer of 1816.
2 The weather was bad because there had been a volcanic eruption that year.
3 Mary had never written anything before.
4 She had a dream that gave her the idea for *Frankenstein*.
5 She started writing *Frankenstein* in July 1816.
6 Before she started writing, she had been reading a book about electricity.
7 Her story was about a monster named Frankenstein.
8 Frankenstein used electricity to bring his creature to life.
9 Frankenstein was proud of the monster that he had made.
10 The monster killed members of Frankenstein's family.

Your response Do you think scientists should try to create artificial life? What are the dangers?

UNIT 2

4 PRONUNCIATION

Count the syllables and mark the stress.

> abandon   artificial   author   chemistry
> childhood   electricity   eruption   horrified
> inspire   interact   investigate   previous   terrified

■ *abandon 3*

🔴 1.19 Now listen and check. Repeat the words.

5 SPEAKING

Look at the picture. Say *what had been happening* before the girl's boyfriend arrived at the coffee shop. Talk about the girl, her boyfriend, the artist, and the waiter using these verbs.

> do   draw   drink   eat   look
> read   run   shop   wait   wash

The girl had been reading a book.

Extension Write three true and two false sentences about what had been happening in the coffee shop before the boyfriend arrived. Read your sentences to another student, who covers the picture and says whether each sentence is true or false.

6 LISTENING

🔴 1.20 Listen to a short biography of another bestselling author and complete the information in the chart.

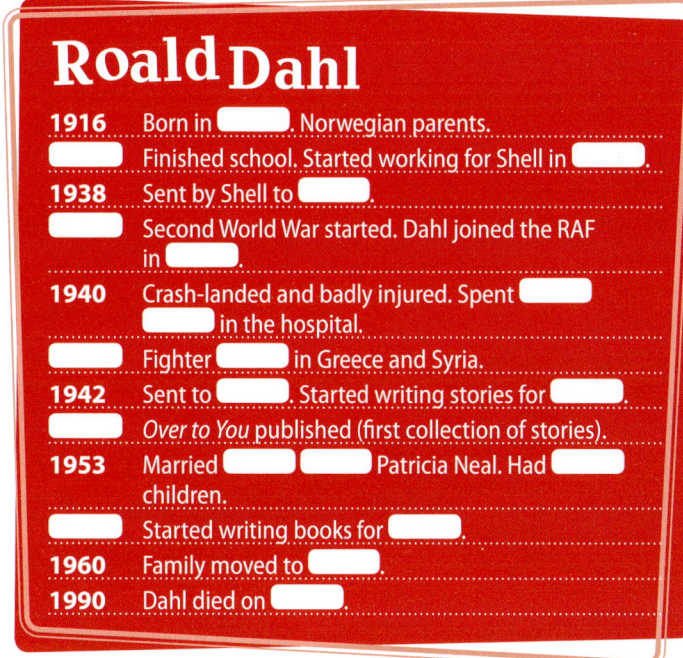

Roald Dahl

1916	Born in ____. Norwegian parents.
____	Finished school. Started working for Shell in ____.
1938	Sent by Shell to ____.
____	Second World War started. Dahl joined the RAF in ____.
1940	Crash-landed and badly injured. Spent ____ in the hospital.
____	Fighter ____ in Greece and Syria.
1942	Sent to ____. Started writing stories for ____
____	*Over to You* published (first collection of stories).
1953	Married ____ Patricia Neal. Had ____ children.
____	Started writing books for ____.
1960	Family moved to ____.
1990	Dahl died on ____.

Now check your answers. Use the simple past perfect and past perfect progressive to link events.

> Dahl was born in Wales in 1916.

> After he'd finished school in 1934, he started working for Shell …

7 WRITING

Find out information about another popular author. Write notes about the author's life, similar to the chart in exercise 6. Then write two or three paragraphs about him/her using the text in exercise 2 to help you.

J. K. Rowling, author of the bestselling Harry Potter books, was born in …

LANGUAGE WORKOUT

Complete.

Past perfect: simple and progressive

| Simple past perfect | Simple past | NOW |

Past perfect progressive -------→

Frankenstein **was** horrified by the creature that he **had made**. He _____ (realize) that he _____ n't _____ (make) a man, he _____ _____ (produce) a monster.
She _____ _____ _____ (think) about her story for some time, when she _____ (have) a dream.
Before Mary _____ (start) writing *Frankenstein*, she _____ _____ _____ (read) a book about chemistry.

We use the simple past perfect to describe the earlier of two past events. We use the _____ _____ _____ to talk about a continuous or repeated earlier activity.

▶ Answers and Practice
Language File pages 113–114

2.4 CREATIVITY
Integrated Skills
Telling a folk tale

The Professor and the Wise Ferryman—
an Indian folk tale

1 OPENER

Every country has folk tales—stories that children often hear from their parents. For example, the Swiss story of William Tell, his son, and the apple is told in many countries. What folk tales are there in your country?

READING

2 Read and complete the text with phrases a–i.

a which he had never learned
b and so had his grandfather before him
c and well-polished shoes
d so I haven't learned any history
e but couldn't understand why people chose to live there
f the countries, mountains, and rivers
g and think about things
h and had been doing it ever since
i and got the same answer

Which words in the phrases helped you to complete the text?

3 Find the highlighted words in the text to match these definitions. The parts of speech in *italics* refer to the highlighted words in the text.

1 important college teacher *n*
2 hurrying, moving very quickly *v*
3 great surprise *n*
4 almost not *adv*
5 with a bright surface *adj*
6 complained *v*

There was once an old ferryman who lived in a hut by the River Ganges in India. For as long as anyone could remember, his family had rowed people across the river. His father had been a ferryman __1__.

Like all the people from his village, the ferryman was poor. The money he made from the ferry was hardly enough to feed his family. He had taken over the job when he was a young boy __2__. Although life was hard, he never grumbled and was pleased to help his passengers.

The ferryman had learned a lot about life by listening to his passengers. He had heard about life in the city, __3__. It seemed to him that city people spent all their lives rushing around with no time to think. The ferryman rowed slowly and was in no hurry. He had time to talk __4__. People said that he was wise and often asked his advice.

One day a well-dressed professor from the city with a shiny briefcase climbed into his boat. He was wearing a nice suit __5__. Slowly the ferryman began to row his passenger across the river. After a while, the professor spoke.

"Have you studied any history?" he asked.

"No, sir," said the ferryman.

"What!" said the professor in surprise. "You haven't studied history? Aren't you proud of your country? Why don't you know any history?"

"Well, sir," the ferryman replied, "I've never been to school. I've been rowing people across the river all my life, __6__."

"There's no excuse for not learning," said the professor. "And I suppose you haven't studied geography either."

"No, sir," the ferryman replied.

"Geography tells us about the world," the professor said almost angrily. "Don't you know anything about the world—__7__?"

"I haven't been to school, sir," the ferryman replied. "I don't know anything about these things."

After a few minutes, the professor asked if the ferryman had studied science, __8__. "You've studied neither geography nor history, and you haven't heard about science!" he shouted in amazement. "Scientists are the most important people in the world today. Look at me. I'm a professor of science. Do you see my briefcase? It's full of important books and papers. If you don't know about science, you don't know about the world. You have learned nothing! And if you don't know anything, you might as well be dead."

The ferryman looked sad. No one had ever spoken to him like this before. He felt terrible. There was so much knowledge hidden in books __9__.

28

4 Linking words: *neither ... nor*

Find an example of *neither ... nor* in *The Professor and the Wise Ferryman*. Rewrite these sentences using *neither ... nor*.

1. The ferryman didn't have a suit or a briefcase.
2. The ferryman hadn't been to school or college.
3. The ferryman hadn't studied history or science.
4. The ferryman and the professor didn't know what was going to happen next.

5 Answer the questions.

1. What do we know about the ferryman and the professor?
2. What reasons did the professor give for learning history, geography, and science? Do you agree?
3. Do you think the ferryman really knew nothing about history, geography, and science? Why/Why not?
4. What do you think will happen next?

6 LISTENING

🔘 1.21 Listen to the end of the story and see if you were right. Answer the questions.

1. What happened to the ferryman and the professor?
2. Does the story have a message? What can we learn from it?

7 SPEAKING

Discuss these questions.

1. Is what you learn in school more important than what you learn out of school? Why/Why not?
2. Which school subjects are the most and least important to you?
3. Some people are said to know a lot, and some are said to be wise. What do you need to know to be wise? What does "wise" mean?

8 GUIDED WRITING

Write a folk tale from your country, using past tenses with time phrases and adverbs to show the sequence of events.

> **Time phrases and adverbs**
> There was once ...   One day ...   In the end ...   after
> as soon as   before   finally   later   then   until   when   while

Now tell other students your tale and say what its message is.

LEARNER INDEPENDENCE

9 Thinking skills: Complete this chart each week to help you think about your learning.

This week the classes were about:
What I learned was:
This week I used my English to:
This week I read these things in English:
This week I made these mistakes when writing:
A problem for me right now is:
I would like to be able to:
Next week I plan to:

10 Word creation: Add the suffix *-ment* to these verbs and use five of them to complete the sentences.

> advertise   amaze   argue   arrange
> equip   move   pay   treat

1. To her _____, she got a job as an extra.
2. I don't want to have an _____, so let's agree to disagree.
3. The agency took 15% of the _____ she received for the work.
4. He was an extra in a TV _____ for a new car.
5. As an artist, he's interested in _____ and light.

11 🔘 1.22 **Phrasebook:** Find these useful expressions in Unit 2. Then listen and repeat.

> It's a complete waste of money!
> Believe it or not ...
> So what's it like?
> No luck yet.
> That's odd!
> after a while
> There's no excuse for ...
> You might as well ...

Which expression means ...?

1. That's strange.
2. some time later
3. It's surprising, but true.
4. I'm still waiting for something to happen.

2 CREATIVITY
Inspired EXTRA!

PROJECT Group magazine

1 Work in a group and make a list of articles about creative subjects that you could contribute to a magazine. For example, articles about interesting people (based on real interviews with people in your school or town, or imaginary interviews with famous people), reviews giving your personal opinion of the best and worst new movies, TV shows, books, concerts, music, etc. Then choose two or three people or topics to write about. You can also include the celebrity interview article you wrote in Lesson 1, the biography of a popular author from Lesson 3, and the folk tale from Lesson 4.

2 Research: Find information for your articles from newspapers, magazines, and the Internet, and take notes:

> **Article about a person**
> - Why do you think the person is interesting?
> - What has he/she done recently?
> - What do you think readers would like to know about the person?
>
> **Review**
> - Describe the movie, TV show, book, CD, etc.
> - What is your personal opinion of it? Would you recommend it to readers? Why/Why not?

Teacher's secret

Everyone knows Ms. Jones (Pam is her first name) as our P.E. teacher and the coach of the school basketball team. But she has a secret. A big secret.

What is it? She's a downhill ski champion. That's right—she loves the fastest and most dangerous kind of ski racing. She has recently been competing in Canada and won her event. "It was great," she told us. "Lots of ice, so it was really bumpy and fast!"

She has even done skiing stunts in movies! So next time you watch skiing on TV or in a movie, look out for Ms. Jones—you may see her on the screen!

3 Work together and write the articles. Read them carefully and correct any mistakes. Find photos from magazines, newspapers, and the internet to illustrate them. Show your magazine articles to other groups, and put them all together make a group magazine.

Game Alibi

Last night, some time between 6 and 10 p.m., a valuable painting was stolen from an art gallery in your town. Police detectives want to interview two suspects who were together yesterday evening.

- Choose two suspects, A and B. The rest of the class are detectives. Look at the notes in the boxes on the right and prepare your roles.
- Suspect B leaves the room. The detectives ask Suspect A questions and write down the answers.
- Then Suspect B returns and the detectives ask the same questions.
- Do the suspects' stories match? The detectives decide whether they are innocent or guilty!

Suspects A and B
You were together from 6 to 10 p.m. last night. The detectives are going to ask you questions about your activities.
Where did you go? What did you do? And after that?
Work together to prepare your alibi in detail.

Detectives
Prepare questions to ask the suspects about what they did last night: ask about places, times, and sequence of events.
Where did you go? What time did you …?
What did you do after you'd …?

UNIT 2

CONSOLIDATION

LESSON 1 Write sentences about yourself using the present perfect progressive with *for* and *since*. Use these phrases to help you.

> learn English   come to this school
> use this book   play (*sports*)   watch (*TV series*)

My favorite sport is basketball. I've been playing basketball for …

LESSON 2 Look at exercise 6 on page 25. Write sentences about things you've done this year, and about things you haven't done yet.

I've seen several movies, but I haven't seen the latest James Bond movie yet.

LESSON 3 Look at your completed chart about Roald Dahl in exercise 6 on page 27 and write a paragraph about his life.

Roald Dahl was born in …

EXTENSION

LESSON 1 Read the paragraphs about artists in exercise 2 on page 22 again. Now find out information about another living artist and write a similar paragraph about his/her work.

LESSON 2 Look at the *Extras Web Forum* in exercise 2 on page 24 again. Imagine you are a movie extra. Write a posting to the forum saying what you have been doing this week.

LESSON 3 Answer these questions using the past perfect progressive. Use your imagination!
1. Why did the police stop the motorcyclist?
2. Why did the man have a black eye?
3. Why was the girl crying?
4. Why was everything white outside?
5. Why were the boys' clothes dirty?
6. Why was the woman angry with her boyfriend?

1 *Because he'd been speeding.*

YOUR CHOICE!

CONSTRUCTION   Past perfect: simple or progressive?

Complete with the correct form of the verbs, using the past perfect progressive where possible.

Superman's first movie appearance was in an animated cartoon series in 1941, but he __1__ (rescue) people for several years before that. The character __2__ (first appear) in comics in 1938. Superman, who __3__ (arrive) on Earth as a baby from the planet Krypton, was created by writer Jerry Siegel and artist Joe Shuster. They __4__ (come) up with the idea in 1933, but it __5__ (take) them five years to sell the story of their superhero.

Superman __6__ (not be) around for long when Batman appeared in 1939. By the end of 1952, Batman and Superman __7__ (meet) each other in a Superman comic story. The two superheroes __8__ (live) separate lives, but now they regularly worked together in a series of adventures.

REFLECTION   Present perfect progressive

Match the examples a–f with language functions 1–3.
The present perfect progressive is used to talk about …
1. a continuous or repeated activity that started in the past and is still continuing
2. a continuous or repeated activity that started in the past and has just finished
3. a completed continuous activity that has present results

a. There you are at last! I've been waiting for ages.
b. We've been living here for 10 years.
c. Her hair is wet because she's been swimming.
d. I can't concentrate with this noise—they've been playing loud music all night.
e. He's been singing so loudly that he's lost his voice!
f. It's been raining since I woke up this morning.

ACTION   Freeze frame game

- Work in a small group.
- You are in a movie on video/DVD. Take turns performing an activity, but don't say what it is. After 5–10 seconds, someone says "Pause!" and you're caught in a freeze frame.
- The rest of the group asks Yes/No questions to find out what you've been doing.
  A Have you been riding a motorcycle?
  B Have you been driving a car?

INTERACTION   It means a lot to me

- Work in a small group.
- Think about a favorite possession that means a lot to you. What's special about it? How long have you had it? How did you feel when you got it?
- Take turns asking and answering questions about each other's favorite possessions.
  A How long have you had your guitar?
  B Who gave it to you?

REVIEW
UNITS 1–2

1 Read and complete. For each number 1–12, choose word or phrase A, B, or C.

Teenage Stunt Driver

Hans __1__ like an ordinary 19-year-old with his mind on sports and studies. But his life is much more exciting than that—he's a movie stunt driver. When directors __2__ a teenage look-alike for one of their stars, they turn to Hans, whose skills also __3__ scuba diving. He __4__ make great movies for years now. "Cars and movies," he says, " __5__ the most important parts of my life."

Hans __6__ cars since he was 12—off the road of course. By the time he got his driver's license, he __7__ driving for five years and __8__ a reputation as a teenage daredevil. "I really enjoy __9__ dangerous stunts," says Hans. "There's nothing I don't want __10__ . I remember __11__ 12 hours a day to learn how to get things right." He smiles. " __12__ fast cars is what my life is about."

1	A looks	B is looking	C was looking
2	A need	B needs	C are needing
3	A includes	B include	C has included
4	A helped	B has been helping	C was helping
5	A are always	B were always	C have always been
6	A drives	B has been driving	C drove
7	A was	B has been	C had been
8	A has	B had	C has had
9	A does	B to do	C doing
10	A to try	B try	C trying
11	A practice	B practicing	C to practice
12	A Drive	B To drive	C Driving

2 Write sentences using the infinitive or gerund of the verbs.

1. I enjoyed (apply) for jobs as a movie extra, but didn't dare (hope) that I would get one.
2. I remember (get) the e-mail asking me to a screen test. Of course I agreed (go).
3. I tried not (look) nervous during the screen test and managed (stay) calm.
4. I can't stand (be) disappointed and really didn't expect (get) the job. But I did.
5. I'll never forget (arrive) at the studio the next day—Zac Efron was there!
6. I pretended not (see) him, but it was no use.
7. The director said he wanted me (double) the role of Zac's co-star in a love scene. Half of me wanted to refuse (do) it—the other half wanted (see) what it would be like.
8. However, I dislike (be) looked at, so I decided (say) no. That was the end of my job as an extra!

3 Complete with the present perfect progressive of these verbs, and *for* or *since*.

collect   consider   get   talk   use   visit   walk

A visitor to a museum has smashed three hugely valuable Chinese vases. The 300-year-old vases had stood in a window on a staircase __1__ over 20 years. Nick Flynn, 42, slipped on the stairs and fell onto the vases. __2__ the accident happened, the museum __3__ the thousands of small pieces. They __4__ a digital camera to photograph the pieces, and they __5__ to experts about repairing the vases. Mr. Flynn was unhurt but angry when he got a letter from the museum asking him not to go there "in the near future." "I __6__ the museum __7__ years," said Mr. Flynn. "It's not my fault that I slipped." The museum says Mr. Flynn misunderstood the letter. "We __8__ lots of calls __9__ the accident from journalists asking for his name—we wanted to protect him," the museum director said. "It was just an accident. People __10__ past those vases __11__ many years and this has never happened before. But __12__ the accident, we __13__ how best to display the vases when they are repaired."

4 Complete with the simple present perfect or present perfect progressive of these verbs.

answer   develop   get   give   let
ring   sell   show   start   win   work

Masa Tateno, 30, the exciting Japanese artist, __1__ his work for over ten years now, but in the last year his paintings __2__ to attract international attention. "I __3__ my own style since I left art school," he says. "Now that I __4__ a few prizes, people are beginning to notice me. Also I __5__ several paintings recently, which __6__ me confidence." Tateno appeared on TV worldwide last month, and since then, he __7__ lots of media attention. "It's hard," he says. "Lots of times I __8__ on a picture when the phone __9__ . Sometimes I __10__ it, and other times I __11__ it ring!"

5 Complete with the simple past perfect or past perfect progressive of the verbs.

Many years ago in Greece there was a painting competition. The judge, who in the past __1__ (be) the best artist in the country, told two artists to paint a picture that was as true to life as possible in three months. The artists returned when they __2__ (finish) their pictures, each of which was covered with a curtain. The judge __3__ (invite) a large crowd, which __4__ (arrive) early in the morning. By noon they __5__ (wait) for several hours when the first painter pulled back his curtain. The picture was of a bunch of grapes and was so beautiful and lifelike that some birds that __6__ (fly) past tried to eat the grapes. Then the judge asked the other painter to pull his curtain back. But the second painter did nothing. The crowd and the judge were impatient because they __7__ (wait) for three months. So the judge tried to pull the curtain. But he couldn't. "There is no curtain here," he said to the crowd. "It is a painting of a curtain." One painting __8__ (fool) the birds and the other __9__ (fool) the people. Which painting did the judge choose? The second one. The crowd cheered because they __10__ (find) out who was the best painter. Or had they?

VOCABULARY

6 Complete with the correct words.

ball/bowl   chop/shop   clouds/crowds
cream/crime   diet/doubt   leaves/lives
math/myth   needles/noodles   poor/power
scenes/screens   sneeze/snooze   taste/toast

1 She was very tired, so she had a quick _____.
2 Mix all the salad ingredients in a large _____.
3 A Greek _____ is a story about gods and heroes.
4 The movie theater is huge—it has 12 _____.
5 The ferryman was _____ because he earned hardly any money.
6 In acupuncture, special _____ are inserted into parts of the body.
7 It was a holiday and there were _____ of people in the street.
8 People often lose weight when they're on a _____.
9 First _____ the onions and then fry them.
10 Firefighters regularly save people's _____.
11 Some people like _____ in their coffee but I prefer milk.
12 You need bread if you're going to make _____.

7 Match the verbs in list A with the words and phrases in list B. Then write sentences using four of the expressions.

A	B
1 beat	a cell phone
2 catch	with cheese
3 charge	the eggs
4 come	vitamins
5 react	up with an idea
6 skip	sight of something
7 sprinkle	a meal
8 take	to pain

8 Match these words with their definitions.

domestic   gang   grater   heritage
margarine   mineral   struggle   tribute

1 yellow substance that looks like butter
2 natural substance in food or in the earth, e.g., iron
3 try very hard to do something difficult
4 something that cuts food into very small pieces
5 important art, buildings, and beliefs from the past
6 something you do to show you respect someone
7 about people's homes and family life

9 Find the word that's different.

1 dried   fresh   frozen   canned
2 mineral   juice   protein   vitamin
3 consist   feel   smell   taste
4 boil   roast   cook   fry
5 fake   false   natural   synthetic
6 agency   commercial   feature film   TV series
7 bronze   gold   iron   wood
8 comic   horror story   folk tale   myth

LEARNER INDEPENDENCE
SELF ASSESSMENT

Look back at Lessons 1–3 in Units 1 and 2.

How good are you at …?	✓Fine	? Not sure
1 Talking about food and drink Workbook pp2–3 exercises 1 and 4–6	☐	☐
2 Describing objects and saying what they're for Workbook p5 exercises 4 and 6	☐	☐
3 Describing a sequence of events Workbook p5 exercise 5	☐	☐
4 Talking about illness and medicine Workbook pp6–7 exercises 1, 2, 4–6, and 9	☐	☐
5 Talking about activities that continue up to now Workbook p14 exercise 2	☐	☐
6 Talking about recent events Workbook pp16–17 exercises 1–3	☐	☐
7 Talking about a sequence of past events Workbook pp18–19 exercises 1–3	☐	☐

Not sure? Take a look at Language File pages 112–114 and do the Workbook exercise(s) again.

Now write an example for 1–7.

1 Margarine and butter contain fat.

PREVIEW

UNITS 3–4

COMMUNICATIVE AIMS
LEARNING HOW TO …

1. Describe and compare the way things happen
2. Make exclamations
3. Express result
4. Talk about future events, schedules, arrangements, and plans
5. Discuss possible future lifestyles
6. Talk about future possibility
7. Talk about imaginary or unlikely situations
8. Express wishes about the present

TOPICS AND VOCABULARY

Science

The world under the ocean

Adjectives

Space flight and tourism

Phrasal verbs with *down*, *on*, and *off*

Medicine

Navigation

Technology

Phrasal verbs with *out*

Global warming

Tourism and travel

Politics

A I wish I could take all my friends.

B

The Earth rotates most quickly at the Equator, more slowly in Paris and London, and doesn't rotate at all at the North or South Pole.

1. Match five of the communicative aims (1–8) with the pictures (A–E).

2. Put the words into categories. There are three extra words that don't fit into the categories.

   Space flight | Medicine | Politics

author   spacecraft   protestor   germs   astronaut   infectious   demonstration   satellite   rabbit   politician   media   vote   pulse   democracy   weightlessness   planet   orbit   statue   bacteria   vaccination   disease

C

People will be living longer and retiring later.

D

I'm flying to Florida today and I'm visiting the Kennedy Space Center tomorrow.

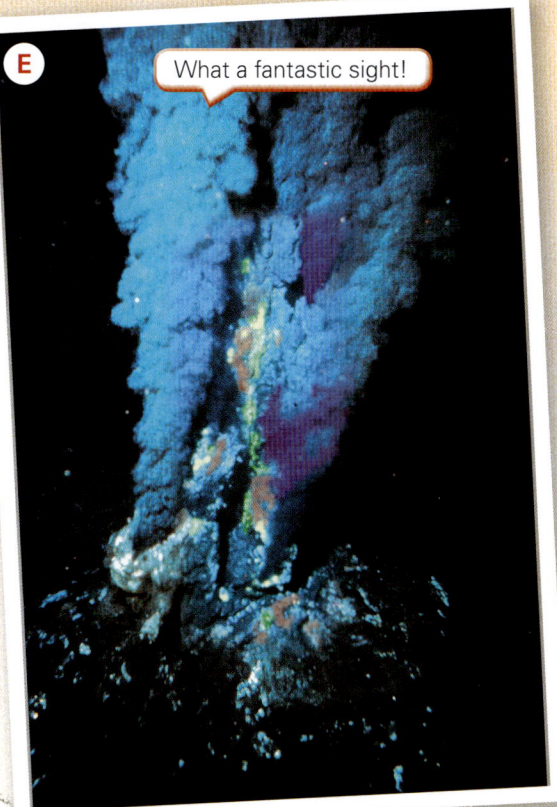

E

What a fantastic sight!

3 🎧 1.23 Listen to extracts 1–3 from Units 3 and 4. Match them with three of the text types A–D.

A A description of an invention
B A debate about political protest
C An interview about travel
D A blog about research under the ocean

4 Do the *Time and Age Survey* with three other students.

TIME AND AGE SURVEY

1 Is it true that time passes more quickly when you're enjoying yourself? Can you think of an example?

2 If you could travel in time, when and where would you go?

3 Would you like to speed up or slow down time?

4 "I'm looking forward to being (*age*)." Say how old and why.

5 "Your schooldays are the happiest days of your life." Do you agree?

6 If someone offered you medicine that would make you live forever, would you take it? Why/Why not?

What interesting or surprising things did you find out? Tell another group.

Believe it or not! Astronauts grow taller in space. After one month in space, they can be up to five centimeters taller. Their spines get longer because there is no gravity. But guess what happens when they return to Earth!

35

3

1 SCIENCE AND DISCOVERY

Light travels incredibly fast

Describing and comparing the way things happen
Comparison of adverbs
Adverbs of degree
Position and order of adverbial phrases

1 OPENER

Have you heard of the Big Bang? What was it and when did it happen?

2 READING

Read and answer the quiz.

3 AFTER READING

▶ 1.24 Read *What on Earth?* and check your answers to the quiz. How well did you do?

Your response Which of the facts in *What on Earth?* do you find the most amazing? Why?

QUIZ How much do you know about the world you live in?

1	Approximately how old is the universe?	A 13.7 million years.	B 13.7 billion years.
2	Which travels faster?	A Light.	B Lightning.
3	When did life on Earth begin?	A Four billion years ago.	B Four million years ago.
4	Which began later?	A Life in the ocean.	B Life on land.
5	Which distance is farther?	A From New York to Moscow.	B From the surface to the center of the Earth.
6	Where does the Earth rotate most quickly?	A At the Equator.	B At the North Pole.
7	Which contains a higher percentage of water?	A A human.	B A potato.

What on Earth?

Scientists disagree about exactly when the Big Bang, which created the universe, happened. But we know that it was between ten and twenty billion years ago. The universe has been expanding extremely rapidly ever since, and is billions and billions of kilometers across. We can also measure distances in space in light years, the distance traveled in one year at the speed of light. And light travels incredibly fast! The speed of light is an amazing 300,000 kilometers a second. Lightning also travels really quickly and can heat the air around it to 28,000°C. But it travels more slowly than light, up to 150,000 kilometers a second.

The Earth itself is four and a half billion years old, and scientists believe that life began suddenly in the ocean soon after that. Life developed extremely slowly after this quick start. It was only four hundred million years ago that organisms began to breathe oxygen and live on land. People believe that apes started to walk on two feet between three and seven million years ago. However, we can say more accurately that the first humans appeared on Earth two million years ago.

It's believed that the Earth weighs an astonishing six billion trillion tonnes. And at 6,380 kilometers, the distance from the surface of the Earth to the center is almost as far as from New York to Moscow. The Earth rotates most quickly at 1,675 kilometers an hour at the Equator, more slowly at about 900 kilometers an hour in Paris and London, and doesn't rotate at all at the North or South Pole.

Maybe we ought to call our planet "Water," because most of its surface is ocean. And animals and plants are largely made up of water—a tomato is 95% water, a potato 80%, and a human 65%.

UNIT 3

4 LISTENING

🔊 1.25 Listen and complete the text.

SPACEFLIGHT RECORDS

- The three astronauts who have been in space longest are all Russian: Sergei Krikalev, with a total of _____ days, Sergei Avdeyev, 747 days, and Valeri Polyakov, _____ days.
- The two astronauts who have flown most often (_____ flights each) are Franklin Chang-Díaz and Jerry L. Ross, both from the U.S.
- The first two spacewalks took place in 1965. In March, Alexei Leonov left his spacecraft for _____ minutes, and in June, Edward White did the same for _____ minutes.
- The first moonwalk was from Apollo 11 on July 21, 1969, when Neil Armstrong and Buzz Aldrin walked on the surface of the Moon for _____ hours, 31 minutes, and 40 seconds. Soon after, on November 19, 1969, Pete Conrad and Alan Bean left their spacecraft, Apollo 12, for a walk that lasted _____ hours, 56 minutes, and three seconds.

Now make sentences comparing the astronauts.

- … was in space longest.
- Krikalev flew in space longer than …
- … have made the most space flights.
- Conrad and Bean walked on the Moon longer than …

5 PRONUNCIATION

🔊 1.26 Listen and repeat.

13.7 billion years   four and a half billion years
300,000 kilometers a second   1,675 kilometers an hour
28,000°C   95%   six billion trillion tonnes
two hours, 31 minutes, and 40 seconds

6 SPEAKING

Ask three other students these questions and write down their answers.

- How fast can you say the alphabet backward in English?
- How far can you throw a tennis ball?
- How high can you reach?
- How far do you travel to school?
- How early do you get up on Saturdays?

Now make comparisons between yourself and the other students.

- Sasha can say the alphabet backward in 45 seconds. That's faster than me.
- I get up at eight on Saturdays. That's earlier than you.

Extension Write five similar questions and interview three different students.

7 WRITING

Look at your notes from exercise 6. Write a paragraph using comparative and superlative adverbs.

Helena and Monika can both reach two meters, but Robert can reach the highest.

LANGUAGE WORKOUT

Complete.

Comparison of adverbs
Lightning travels _____ slowly than light.
Which began _____: life in the ocean or on land?
Where does the Earth rotate _____ quickly?

Adverbs ending in -*ly* take *more/most*. Adverbs with the same form as adjectives add -*er*/-*est*.

Irregular forms
well	better	_____
badly	worse	worst
far	farther	farthest

Adverbs of degree
extremely incredibly pretty really very
The universe has been expanding _____ rapidly.
Lightning also travels _____ quickly.

Position and order of adverbial phrases
Life began suddenly in the ocean after that.
   Manner → Place → Time

▶Answers and Practice
Language File page 114

3 SCIENCE AND DISCOVERY

2 What a fantastic sight!

Making exclamations
Expressing result
What (a/an) …! so/such (a/an) …
Result clauses: *so/such … that*
Order of adjectives

1 OPENER

Read *Deep Sea Fact File*. Do any of the facts surprise you?

2 READING

🔊 1.27 Read scientist Petra Hardy's blog. What is so unusual about the Rainbow Vents?

DEEP SEA FACT FILE

About 97% of all the water on Earth is in the ocean and the average depth is 3.86 kilometers. But until recently what was beneath the waves was a mystery. In 1930, Charles William Beebe and Otis Barton set a world record by descending 183 meters. Beebe wrote, "As I peered down, I realized I was looking toward a world of life almost as unknown as that of Mars."

Thirty years later a two-man U.S. Navy team in the *Trieste* dived 10,916 meters to the Challenger Deep in the Mariana Trench in the western Pacific, the deepest underwater point on Earth. It was so deep that they didn't expect to see any life, but when their submersible touched the bottom, it disturbed a fish.

Greetings from a research ship in the Azores in the western Atlantic. One of science's great questions is why the ocean doesn't get saltier when millions of liters of water evaporate every day. The answer lies 2,400 meters below me on the ocean floor and I'm going down in a submersible to see it. I'm taking my laptop with me and will continue the blog underwater.

We're diving in a comfortable, spacious, modern, Russian submersible. The three of us—the pilot, myself, and another observer—are having such an amazing time as we go deeper and deeper! We're heading toward hydrothermal vents called the Rainbow Vents—they're a kind of underwater volcano.

We're over 2,000 meters down now, and everything is dark because no sunlight comes this far. Now we're near the ocean floor. The pilot puts on the submersible's lights and we can see the Rainbow Vents. What a fantastic sight! It's so unexpected! The bottom is covered with "chimneys" up to 20 meters high, and from the chimneys comes black, white, and clear water. The chimneys themselves are yellow, red, orange, green, blue, and black—you can see why they are named rainbows.

The most incredible thing is that the water from the chimneys is at a temperature of 400°C, while the rest of the water down here is only 1°C. People had thought that the water was so cold that nothing could live at this depth. But thousands of shrimp, crabs, mussels, and fish live around the chimneys. There are so many different kinds that I can't count them. I've just seen a beautiful, small, flat, blue fish and I'm sure it's a new species.

What does this have to do with salt? Well, there are hydrothermal vents all over the world where new rock has pushed up the ocean floor. Water goes slowly down through tiny cracks in the ocean floor. Then, a kilometer below the ocean floor, the water meets molten rock, is heated, and comes back up again. During this process, the salt is removed. It's not quick though—it can take ten million years. And, until 1977, no one knew that hydrothermal vents existed! What a discovery!

Today, I've seen the vents for myself, and after ten hours we're returning to the surface. It's been such an exciting dive that I haven't noticed the time. But now I'm starting to get hungry!

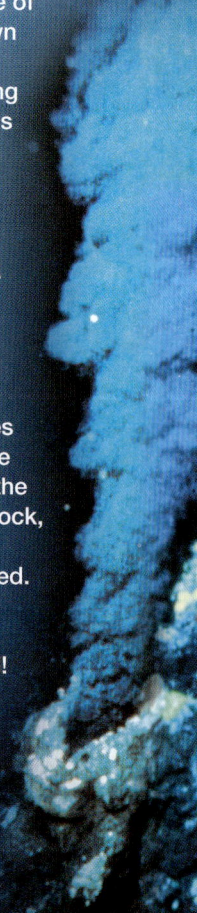

3 AFTER READING

Complete the questions with *What, When, Where, How,* or *How many.* Then match the questions with the answers.

1 _____ is the research ship?
2 _____ is one of science's greatest questions?
3 _____ meters below the ship is the ocean floor?
4 _____ people are there in the submersible?
5 _____ did the Rainbow Vents get their name?
6 _____ temperature is the water in the chimneys?
7 _____ far below the ocean floor is the hot rock?
8 _____ is removed from the water in the hydrothermal vents?
9 _____ were hydrothermal vents first discovered?
10 _____ hours did Petra's dive last?

a 2,400.
b 10.
c 400°C.
d Salt.
e In the Azores.
f Three.
g In 1977.
h They are multicolored.
i One kilometer.
j Why doesn't the water in the ocean get saltier?

Your response Would you like to dive 2,000 meters underwater in a submersible? Why/Why not?

4 VOCABULARY

Write these adjectives under the correct headings.

Word Bank Adjectives

ancient average beautiful blue Brazilian
Chinese comfortable enormous fantastic
flat French giant green gray huge
incredible Italian long modern narrow
new old purple recent red round
Russian small spacious Spanish square
thin tiny unknown white young

Opinion	Size	Age	Shape	Color	Origin

Extension Think of something and describe it using at least three adjectives. Can other students guess what it is?

— It's a small round red fruit.
— A tomato!

5 PRONUNCIATION

🔊 1.28 Listen and repeat.

Exclamations
What a fantastic sight!
What a discovery!
It's so unexpected!
We're having such an amazing time!
It's such a high temperature!
It's been such an exciting dive!

6 SPEAKING

Write notes about real or imaginary exciting events in your life and the life of someone you know. Tell another student about the events: say what happened and what the reactions were.

— I was out shopping, and a TV crew wanted to interview me about clothes. I got so excited that I couldn't think of anything to say!

— I was with Paula when she heard that she had passed the exams. She was so happy that she cried.

7 WRITING

Use your notes from exercise 6 to write descriptions of five exciting events.

LANGUAGE WORKOUT

Complete.

What (a/an) ... so/such (a/an) ...
_____ a discovery!
The three of us are having _____ an amazing time!
It's _____ unexpected!

Result clauses: so/such ... that
It was _____ deep _____ they didn't expect to see any life.
It's been _____ an exciting dive _____ I haven't noticed the time.

Order of adjectives
I've just seen a _____ , _____ , _____ , _____ fish.
 Opinion Size Shape Color
... a _____ , _____ , _____ , _____ submersible.
 Opinion Size Age Origin

Usual Order:
Opinion → Size → Age → Shape → Color → Origin

▶ **Answers and Practice**
Language File page 114

UNIT 3

39

3 SCIENCE AND DISCOVERY

3 It won't be cheap

Talking about future events, schedules, arrangements, and plans
Future review: simple future, simple present, present progressive, and *going to*

All you ever wanted to know about ...
Space Tourism

People have been talking about space tourism ever since astronauts first landed on the Moon. Will the dream ever become reality?

Believe it or not, we're counting down to the first space tourist flight. The Virgin Galactic Spaceship Enterprise is due to take off soon, and there are rumors that Angelina Jolie and Brad Pitt are among the 370 people who have put their names down to fly.

How exciting! I'm going to make a reservation!

Hold on, it won't be cheap—each passenger will pay $200,000 for the two-hour flight.

One hundred thousand dollars an hour—that's extremely expensive!

Yes, but the space tourists will fly at three times the speed of sound, they'll experience six minutes of weightlessness, and they'll be able to look down on Earth. "Every passenger will have a spectacular view; they will have large windows and luxurious seats," says Virgin boss Sir Richard Branson, who's going to travel on the first flight with members of his family. And the vacation will include three days of preflight training at the new Spaceport America in New Mexico.

And what about people who don't have thousands of dollars?

I'm sure the cost of space flights will come down, and one day ordinary travelers will be able to go on trips into space. So maybe our grandchildren will spend their vacations on the Moon, and have honeymoons in a hotel orbiting Venus. But meanwhile, you can reserve a spaceship flight online at www.virgingalactic.com with a deposit of $20,000.

Forget it! I have to go—I'm flying to Florida today and I'm visiting the Kennedy Space Center tomorrow. The tour starts at 9:45 a.m. ...

1 OPENER

You are going to read about space tourism. Which of these words do you expect to find in the text?

astronaut   flight   helicopter
honeymoon   lightning
orbit   passenger   spaceship
speed   weightlessness

2 READING

1.29   Read the text. What is the most surprising information?

3 AFTER READING

Answer the questions.

1. What will be the highlights of the Virgin Galactic spaceship flight?
2. What else will the $200,000 fare include?
3. Who are going to be among the first passengers?
4. How will ordinary travelers be able to afford space tourism?
5. The man says "Forget it!"—what is he not going to do?

Your response Do you think you will be a space tourist one day? Why/Why not?

UNIT 3

4 LISTENING

🔊 1.30 Listen and complete the tour schedule with the times.

Now imagine you are going on the Kennedy Space Center Tour. Ask and answer questions about the schedule using the simple present.

> What time do we arrive at the Space Center?

Kennedy Space Center Tour

9:45 a.m.	Arrive at the Kennedy Space Center
_____ a.m.	See an IMAX space movie
_____ a.m.	Visit the Astronaut Hall of Fame and ride a space flight simulator
_____ p.m.	Meet an astronaut during lunch at the Space Center
_____ p.m.	Take the NASA bus tour, which stops at the International Space Station
_____ p.m.	Return to the Kennedy Space Center
_____ p.m.	Depart from the Kennedy Space Center

5 PRONUNCIATION

Complete the exclamations with *cold, exciting, expensive, fast*.

> It costs over a million dollars.
> That's extremely _____!
> It flies at three times the speed of sound.
> That's incredibly _____!
> The temperature is minus 30°C.
> That's terribly _____!
> We're going to meet an astronaut.
> How _____!

🔊 1.31 Now listen and check. Repeat the exclamations.

6 SPEAKING

Below are some predictions about space travel in the future. Do you agree or disagree with the predictions? Say what you think about them.

A Do you think there'll be a hotel in space by 2020?
B Yes, it's possible. The Russians say they're going to build one. But I'm not going to stay in it because it'll be too expensive.

SPACE TRAVEL IN THE FUTURE

2020	First hotel in space
2025	Astronauts on the Moon again
2030	Mining on the Moon for aluminum
2030s	First spaceship goes to Mars
	Space factories start production
2035	Space elevator takes people to the Moon
2040s	Moon base the size of a small village
	Humans live on Mars
From 2051	Contact with aliens

Extension Make predictions about changes in life on Earth between now and 2050. Discuss your predictions with another student.

7 VOCABULARY

Find these phrasal verbs in the text about space tourism and match them with their meanings.

Word Bank Phrasal verbs

come down   count down   hold on
look down   put down   take off

1 wait a minute   4 opposite of *land*
2 fall/become less   5 10-9-8-7-6-5-4-3-2-1!
3 write someone's name 6 drop your eyes
  on a list

8 WRITING

You are on a spaceship that has been away from Earth for ten years. Now you are returning to Earth and will land there tomorrow.

What are you going to do when you land? Write about your plans.

What changes do you think there will be on Earth? Think about your family and friends, and your city.

LANGUAGE WORKOUT

Complete.

Talking about the future

We use the simple future (*will/won't*) to give information about future events and to make predictions.
Every passenger _____ have a spectacular view.
I'm sure the cost of space flights _____ come down.
It _____ be cheap.
_____ the dream ever become reality?

We use the simple present to talk about schedules and timetables.
The tour _____ at 9:45 a.m.

We use the present progressive to talk about fixed future arrangements.
I _____ _____ the Kennedy Space Center tomorrow.

We use *going to* to talk about plans and intentions.
Branson _____ _____ to travel on the first flight.
I _____ _____ to make a reservation!

▶Answers and Practice
Language File page 115

3 SCIENCE AND DISCOVERY

4 Integrated Skills
Describing events and consequences

1 OPENER
This lesson is about people who changed the world. Which people do you think changed the world?

READING

2 Read *People who Changed the World* and complete the text with six of the phrases a–h. There are two extra phrases.

a and to reduce environmental damage
b which led to his "germ theory" of disease
c since the beginning of the century
d in the air, and at sea
e by boiling and then cooling the liquid
f published in 1962
g which will be extremely difficult
h from England to France in 1899

Which words in the phrases helped you to complete the text?

3 Find words in the text to match these definitions. The parts of speech in *italics* refer to the words in the text.

1 disease that can pass from one person to another *adj*
2 idea that explains how or why something happens *n*
3 causing discussion and disagreement *adj*
4 chemicals used to kill insects *n*
5 effect *n*
6 damage caused to the air, water, or land, e.g., by chemicals *n*
7 growing crops on farms *n*
8 someone who studies physics *n*
9 across the Atlantic Ocean *adj*
10 send out an electronic signal *v*

People who Changed the World

The French chemist and biologist Louis Pasteur (1822–1895) made one of the most important discoveries in medical history. He discovered that there were germs called bacteria in the air that caused liquids to turn sour, so he developed the process called "pasteurization": killing the bacteria ___1___. Because of Pasteur's research, most dairy products today are pasteurized. Pasteur then realized that most infectious diseases are caused by germs in the air, ___2___. He used this theory to explain how vaccination worked and showed how doctors could prevent some illnesses by injecting weak forms of the disease. Pasteur's pioneering work has protected millions of people from disease, thanks to pasteurization and vaccination.

The American writer and biologist Rachel Carson (1907–1964) started the modern environmental movement when she wrote a controversial book about the destructive effects of pesticides on the chain of life. *Silent Spring*, ___3___, is one of the few books that have changed the way people view the natural world. Its impact was so enormous that it was compared with Charles Darwin's theory of evolution. As a result, Carson was attacked by the chemical industry, but *Silent Spring* also caused a massive protest against environmental pollution. Consequently, the U.S. government started to take action to control the use of pesticides in agriculture ___4___. And thanks to Rachel Carson, there is now a worldwide movement to protect the environment.

The Italian physicist Guglielmo Marconi (1874–1937) made the first-ever transatlantic radio transmission on December 12, 1901. A transmitter in southwest England signaled the letter S—three dots in Morse code—and the signal was picked up in Newfoundland, 3,500 kilometers away. This achievement was so extraordinary that at first people didn't believe it. Marconi had already successfully transmitted a message over 50 kilometers ___5___. But most scientists believed that radio waves would not follow the curve of the Earth and could, therefore, never transmit signals across an ocean. It was such a long way that it seemed completely impossible. Marconi proved them wrong. As a result of his achievement, we have seen the development of broadcasting, communications satellites, radar, the telephone, and the Internet. Marconi's genius has also helped to save thousands of lives on land, ___6___—when the *Titanic* sank in 1912, an estimated 700 lives were saved thanks to SOS signals from a Marconi transmitter.

42

4 Linking words: expressing cause and result

We can use these phrases to express reason or cause.

> as a result of …   because (of) …   thanks to …

We can use these words and phrases to express consequence or result.

> as a result   consequently   so   so … that
> such … that   therefore

Find examples of all these words and phrases in *People who Changed the World* and notice how they are used.

5 LISTENING

🔊 1.32 There are ten mistakes in the text. Read the text and guess what they are. Then listen and correct the mistakes.

The English engineer John Harrison (1693–1776) solved a major scientific problem. Ships sailing across rivers didn't know their exact position at sea because they couldn't measure longitude—the distance east or west from an imaginary line (called the meridian) from the top of the Earth to the middle. Longitude is measured in degrees, and for every 15 degrees that you travel east, the local time is one hour ahead. If you travel west 15 degrees, the local time is one minute behind. Therefore, if we know the exact time at two points, we can figure out who we are. But early sailors couldn't do this because the movement of the Earth made their clocks inaccurate.

In 1714, the British government offered a prize of £20,000 (a small amount then) for a clock that would tell the time accurately at sea. Thanks to John Harrison, the "longitude problem" was solved, but it took him most of his life. His last attempt was a clock called H1, which he built between 1730 and 1735. His next attempts, from 1737 to 1759, resulted in H4, a bigger pocket watch. This was tested on a voyage to the West Indies in 1764 and worked perfectly. But Harrison was given only half the prize and told to make ten more watches. This he did, and, as a result of complaining to the King and Parliament, received the rest of his money in 1773, at the age of 100!

6 SPEAKING

Which of the people in this lesson changed the world the most? Tell each other your opinion and give reasons for your choice.

7 GUIDED WRITING

Find out information about another person who you think changed the world and make notes.

- What did the person do and when?
- Why was his/her achievement so important?
- What were the consequences?

Now write one or two paragraphs about the person. Use the texts in exercises 2 and 5 to help you, and some of the linking words and phrases from exercise 4.

LEARNER INDEPENDENCE

8 Thinking skills: Look at this list of nouns for two minutes and try to remember them all.

> satellite   astronaut   shrimp
> spaceship   chimney   damage
> theory   distance   solution   impact

Now cover the list and write down all the words you can remember. Then compare your list with another student. Which words were easier to remember?

Nouns that refer to things you can see or touch are often easier to remember than abstract nouns—words for ideas, feelings, or qualities. Try to associate abstract nouns with things you can see or touch, e.g., *damage—car*.

9 Word creation: Make nouns ending in *-sion* or *-tion* from these verbs and use six of them to complete the sentences.

> act   create   decide   discuss
> evolve   pasteurize   permit
> pollute   possess   produce   solve
> suggest   transmit   vaccinate

1 Cars cause serious _____ in cities.
2 The class had an interesting _____ about the media.
3 My arm hurts because I've just had a _____.
4 You should ask the teacher for _____ to leave early.
5 Broadband _____ makes Internet use faster.
6 Everyone can take _____ to protect the environment.

10 🔊 1.33 **Phrasebook:** Find these useful expressions in Unit 3. Then listen and repeat.

> What a fantastic sight!
> It's so unexpected!
> The most incredible thing is …
> What does this have to do with …?
> How exciting!
> Hold on.
> Forget it!

Now think of other situations where you could use each of the four exclamations.

"What a fantastic sight!"
Looking at Earth from space.

3 SCIENCE AND DISCOVERY
Inspired EXTRA!

LANGUAGE LINKS

Match the headings A–F from the box with the instructions below, and then label the coffee pot in English, French, and German.

A Entretien de votre cafetière
B Instructions for use
C Pflege der Stabfilterkanne
D Caring for your coffee pot
E Instructions d'utilisation
F Bedienungsanleitung

What words helped you choose the correct headings? One of the languages gives slightly different instructions. Which language is it and what is the difference?

___
Geben Sie einen gehäuften Teelöffel gemahlenen Kaffee pro Tasse in die Kanne. Füllen Sie die Kanne bis 2,5 cm vor dem Rand mit heißem, nicht kochendem Wasser. Lassen Sie den Kaffee mindestens fünf Minuten ziehen. Drücken Sie den Stempel langsam nach unten.

Reinigen Sie die Kanne, den Deckel und den Filterteller in warmem Seifenwasser.

___
Add one heaping teaspoonful of ground coffee per normal-sized cup. Fill the jug, leaving a 2.5 cm space at the top, with water that is very hot but not boiling. Let it stand for at least four minutes. Push the plunger down slowly.

Wash the jug, lid, and filter in warm soapy water.

___
Ajoutez une bonne cuillère de café moulu par tasse de taille normale. Remplissez le pichet jusqu'à 2,5cm du haut avec de l'eau très chaude mais non bouillante. Laissez passer un délai minimum de quatre minutes. Poussez doucement le piston vers le bas.

Lavez le pichet, le couvercle et le filtre à l'eau chaude et savonneuse.

SKIT Space Talk

🔴 1.34 Read and listen.

CAPTAIN What a great day, Number 1. Today we're going to break the world spacewalk record.
NUMBER 1 Excuse me, sir, but don't you mean the space spacewalk record? After all, we are in space, not on Earth. And what's all that equipment for?
CAPTAIN Number 1. I know best—that's why I'm the captain. I need this equipment to show that we broke the record. I'll go first. Oh, no! I can't get through the door. Give me a push.
NUMBER 1 I can't, sir. We're weightless. There's nothing to push against, sir.
CAPTAIN Put your back against the door so that you can push me out.
NUMBER 1 But, sir, what will happen when you …
CAPTAIN Push! There, you see, it worked! Now come and join me.

* * *

CAPTAIN Right, Number 1. That's a new world record!
NUMBER 1 Yes, sir. Now, it's time to get back in the spaceship.
CAPTAIN Not yet, Number 1. We're going to set a record that no one can beat.
NUMBER 1 But, sir, in a few minutes the computer will close the door and fire the rockets to return to Earth.
CAPTAIN Oh, very well then. But I can't get through the door!
NUMBER 1 Let me get in first, sir, and I can pull you in.
CAPTAIN Good idea, Number 1. There, you go in first. Now take my hands and pull.
NUMBER 1 Oh, no, sir! The computer's closing the door. It's going to fire the rockets. I'll have to let you go. I'm sorry, sir. The next spaceship will be here in a week's time. Goodbye, sir!
CAPTAIN Help! Help …
NUMBER 1 Spaceship to Ground Control. Can you hear me? Returning to Earth now. Captain is staying in space to attempt a new record.

Now act out the skit in pairs.

Game Mystery word

- Play in pairs. The object is to discover the other player's mystery word.
- Student A writes down a four- to six-letter word from this unit, and says how many letters the word has.
- Student B tries to guess the word by saying a word with the same number of letters.
- Student A then says how many letters are the same as in the mystery word and what those letters are. For example, if the mystery word is *flight* and Student B says *planet*, Student A replies "Two letters: *l* and *t*."
- The game continues until Student B guesses the word. If Student B hasn't guessed the word after ten tries, Student A wins. Then Student B writes down a mystery word.

CONSOLIDATION

LESSON 1 Look at the questionnaire and *What on Earth?* text on page 36. Write five similar questions about the text and ask another student to answer them.

1 How big is the universe?
   a) twenty billion kilometers across
   b) billions and billions of kilometers across

LESSON 2 Choose six words from the blog in exercise 2 on page 38, and use your dictionary to help you write definitions. Ask another student to match your words with your definitions.

LESSON 3 Look at exercises 2 and 3 on page 40. Write five more questions about the space tourism text and answer them.

How much will each passenger pay for the Virgin Galactic Spaceship flight?
$200,000.

EXTENSION

LESSON 1 Look at *Spaceflight Records* on page 37. Write five questions about the text beginning with *Who, When, How long, What,* and *Where.* Ask another student to answer the questions.

LESSON 2 Look at the blog in exercise 2 on page 38. When Petra gets to the surface, she calls a friend in the U.S. and describes her dive. Her friend asks lots of questions. Write the conversation between Petra and her friend.

Petra   Hi! I've just had such a fantastic experience.
Friend   Really? What have you been doing?

LESSON 3 Write about your future. What are you doing next week?
Write about your arrangements.
What are you going to do in the next five years?
Write about your plans.
What else do you think you'll do in the future?

YOUR CHOICE!

CONSTRUCTION Order of adjectives
Put the adjectives in the right order.

1. The first submersible was Beebe's (round/small/uncomfortable) "bathysphere."
2. The *Alvin* is the (American/modern/round) submersible that explored the wreck of the *Titanic*, the (famous/old) passenger ship.
3. Around the hydrothermal vents there are (long/red and white/spectacular) worms, (pink/small/strange) fish, and (unusual/white) crabs.
4. By the hot vents there are also (black/giant/unknown) mussels and (5 cm-long/white) shrimp.

ACTION Move in order
- Work in two groups of five or six.
- Each group chooses a different lesson from this unit, and then chooses a paragraph from the text(s). They copy the first few sentences, each on a separate piece of paper.
- Group A gives their mixed-up pieces of paper to group B, one to each student.
- The members of group B read their sentences aloud.
- Then they try to stand in a line to show the order of the sentences in the paragraph.
- When group B is ready, group A shows them the original paragraph. Then group B gives group A their mixed-up pieces of paper.

REFLECTION *so* or *such*?
Complete.

- We use _____ before a/an + _____ + noun:
  It was such a deep dive.
- We don't use _____ after _____:
  It was a ~~so~~ huge ship.
- _____ is followed by an adjective without a noun:
  It was _____ dark that they didn't expect to find anything.
- _____ can be followed by a/an + noun, or by a/an + adjective + noun:
  It was _____ a (big) surprise that she couldn't believe it.

INTERACTION Fortune teller
- Work in a small group.
- Each student writes three questions to ask the fortune teller: one each about his/her life one, three, and ten years from now.
- One student plays the role of the fortune teller and the other students ask their questions. The fortune teller always replies in the same way.

Fortune teller: What do you want to know about your life three years from now?
Student: Will I be in college?
Fortune teller: Tell me the answer you want and it will come true.
Student: I want to go to college and study English.
Fortune teller: Yes, you will go to college and you will study English.

3 Culture

YOUNG SCIENTISTS

Since 1989, the European Union has organized an annual Contest for Young Scientists. Each country can submit three projects, which must have won a national competition. Competitors have to be aged between 14 and 21. They show a display of their work and answer questions from a scientific jury. At the 22nd contest in Lisbon, Portugal, there were 45 female participants and 80 male, making a total of 125. Here are some of the competitors and their projects.

Hanne Binder Denmark
Whales and wings

Hanne's project looked at the flippers of the humpback whale to see if they could help with the design of wings for aircraft. Humpback whales have evolved over millions of years and use their flippers in water like wings. Humans have only been trying to make efficient wings for a hundred years. Hanne compared the performance of a traditional wing and one inspired by the humpback's flippers. The results were very clear—guess which was best!

Nassira El Hadri El Yousfi Spain
Stories from Morocco

This social science project focused on stories from the north of Morocco, where there is a tradition of oral story telling. The object was to make these stories accessible to children of Moroccan origin living in Spain, so that they did not lose touch with their cultural heritage. Nassira collected the stories, and ten were recorded in both Catalan and Spanish, and issued on a CD.

Olga Gavrina Russia
Eye cataracts and digital cameras

As people get older, some develop what are called "cataracts" in their eyes, which prevent them from seeing properly. The normal way of detecting cataracts involves special equipment in a hospital. However, Olga developed a way of detecting cataracts using the "red eye" effect produced by a digital camera. She compared her discovery with the standard method, and in more than 95% of cases, the results were the same. Olga's method is simple, quick, and you can do it at home!

Culture

Fatih Koç and Furkan Esen
Turkey
Surfaces that always stay dry

When surfaces are described as "hydrophobic," it means that they can't get wet. Water can't stay on these surfaces, so they are always dry—like the leaves on some plants. Fatih and Furkan coated glass with two substances that made it hydrophobic and compared the results. Applications of this technique could include car windshields without wipers, and paintwork on buildings that cleans itself.

Christian Meier and Thomas Vögeli
Switzerland
A magnetic transportation system

Christian and Thomas designed a way of transporting flat pieces of steel without any contact. They used four electromagnets to lift the steel plate and work against gravity. Optical sensors measure the distance between the magnets and the plate, and the whole system is computer-controlled. Christian and Thomas designed all the important components and the software themselves. A system like this could be useful when steel is being painted or is contaminated in some way.

1 READING

Read *Young Scientists* and answer the questions.

1 What is the similarity between a humpback whale and an aircraft?
2 What was the result of Hanne's project?
3 Why did Nassira collect stories for Spanish children with a Moroccan background?
4 What happened to the stories that Nassira collected?
5 How are cataracts usually discovered?
6 How successful was Olga's method compared to the normal one?
7 What natural things are hydrophobic?
8 What wouldn't cars need if they had hydrophobic glass?
9 How did Christian and Thomas overcome the force of gravity?
10 What two uses are possible for the magnetic transportation system?

2 VOCABULARY

Find the highlighted words in the text to match these definitions. The parts of speech in *italics* refer to the highlighted words in the text.

1 spoken *adj*
2 covered *v*
3 proving that something is present *v*
4 changed and developed over a long period of time *v*
5 normal, usual *adj*
6 stop *v*
7 moving *v*
8 uses *n*
9 to do with sight or light *adj*

3 SPEAKING

Discuss these questions.

1 Which of the participants' projects is most interesting and why?
2 Does science always have to be "useful"?
3 What are the advantages and disadvantages of doing a project alone rather than with someone else?
4 What do you think the benefits are for participants in the Contest for Young Scientists, even if they don't win a prize?
5 If you entered the Contest for Young Scientists, what would your project be?

4 MINI-PROJECT
Women and science

36% of the participants in the 22nd Contest for Young Scientists were female. In 1989, the figure was less than 10%. Work with another student and discuss male and female attitudes to science. Think about:

- The contest: why do you think the percentage of female participants has increased?
- Your school: do as many girls as boys study science?
- Higher education: do as many women as men study science in college?
- Society: how easy is it for women to get scientific jobs?

Work together and write about your views on *Women and science*. Read your work carefully and correct any mistakes. Then show it to other students.

4 GETTING IT RIGHT

1 Some things won't have changed

Discussing possible future lifestyles
Future progressive
Future perfect

2020 Vision

Earrings that read our pulse rates, or a life expectancy of 120, and cats that glow in the dark? Different experts have different views on how we'll be living in 2020. Some things won't have changed much—people will still have to work, but they'll be working longer and retiring later. Other areas of our life will have changed completely.

Craig Cormick, of Biotechnology Australia, believes that people will live until they're 120, thanks to advances in medicine. "The main difference between life now and then," he says, "is that doctors won't be treating diseases anymore." Cormick sees a world where we'll be able to wipe out disease by eating a banana. "We'll be growing crops with vitamins and vaccines in them to prevent health problems."

"You'll also be able to change the color of your cat or dog. We can already carry out operations to put genes into rabbits and fish, and make them glow," Cormick points out. "So it will be perfectly possible to create a glow-in-the-dark cat or a designer dog."

Almost all researchers agree that wireless technology will have continued to develop. Anything large enough to carry a microchip will have one, and microchips will have become much smaller. Scientists will have invented earrings that take our pulses, and instead of watches, we'll be wearing gadgets that will combine the functions of a phone, camera, MP3 player, and computer. In the home, household equipment will have improved and will be linked by wireless networks. On the road, we won't have gotten rid of cars, but we will have keyless electric cars that we can talk to.

Will we get the balance right? Will we have created a bright new future, or will we all be living longer, but no more happily? Only time will tell.

1 OPENER

Is it possible to predict the future? Here are some famous "bad" predictions.

What do you think life will be like in 2020?

Radio has no future. Heavier-than-air flying machines are impossible. X-rays will prove to be a hoax.
Lord Kelvin, British scientist, 1899

There is not the slightest indication that nuclear energy will ever be obtainable.
Albert Einstein, 1932

There will never be a bigger plane.
Boeing engineer after the first Boeing 247 flight, 1933

We don't like their sound, and guitar music is on the way out.
Decca Records executive who missed out on signing the Beatles, 1962

2 READING

🔊 1.35 Read *2020 Vision* and see if your predictions are the same as those of the experts.

3 AFTER READING

Answer the questions.

1. What won't have changed in 2020?
2. Will people be retiring earlier in 2020?
3. What won't doctors be treating then?
4. How will food keep people well?
5. What idea is shared by most thinkers about the future?
6. What will we be wearing on our wrists in 2020?
7. How will improved household equipment communicate?
8. What won't the cars of the future have?

Your response Do you believe these predictions? Which are the most and least likely to happen?

4 VOCABULARY

How many of these phrasal verbs can you find in this lesson? Match the verbs with their meanings.

Word Bank Phrasal verbs with *out*

carry out   figure out   miss out on
point out   wipe out

1. calculate
2. destroy
3. do a particular piece of work
4. fail to take the chance to do something
5. tell someone something they should know

5 PRONUNCIATION

🔊 1.36 Listen and repeat this sentence, copying the stress and intonation closely.

> Life in 2020 will have changed because of better medicine, later retirement, less disease, fewer health problems, wireless technology, more microchips, and improved household equipment.

SPEAKING

6 Ask two students these questions and write down their answers. If the answer is *No*, ask *So what/who will you be ...ing?*

> What will you be doing in three months' time?
> Will you be ...

- wearing the same clothes?
- listening to different music?
- texting the same friends?
- watching the same TV shows?
- supporting a different sports team?
- looking forward to vacation?
- eating different food for breakfast?
- worrying about your exams?
- feeling happier than you are now?

7 Ask two different students these questions and write down their answers.

> What will you have done in three months' time?
> Will you have ...

- been on a vacation? Where?
- learned a new skill? What?
- saved some money? How much?
- been to a party? Whose?
- taken a trip? Where?
- bought something new? What?
- given someone a gift? What?
- done something you've always wanted to? What?
- done something you haven't wanted to do at all? What?

Extension Write more questions beginning *Will you be ...?* and *Will you have ...?* and interview two more students about their lives in five years' time.

8 WRITING

Look at the questions in exercises 6 and 7 again. Write two paragraphs about yourself saying what you will be doing in three months' time and what you will have done in three months' time.

LANGUAGE WORKOUT

Complete.

Future progressive
They _____ _____ _____ (work) longer.
Doctors _____ _____ _____ (treat) diseases anymore.
_____ we all _____ _____ (live) longer?

Future perfect
Scientists _____ have _____ (invent) earrings that take our pulses.
We _____ _____ _____ (get) rid of cars.
_____ we _____ _____ (create) a bright new future?

We use the future _____ to talk about events that will be in progress at a particular time in the future.
We can also use the future progressive to talk about future arrangements.
We use the future _____ to talk about something that *will/won't* have finished by a certain time in the future.

▶**Answers and Practice**
Language File page 115

4 GETTING IT RIGHT

2 We won't halt global warming until ...

Talking about future possibility
First conditional with *if* and *unless*
Future time clauses with *when*, *as soon as*, and *until*

1 OPENER

Look at the title of the lesson. Which of these words and phrases do you expect to find in it?

> atmosphere   carbon dioxide   childhood
> climate change   carbon emissions
> global warming   greenhouse gases
> longitude   pollution   rainbow

2 LISTENING

🔊 1.37 Read statements 1–3 below. Then listen to Adam, Tami, and Nicole, and put a check or a cross in the chart to show whether they agree or disagree with each statement.

1. Unless we do something about global warming soon, it will be too late.
2. It won't make any difference to global warming if I travel by plane.
3. It doesn't make sense to fly food halfway around the world.

	Adam	Tami	Nicole
1			
2			
3			

Now complete the chart for another student: does he/she agree with statements 1–3?

A Question of Balance

Climate change is no longer a threat—it is a reality, as a result of global warming. Most global warming has been caused by the production of greenhouse gases, in particular, carbon dioxide (CO_2). Whenever we turn on the TV, drive a car, or take a flight, we add more CO_2 to the atmosphere. Today, we talk to environmental campaigner Gina Freeman about carbon emissions.

Is it too late to do something about carbon emissions?
No, it isn't. And as soon as carbon emissions decrease, air pollution will decrease. But unless we take action now, we won't reduce the impact of global warming.

You're particularly concerned about the increase in air travel—why?
Air travel is a major source of carbon emissions. It's estimated that by 2020 it will be the single biggest cause of global warming. I believe that we won't halt global warming until we stop flying everywhere. If we don't fly so much, we'll reduce carbon emissions. And if we travel by train, we'll only produce 12.5% of the emissions of a flight.

But what if I have to fly?
One solution is to "offset," or balance, carbon emissions. If you pay an organization to reduce CO_2 in the atmosphere by the same amount as your flight creates, you will offset your carbon emissions. There are several organizations that fund carbon offset projects, for example, by planting trees, which absorb CO_2 from the atmosphere.

We import a lot of food by air. I imagine you're against that too.
Not necessarily—it depends. Many communities rely on food exports for a living. If we stop buying from them, we'll make poor people even poorer. Producing fruit and vegetables in cool climates can require a lot of heat and fertilizer, and these create greenhouse gases. So I suspect it doesn't make much difference where our food comes from.

Will carbon offset projects and flying less solve the problem of global warming?
No, they won't. But the situation won't improve unless we all work together. And the future will look brighter when all governments agree to reduce carbon emissions.

3 READING

🔊 1.38 Read *A Question of Balance*. Which statements in exercise 2 does Gina Freeman agree with?

4 AFTER READING

True or false? Correct the false sentences.

1. Air pollution will increase when carbon emissions decrease.
2. We will reduce the impact of global warming if we take action now.
3. We won't reduce carbon emissions if we fly less often.
4. If we travel by train, we'll only produce a quarter of the emissions of a flight.
5. If you have to fly, you can offset your carbon emissions.
6. Many poor communities will suffer if they can't sell food exports.
7. Carbon offset projects and flying less will solve the problem of global warming.
8. The situation will improve if we all work together.

Your response What can you personally do to reduce global warming?

5 PRONUNCIATION

Many English words are both nouns and verbs. The following two-syllable words have first-syllable stress when they are nouns and second-syllable stress when they are verbs.

| decrease | desert | export | import |
| increase | permit | produce | suspect |

Mark the stressed syllable on the highlighted words in these sentences.

1. There will be a decrease in pollution when carbon emissions decrease.
2. Our problems increase with the increase in global warming.
3. The soldier deserted the army in the desert.
4. The U.S. imports a lot of food but also sells food exports.
5. The police suspect the money was stolen and are questioning a suspect.
6. You aren't permitted to work there without a work permit.

🔊 1.39 Now listen and check. Repeat the sentences.

Extension How many of these words can you find in this lesson? Are they nouns or verbs?

6 ROLE-PLAY

Act out a conversation about travel plans.

A
- Say you want to fly to (*place*).
- Ask why you shouldn't fly.
- Say why you want to go to (*place*).
- Say why you have to fly.
- Reply.

B
- Suggest A avoids flying.
- Explain about carbon emissions.
- Suggest another means of transportation.
- Explain how to offset carbon emissions.

7 WRITING

Complete this paragraph in your own words to explain why we should reduce carbon emissions.

Climate change will continue unless … . Global temperatures will increase if … . The polar ice caps will melt if … . The sea level will rise when … . Many islands will disappear if … . There will be droughts and floods unless … . As soon as there is a serious energy crisis … . We won't reduce global warming until … . We'll save the planet if … .

LANGUAGE WORKOUT

Complete.

First conditional
if/ unless + simple present, simple future
If we _____ (not fly) so much, we _____ (reduce) carbon emissions.
If we _____ (stop) buying from them, we _____ (make) poor people even poorer.
The situation _____ (not improve) unless we all _____ (work) together.

Future time clauses
when/ as soon as/ until + simple present, simple future
The future _____ (look) brighter when all governments _____ (agree) to reduce carbon emissions.
As soon as carbon emissions _____ (decrease), air pollution _____ (decrease).
We _____ (not halt) global warming until we _____ (stop) flying.

▶ Answers and Practice
Language File page 115

4.3 GETTING IT RIGHT
If you could choose ...

Talking about imaginary or unlikely situations
Expressing wishes about the present
Second conditional
wish/if only + simple past

1 OPENER

You are going to read about travel. Which of these words do you expect to find in the text?

> autograph   guesthouse   hostel
> microchip   out-of-date
> overland   performance   satellite
> scenery   traditional   trekking

2 READING

🔊 1.40   Read the text. Has Vic been to Nepal before?

3 AFTER READING

Match the beginnings with the endings. There are three extra endings.

1. Hippies used to travel
2. It's still possible to travel
3. Vic has visited
4. He would stay
5. He wishes that people
6. He wouldn't stay
7. Nepal is a great place
8. Vic wouldn't take

a. in New York drank a lot of tea.
b. his friends with him.
c. to meet crazy people.
d. Kathmandu at least once before.
e. in Kathmandu if he was on a long visit.
f. overland to Nepal, but it isn't very safe.
g. to Nepal lots of times.
h. if you like walking long distances.
i. in New York lived at a slower pace.
j. in the same hostel because of the garden.
k. overland to Nepal in the 1960s.

Your response   Do you think Nepal sounds like "paradise on earth"? Why/Why not? What's your idea of paradise on earth?

If you could choose ...

Vic Gerrard, student, New York

If you could choose ... where would you be now?

In Kathmandu, in Nepal. It's a magical place, with the world's highest mountains and some of the most beautiful scenery. Nepal is paradise on earth!

how would you get there?

If I had enough time, I'd travel overland. That's the way the hippies went there in the 60s. And, in theory, you could still do it—fly from New York to Paris, then 18 weeks from Paris to Kathmandu—if you really wanted to. But these days, it would be safer to fly to India and go overland from there.

where would you stay?

I'd stay in the International Hostel, which is where I stayed last year. It's a traditional Nepali guesthouse—lots of hand-carved wood, endless tea, and no TV. If I could, I'd go back there because it has a beautiful garden. And the guy who runs it always has time for tea and conversation. If only people were like that in New York!

what would you do?

If I was in Nepal for a short time, I wouldn't leave Kathmandu—it's a crazy mixture of East and West, and you meet the most amazing people. But, if I had more time, I'd definitely go trekking—Nepal has some fantastic walking country.

who would you take with you?

I wish I could take all my friends! No, not really. When you travel, the whole point is meeting new people. So if I took all my friends, I'd spend all my time with them and not meet anyone new.

4 LISTENING

🔊 1.41 Listen to a radio call-in show called *Secret Wishes* and complete the chart.

Name	Problem	Secret Wish: would like …
Karen	People don't talk to _____. They all talk to her _____.	to be an _____ _____.
Will	Spends all his time on _____. Feels sick when he _____ _____ _____.	to _____ _____ _____ _____.
Alice	Has too many _____. Never has time for _____.	to be _____ _____.
Sally and Frank	Their _____ aren't happy with their relationship.	them to _____ what they mean to each other.

Now tell another student what the callers' secret wishes are.

> Karen wishes she was …

Then tell each other what the callers believe. Do you agree?

> Karen believes that if she was … people would …

Extension Complete the presenter's final sentence to each caller.
To Karen: Have you tried discussing this with …?
To Will: Is there another …?
To Alice: Well, have you thought of …?
To Sally and Frank: It's very difficult when …

5 SPEAKING

Complete these sentences with your own ideas—real or imaginary—and tell another student.

- I wish I could …
- If I had more …
- I wish I lived …
- If only my friends were …
- I wish I was …

> I wish I could fly! If I could fly, I could go anywhere in the world.

6 PRONUNCIATION

🔊 1.42 Listen and repeat these sentences from exercise 4. Mark the stressed words.

> It's hard. Really hard.
> It takes ages. Absolutely ages.
> It sounds silly. Extremely silly.
> They get angry. Very angry.

7 SPEAKING

Interview three other students using these questions from the text and take notes.

If you could choose, …
- where would you be now?
- how would you get there?
- where would you stay?
- what would you do?
- who would you take with you?

8 WRITING

Use your notes to write one paragraph each about two of the interviews.

If Sylvia could choose, she'd be in Cozumel now. She'd travel there in a van with lots of friends.

LANGUAGE WORKOUT

Complete.

Second conditional
If I _____ enough time, I _____ travel overland.
If I _____ in Nepal for a short time, I _____ (not) leave Kathmandu.
If you _____ choose, where _____ you stay?

wish + simple past
I wish I _____ take all my friends!

if only + simple past
If only people _____ like that in New York!

We use the _____ conditional to talk about imaginary present or unlikely future situations.
We use _____ *only* or _____ + simple past to express a hope or desire for something in the present to be different.
With the verb *be*, we can use either *was* or *were* after *I/he/she/it*.

▶ **Answers and Practice**
Language File pages 115–116

4 GETTING IT RIGHT

4 Integrated Skills
Debating an issue

1 OPENER

What's happening in the photo? What other issues do people protest about?

READING

2 Read and complete the text with six of the phrases a–g. There is one extra phrase.

a who are too young to vote
b as has happened in anti-globalization demonstrations
c have to take notice
d and not on the streets
e and attacked the police
f who feel strongly about a particular issue
g and generated enormous publicity

Which words in the phrases helped you to complete the text?

3 Find the highlighted words in the text to match these definitions. The parts of speech in *italics* refer to the highlighted words in the text.

1 to do with right and wrong *adj*
2 take control of something e.g., a plane illegally *v*
3 protests in the streets by a large number of people *n*
4 extremely important *adj*
5 with changed genes *adj*
6 protests where people refuse to eat for a long period *n*
7 start fighting *v*
8 separation of black and white people *n*
9 well balanced *adj*
10 protests where people take over a building *n*

4 Do you agree with the ideas in the quotations from Gandhi, Pankhurst, and King?

5 Linking words: adding information and giving examples

Find *also, in addition, what's more* in the text. Which two of these expressions usually come at the start of a sentence?

Find *for example, for instance, such as* in the text. Which one of these expressions can't come at the start of a sentence?

DIRECT ACTION

For three famous people, Mahatma Gandhi, Emmeline Pankhurst, and Martin Luther King, Jr., direct action was the only way to achieve their goals. They organized demonstrations and marches, sit-ins, and hunger strikes, __1__. Largely as a result of their direct action, India became independent (1947), women in Britain got the vote (partly in 1918 and fully in 1928), and racial segregation ended in the United States (1964 and 1965).

"Happiness is when what you think, what you say, and what you do are in harmony."
Mahatma Gandhi

"Nonviolence is the answer to the crucial political and moral questions of our time." *Martin Luther King, Jr.*

"We have to free half of the human race, the women, so that they can help free the other half."
Emmeline Pankhurst

So what are the arguments for and against direct action?

Supporters of direct action say that their methods get results. For example, they claim that anti-GM food demonstrations have made people aware of the dangers of genetically modified food. And the world knows about the cruelty of whale hunting thanks to direct action against Japanese and Norwegian whaling ships. They also argue that direct action involves people who can't or don't vote in elections, such as those who are not registered or __2__. What's more, they say that when the media reports direct action, for instance a million people on an anti-war march, politicians listen __3__.

Opponents of direct action point out that nonviolent protest can lead to violence when protestors and police clash, __4__. They also claim that it is easy for small groups of protestors __5__ to "hijack" demonstrations. In addition, they argue that the whole point of a democracy is that we elect representatives to make decisions for us. If we feel strongly about an issue, we should make our case with the elected representatives __6__.

6 LISTENING

🔊 1.43 Listen to a debate about the environment. What is the result? Then listen again and complete the speakers' notes and the details of the voting.

Introduction

CHAIR Hello, my name's Jan and I'm chairing this debate. The motion today is: "If necessary, we should take direct action to protect the environment." Tim is proposing the motion and Helen is opposing it. Tim, would you like to start?

Tim's notes for the start of his speech

> What I'm going to argue is that direct action can be necessary. First, because big business is so __1__ that even governments can't stop it. Second, because direct action makes people aware of problems, take __2__ for example. And third, because it is often the only way to save an animal or the environment before it is __3__.

Helen's notes for the end of her speech

> What I've argued is this. First, if __4__ looked after their own environment, we wouldn't need direct action. Second, many protesters are better at getting __5__ than actually changing anything. And third, that political action is better than direct action—the environment is too important to be left to __6__.

Conclusion

CHAIR Thank you both very much. Now you have one sentence each to sum up your argument before we have a vote.
TIM We only have one world. Let's use direct action to save it.
HELEN Show by the way you live your life that you care about the environment.
CHAIR And now raise your hands to vote. Those in favor of the motion? Thank you. And those against? Thank you. The result is __7__ votes for the motion and __8__ votes against.

7 SPEAKING

Have a class or group debate. Choose a chair and two speakers. Look at exercise 6 again and use this structure:

The Chair says what the motion is and introduces the speakers.
Each speaker:

1 says what he/she is going to say.
2 makes three points about the motion.
3 summarizes what he/she has said.

The Chair asks each speaker for a one-sentence summary of their views and then there is a vote.

Choose your own topic or one of these:

- People should be able to vote when they are 16.
- Cell phones are dangerous and should be banned.
- A woman's place is in the home.

8 GUIDED WRITING

Write two paragraphs giving a balanced description of the arguments for and against the topic of your debate, or of one of the topics in exercise 7. Use the text in exercise 2, the linking words in exercise 5, and the notes in exercise 6 to help you.

UNIT 4

LEARNER INDEPENDENCE

9 Thinking skills: Learning new words and phrases

- Write the new words and phrases on cards and place them around your room.
- Walk around the room looking at each card. Say each word or phrase aloud and remember its position. Look at the cards the next time you move around the room.
- Take the cards away. The next day, walk around the room and try to remember what was on each card.

10 Word creation: Add the prefix *anti-* or *non-* to these words and complete the sentences.

> fiction   iron   spam
> terrorism   violent   war

1 The government has introduced new _____ laws.
2 This new shirt is great—it's completely _____.
3 I read some novels, but I prefer _____.
4 Gandhi was in favor of _____ protest.
5 There was a large _____ demonstration on Saturday.
6 I have a new _____ program for my computer.

11 🔊 1.44 **Phrasebook:** Find these useful expressions in Unit 4. Then listen and repeat.

> Only time will tell.
> But what if I …?
> Not necessarily.
> If only people were like that.
> You meet the most amazing people.
> The whole point is …
> It takes ages.
> It sounds silly.
> What's more …

Now write a five-line dialogue using three of the expressions.

55

4 GETTING IT RIGHT
Inspired EXTRA!

PROJECT Future predictions

1 Work in a group and make a list of aspects of our lives that will probably be different in the future, for example: transportation, environment, fashion, music, food, money, communications, education, work. Choose a year in the future, and choose two or three topics to make predictions about.

2 Research: Use the Internet or your library to get ideas and write notes about each topic:
- What will we be doing in (year)?
- What will we have stopped doing?
- What will we have invented/discovered/built?
- Will our lives be better or worse because of these changes? Why?

3 Work together and write your future predictions. Read your work carefully and correct any mistakes. Draw pictures or use illustrations from magazines or newspapers. Show your work to the other groups.

Future predictions
In 2050, we'll all be using electric vehicles. We'll have stopped using gasoline and diesel engines because oil will have run out or become too expensive to use as a fuel. The good news is that we'll have invented much better batteries, so the electric vehicles will be able to go much faster over longer distances. This change will improve our lives considerably because electric vehicles don't produce greenhouse gases.

Game Word square

- Work in pairs.
- Write down as many English words as possible using pairs of letters from anywhere in the square, e.g., FU + TU + RE, FU + EL.
- Score 1 point for a four-letter word, 2 points for a six-letter word, 4 points for an eight-letter word.
- The pair with the most points is the winner.

FU	LL	EL	CO	AL
TU	LI	FE	HE	AT
RE	AC	TI	ON	NA
PO	RT	ME	TE	ST
TH	EN	ER	GY	CA

CONSOLIDATION

LESSON 1 Look at the notes you took in exercises 6 and 7 on page 49. Write sentences about one of the students you interviewed.

In three months' time, Juan won't be wearing the same clothes. He'll have bought new jeans.

LESSON 2 Look at your completed chart in exercise 2 on page 50. Write sentences about Adam, Tami, and Nicole.

Tami thinks that unless we do something about global warming now, it will be too late.

LESSON 3 Look at your completed *Secret Wishes* chart in exercise 4 on page 53.

What did the callers say? Write two or three sentences for each person.

Karen: People don't talk to me. I wish I was an only child. If my sister wasn't there, people would talk to me.

EXTENSION

LESSON 1 Imagine yourself in ten years' time. Write two paragraphs saying what you will be doing and what you will have done.

In ten years' time, I'll be working ...

LESSON 2 Complete these sentences about yourself.

1. When I finish school, I ...
2. If I go to college, I ...
3. ... unless I work hard.
4. As soon as I have enough money, ...
5. I won't get married until ...

LESSON 3 Imagine you're alone in a strange place with no map or cell phone. You're hungry and thirsty, but you don't have any money. Write sentences:

I wish/If only ...   If I ..., I would(n't) ...

I wish I wasn't alone. If I wasn't alone, I wouldn't feel so nervous.

YOUR CHOICE!

CONSTRUCTION Conditional sentences with *if* and *unless*

Rewrite the sentences with the verbs in the negative.

1 You won't catch the train if you don't run.

1. You'll catch the train if you run.
2. I'd buy a car if I passed my driving test.
3. We'll have a picnic if the weather is nice.
4. They'll see the Pyramids if they go to Cairo.
5. He'd take Spanish lessons if he went to Mexico.
6. I'll call you if I need help.
7. She'll go to the party if she feels better.
8. They'd call the police if they were really worried.

Now rewrite the sentences using *unless*.

1 You won't catch the train unless you run.

ACTION Mime game

- Work in a small group.
- Take turns choosing a word from Unit 4. Say the number of letters in the word, but don't say what it is! Then act out words that begin with each letter in your chosen word. For example, if your word is *HALT*, you could mime *Happy, Angry, Love, Tired*. You can make sounds, but don't say anything.
- The rest of the group guesses and writes down each letter until they have the complete word.

REFLECTION Present or past?

Complete the rules and examples.

- We form the future progressive with *will/won't be* + _____ participle: This time tomorrow, she'll be on a plane. She'll _____ _____ to Australia!
- We form the future perfect with *will/won't have* + _____ participle: I'm sorry, but I won't _____ _____ my homework by tomorrow.
- In first conditional sentences, the verb in the *if* clause is in the _____ tense: If you _____ at people, they'll smile back at you.
- In second conditional sentences, the verb in the *if* clause is in the _____ tense: We wouldn't be lost if we _____ a map.

INTERACTION I wish ...

- Work in a small group.
- Tell each other about:
  someone you wish you could meet.
  something you wish you had.
  something you wish you didn't feel.
- Explain why you wish these things and answer other students' questions.

REVIEW
UNITS 3–4

1 Read and complete. For each number 1–10, choose word or phrase A, B, or C.

Expanding Cities

This boy lives in Mumbai, India, where hundreds of people arrive every day from the countryside. They come to look for work. But they also need somewhere to live. While Mumbai is expanding really quickly, other cities are growing even __1__. Where are all these new arrivals __2__? Until we take this question seriously, the problem __3__ worse.

Every day almost 180,000 people around the world move into cities from the countryside—that's about 70 million people a year. A recent report predicts that two billion more people __4__ to cities by 2030. __5__ something is done, up to half of these __6__ in the worst kind of housing: slums. In 2005, one billion people were living in slums worldwide—about a third of the people who live in cities. By 2030, it is predicted that another billion __7__ in slums.

If people were more aware of the situation, they __8__ their governments to take action. But poor housing receives little media attention. If only the TV and newspapers __9__ as much attention to world poverty as they give to sports. Until they __10__, the situation can only get worse.

	A	B	C
1	more rapid	more rapidly	rapid
2	live	living	going to live
3	will get	is getting	gets
4	have moved	are moving	will have moved
5	Unless	As long as	If
6	live	will live	will have lived
7	live	are living	will be living
8	will ask	would ask	will have asked
9	gave	give	are giving
10	are doing	do	will do

2 Complete with the correct adverbs, using the information in *Expanding Cities* where necessary.

1 The number of new arrivals in Mumbai has been growing _____ _____. (incredible/quick)
2 But other cities are expanding even _____ than Mumbai. (fast)
3 We must take this problem _____ than we do. (serious)
4 "Which city in Africa is growing _____?" "Lagos." (rapid)
5 Nearly half the people of Jakarta, the capital of Indonesia, are living _____ _____ in slums (extreme/miserable).
6 The media could be _____ at informing people about poor housing. (good)

3 Complete with *so* or *such* and match the beginnings with the endings.

1 The ocean floor is _____ dark that
2 Submersibles are _____ expensive things to build that
3 The water around a "chimney" is _____ different from the rest of the ocean that
4 The molten rock deep in the Earth is _____ hot that
5 Hydrothermal vents are _____ a recent discovery that

a we still don't know how many new species there are around them.
b salt is removed from the water.
c the animals that live around it are unique.
d there are still only a few of them in the world.
e submersibles need to have powerful lights.

4 Complete with the most suitable form of the verbs: simple future, simple present, or present progressive.

One day, spaceships __1__ (fly) from California to France in 30 minutes. People __2__ have conversations like this:

KIM What __3__ (you/do) this afternoon?
CATHY Oh, I __4__ (fly) to France after lunch on one of the new spaceships.
KIM When __5__ (it/leave)?
CATHY At three o'clock, and it __6__ (get) there at 3:30 our time.
KIM But what time __7__ (it/be) in France when you arrive?
CATHY 12:30 a.m.
KIM So all the stores __8__ (be) closed, and everyone __9__ (be) asleep.
CATHY I know. But I __10__ (only go) for the ride. I __11__ (come) back on the next flight.
KIM And when __12__ (that/leave)?
CATHY At 1 a.m. French time. So it __13__ (arrive) back here at 4:30 our time.
KIM I see. So what __14__ (you/do) this evening?

5 Complete with the future progressive or future perfect of the verbs.

• "Louis Pasteur's theory of germs is ridiculous fiction. Soon we __1__ (inject) ourselves with diseases in order to get better! Whatever next!" *French professor, 1872*
• By the time he is 70, the average American __2__ (eat) 2,400 animals—2,287 chickens, 70 turkeys, 31 pigs, and 12 cows.
• The average teenager __3__ (eat) his or her own weight in additives—things added to food to make it look or taste good—by the time she or he is 17.
• "The 'telephone' has too many problems for us to take it seriously. In 100 years' time we __4__ (still send) messages by hand." *U.S. company executive, 1876*
• Worldwide, the number of robots in people's homes __5__ (pass) twenty million by 2020.
• "We __6__ (not use) planes to fight wars in the future—they are just interesting things to play with." *French general, 1898*

6 Complete with the simple past of the verb or *would*, and answer the questions for yourself.

Everyday nightmares
1. What _____ (you/do) if you _____ (drop) your cell phone down the toilet?
2. If the police _____ (arrest) you, who _____ (you/call) from the police station?
3. How _____ (you/get) home if you _____ (not have) enough money for the bus?
4. If you _____ (have to) choose, which _____ (you/give up): being able to see or being able to hear?
5. If you _____ (be) on vacation and lost your passport, who _____ (you/ask) for help?
6. What _____ (you/do) if you _____ (be) in a store and there was a robbery?
7. If you _____ (have to) go to the hospital, what three things _____ (you/take) with you?
8. What problems _____ (you/have) if you always _____ (have to) tell the truth?
9. What _____ (you/say) if a stranger _____ (ask) you for money?
10. _____ (you/panic) if _____ (you/be) at home alone and _____ (hear) footsteps?

7 Complete with the correct form of these verbs.

| be | can | grow | have | realize | spend | try |

Six wishes for a better world
1. I wish people _____ to understand each other better.
2. Everyone wishes there _____ peace on Earth.
3. We wish that we _____ do more to help people suffering from AIDS.
4. If only countries _____ less money on guns and _____ more food.
5. If only people _____ that the future of the world is in their own hands.
6. We wish that everyone _____ enough to eat and somewhere safe to sleep.

VOCABULARY

8 Complete with nine of these words.

atmosphere	balance	carbon	expectancy
flood	gadget	march	politician	protestors
retire	rotate	source	wireless

1. Women have a longer life _____ than men.
2. There were lots of _____ at the anti-war demonstration.
3. Air travel causes serious pollution in the _____.
4. My computer is _____, so I can use it anywhere.
5. In the U.S., many people will have to _____ from work at a later age.
6. How fast does Earth _____ at the Equator?
7. There is a _____ in Washington, D.C. today to protest about GM food.
8. After the heavy rain, the river rose and there was a _____ in the town.
9. You can _____ or offset your carbon emissions by planting trees.

9 Match these words with their definitions.

| absorb | crisis | decrease | glow | hoax | pulse |

1. trick to make you believe something that isn't true
2. take in, e.g., gas or liquid
3. regular movement of blood around the body
4. difficult or dangerous situation
5. shine with a soft light
6. become less, get smaller

10 Match the verbs in list A with the words and phrases in list B. Then write sentences using four of the expressions.

	A	B
1	achieve	publicity
2	fund	a case
3	generate	in an election
4	make	a goal
5	play	a project
6	vote	a part

REVIEW

LEARNER INDEPENDENCE
SELF ASSESSMENT

Look back at Lessons 1–3 in Units 3 and 4.

How good are you at …?	✓ Fine	? Not sure
1 Describing and comparing the way things happen Workbook pp26–27 exercises 1–4	☐	☐
2 Making exclamations Workbook p28 exercise 2	☐	☐
3 Expressing result Workbook pp28–29 exercises 1–3	☐	☐
4 Talking about future events, schedules, arrangements, and plans Workbook pp30–31 exercises 1–3	☐	☐
5 Discussing possible future lifestyles Workbook pp38–39 exercises 1–4	☐	☐
6 Talking about future possibility Workbook pp40–41 exercises 1–5	☐	☐
7 Talking about imaginary or unlikely situations Workbook pp42–43 exercises 1–3	☐	☐
8 Expressing wishes about the present Workbook p43 exercise 4	☐	☐

Not sure? Take a look at Language File pages 114–116 and do the Workbook exercise(s) again.

Now write an example for 1–8.
1. *Life developed extremely slowly.*

PREVIEW
UNITS 5-6

COMMUNICATIVE AIMS
LEARNING HOW TO ...

1. Talk about unreal or imaginary past events
2. Express regret about the past
3. Express obligation and lack of obligation
4. Make deductions and speculate about the past
5. Report what people said
6. Report what people asked
7. Ask for agreement and check information

TOPICS AND VOCABULARY

Historical events
Routines
Qualifications
Aviation
Phrasal verbs with *up*
Sports
Travel
Restaurant
Food
Buildings
Vacations

A

The team needs to clean the inside of the tank walls regularly so that visitors can see the fish clearly.

B

You'd like to stay there, wouldn't you?

1. Match six of the communicative aims (1–7) with the pictures (A–F).

2. Complete the words on the right and put them into categories.

Aviation   Restaurant   Sports

a_rcraft   cl_b   fl_ght   f_rk
g_me   gl_ss   g_al   l_nding
m_nu   p_ssenger   p_lot
pl_ne   pl_te   pl_yer   sc_re
s_up   t_am   w_itress

60

PREVIEW

C I promised to send lots of e-mails.

F  The waitress wanted to know if she could get me anything else.

D If only they had filled all the lifeboats!

E Some people think that Earhart and Noonan may have been U.S. spies on a secret mission.

4 Do the *Extraordinary People Survey* with three other students.

Extraordinary People Survey

1 Who's the oldest person you've met? How did you meet? What was he/she like?

2 Who's the youngest person you know? Describe him/her.

3 Who's the most intelligent person you've spoken to? What did he/she say?

4 Who's the most interesting person you know? What's interesting about him/her?

5 Who would you most like to meet? Why?

What interesting or surprising things did you find out? Tell another group.

Believe it or not! Members of the *Most Traveled People* club estimate that there are 872 countries, independent regions, and separate island groups in the world. Charles Veley of San Francisco claims to have visited 822 of them and traveled 2,710,075 kilometers to do so—he still has 50 more left to visit.

3 🔘 2.02 Listen to extracts 1–3 from Units 5 and 6. Match them with three of the text types A–D.

A An article about a famous woman
B An interview about vacations
C A radio show about jobs
D A description of a building

61

5 EXTRAORDINARY PEPLE

1 If the ship hadn't hit an iceberg ...

Talking about unreal or imaginary past events
Expressing regret about the past
Third conditional
wish/if only + past perfect

1 OPENER

Look at the pictures on this page. Which of these words do you expect to find in the text?

binoculars crew chemistry deck disaster
iceberg lifeboat lightning lookout
passenger sculpture survivor voyage

2 READING

🔘 2.03 Read *The "unsinkable" Titanic*. Why is "unsinkable" in quotation marks?

The "unsinkable" Titanic

The *Titanic* was the largest ship ever built when it left England in April, 1912, on its first voyage across the Atlantic Ocean to New York City. It was said to be "unsinkable." But at 11:40 p.m. on April 14, the luxury ship hit an iceberg south of Newfoundland, and it sank less than three hours later. Over 1,500 passengers and crew drowned or froze to death in the icy water, and there were only 705 survivors.

But this terrible disaster could have been avoided. Captain Edward J. Smith knew that there was a major risk of icebergs in the north Atlantic, but he didn't reduce the ship's speed. So by the time the lookouts saw the iceberg, the ship was moving too fast to avoid it. If the ship had slowed down earlier, there would have been time to change course.

On the night of April 14, there was no moon, and it was difficult to see icebergs in the dark. "I wish we had had binoculars," said a surviving lookout. "If we had had binoculars, we would have seen the iceberg in time to save the ship."

Another problem was the number of lifeboats. The *Titanic* was designed to carry 64 lifeboats, but it had only 20 to save space on deck. Only 18 lifeboats were launched, and most of these were not full. The crew hadn't even had a lifeboat drill. If only they had filled all the lifeboats! They would have saved 500 more lives if the lifeboats had been full.

Most of the survivors lost family members, and wished they had never set sail on the *Titanic*. There were hundreds of heroes that night who gave their lives to save others. Most extraordinary of all, the eight musicians of the *Titanic* band continued playing until the ship went down. None of them survived.

3 AFTER READING

Match the beginnings with the endings. There are two extra endings.

1 The *Titanic* sank
2 If the ship hadn't hit an iceberg,
3 Over two-thirds of the passengers and crew
4 The *Titanic* would have had time to change direction
5 The lookouts didn't have binoculars
6 There would have been more survivors
7 If all the lifeboats had been full,
8 The *Titanic* band played

a more people would have survived.
b because the crew hadn't had a lifeboat drill.
c in the early hours of April 15, 1912.
d if there had been more lifeboats.
e so they didn't see the iceberg in time.
f until the ship sank.
g it wouldn't have sunk.
h if it had reduced its speed.
i if they hadn't been on the voyage.
j died in the disaster.

Your response Do you think the *Titanic* musicians were heroes? Why/Why not? What do you think was the main reason so many people died in the *Titanic* disaster?

4 WRITING

Complete the quotations with the correct form of the verb: past perfect or would(n't) have.

1 "If God _____ (intend) us to fly, he _____ (give) us wings."
   Father of Orville and Wilbur Wright
2 "If I _____ (know) I was going to live this long, I _____ (take) better care of myself."
   Eubie Blake, jazz musician
3 "If I _____ (not start) painting, I _____ (raise) chickens."
   Grandma Moses, artist
4 "If it _____ (not be) for the Cold War, Russia and America _____ (not send) people into space."
   James Lovelock, scientist
5 "I don't know what _____ (happen) to me if I _____ (not be) able to hear."
   Ray Charles, singer
6 "If I _____ (not be) President of the United States, I probably _____ (end) up a piano player."
   Harry S. Truman, U.S. president

5 PRONUNCIATION

2.04 Listen and repeat the first two sentences in exercise 4. Mark the stressed words in each sentence. What happens to *have* and *had* in these sentences?

6 SPEAKING

What are these people thinking? Complete using the past perfect.

Extension Complete these sentences about regrets and tell another student.

I wish I'd known/listened to/seen …
If only I hadn't forgotten/lost/missed …

7 LISTENING

2.05 Two years ago, Sally King won the lottery. Listen to her talking about how her life changed. Check the things she actually did, and put a cross by the things she didn't do.

a give up her job
b continue working
c sell her apartment
d buy a farmhouse
e stay in Chicago
f move to Italy
g meet Giorgio
h take up painting

Now check your answers with another student.

A She gave up her job.
B She wouldn't have given up her job if she hadn't won the lottery.

8 WRITING

If the *Titanic* hadn't hit an iceberg, it wouldn't have sunk. Choose another significant event, and write sentences saying what would and wouldn't have happened if things had turned out differently.

If Columbus hadn't sailed across the Atlantic Ocean, …

If someone hadn't invented the wheel, …

LANGUAGE WORKOUT

Complete.

Third conditional
If the ship _____ slowed down, there _____ _____ been time to change course.
If the ship _____n't hit an iceberg, it _____n't _____ sunk.

wish/if only + past perfect
I wish we _____ had binoculars.
Most of the survivors wished they _____ never _____ sail on the *Titanic*.
If only they _____ _____ all the lifeboats!

We use the _____ conditional to talk about unreal or imaginary past events.
We use _____ *only* or _____ + past perfect to express regret about the past.

▶ Answers and Practice
Language file page 116

5 EXTRAORDINARY PEOPLE

2 You have to be careful

Expressing obligation and lack of obligation
must, can't, have to, and *need to*
don't have to and *don't need to*

The world's weirdest jobs!

Meet three people who work at three great tourist attractions.

Alan Lopez, snake milker

Alan Lopez works at a snake farm called Snake Town. He collects venom from poisonous snakes. Snake venom is used to make anti-venom serum, and medical researchers are studying snake venom as a possible treatment for disease.

Alan says, "I don't have to collect the venom from each snake every day—every two weeks is enough. I hold the snake's head tightly to make the fangs appear. Then I make the snake bite through a thin rubber cover on a glass jar. I use pressure, and the venom comes out. And that's it."

Visitors to Snake Town can watch the procedure, but they must stand in another room and watch through a window. Alan has to concentrate, so he doesn't have to explain the procedure to the visitors. A guide does that.

Alan was bitten once, and he says, "Once is enough!"

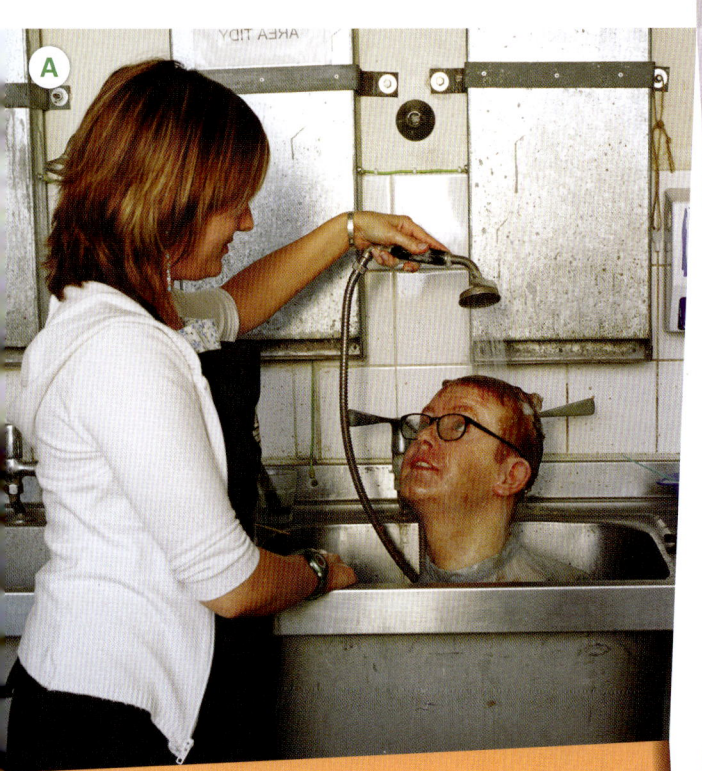

Jo Kinsey, hair and color artist

In the quiet afternoon sunshine, Jo Kinsey, 28, runs her hands over Gérard Depardieu's hair. A radio plays softly somewhere, and a cup of coffee sits half-drunk on the table. As Kinsey stands in front of Gérard, Richard Branson looks on, his eyes not moving.

Kinsey works at Madame Tussauds in London. Starting at 7:30 a.m., two hours before the crowds arrive, she moves through the museum, checking that all the models are undamaged. "Richard Branson had a broken nose this morning," she says. "And Hitler had a broken ear. He's had several lately, I don't know why."

Her main responsibility is hair. If the hair looks dirty, she takes off the head and washes it. "I put it in the sink, use the shower, then dry it—not too hot, of course, because of the wax. We don't want to melt it." This week, she's working on Depardieu, Branson, and Chris Evans.

"It's usually ones with elaborate hairstyles that need work," says Kinsey. Each model has a reference file with 400 photographs and measurements. It costs around $100,000 to make a model, and the hair alone takes up to five weeks.

Jeanette Ewart, shark tank cleaner

"Sharks definitely have characters," Jeanette Ewart says firmly. "We work with them every day, so we get to know them. You have to watch their swim patterns and notice any changes. George is the largest shark in there—she's the boss of the tank—and sometimes when you're diving, you notice her dropping lower in the water and looking right at you."

"The first day I went into the shark tank, I was excited but nervous. I had to tell myself to stay calm. But we're always careful—there are strict guidelines for aquarium diving, so there's always a diver, a stand-by diver in the tank, and someone supervising from the edge. You don't need to worry about me—I've never had any scary moments."

For 18 months, 23-year-old Ewart has been part of a team that keeps the aquarium clean and the fish healthy and well-fed (the sharks are fed three times a week). The team needs to clean the inside of the tank walls regularly so that visitors can see the fish clearly.

"Where else can you work in a city and scuba dive for a living?" Ewart asks, grinning.

UNIT 5

1 OPENER

Look at the photos of people working at three famous tourist attractions. Match them with these places.

> Snake Town   An aquarium
> Madame Tussauds

2 READING

Read *The world's weirdest jobs!* Which of the jobs are dangerous?

3 AFTER READING

Answer the questions.

1. Why don't Richard Branson's eyes move?
2. What does Jo do on arrival at work every morning?
3. Why can't Jo use a very hot hairdryer?
4. Does Alan have to collect snake venom every day?
5. How does he make venom come out of a snake's fangs?
6. Why doesn't Alan have to explain the procedure to visitors?
7. What is unusual about the largest shark's name?
8. Why does Jeanette say we don't need to worry about her?
9. Why does the team have to clean the tank wall regularly?

Your response Which of the three jobs would you most/least like to do?

4 PRONUNCIATION

🔊 2.06 Make sentences correcting these statements about *The world's weirdest jobs!* and say them aloud. Then listen and check the stress.

> Jo Kinsey works in <u>London</u>, not <u>New York</u>.

1. Jo Kinsey works in New York.
2. Richard Branson had a broken leg.
3. There are 200 photographs of each model.
4. Alan Lopez milks cows.
5. George is the smallest shark.
6. Jeanette Ewart is 25 years old.

Extension Write another sentence about each job containing one false fact. Ask another student to correct your sentences orally.

5 LISTENING

🔊 2.07 Look at the chart and try to guess which qualifications are necessary for each job. Then listen and check, and complete the chart.

have to ✓
can't ✗✗
don't have/need to ✗

JOB QUALIFICATIONS	Flight attendant	Yacht crew	Human cannonball
Be over 21 years old			
Be over 1.5 meters tall			
Be over 1.88 meters			
Be physically fit			
Have a driver's license			
Speak a foreign language			
Have a degree			
Have safety training			
Be willing to travel			

Now talk about the qualifications for the three jobs.

> Flight attendants can't be under 21, and they have to be over 1.5 meters tall.

6 WRITING

Write two paragraphs about the qualifications needed for two of the jobs in exercise 5.

Flight attendants have to be over 1.5 meters tall.

LANGUAGE WORKOUT

Complete.

Obligation
must, can't, have to, and *need to*
Why _____ Jo be very careful?
You _____ _____ watch their swim patterns.
The team _____ _____ clean the tank walls regularly.

can't means that something is not allowed.

Past forms: *had to* and *needed to*
I _____ _____ tell myself to stay calm.

Note that *need* can also be followed by an object:
The elaborate hairstyles need work.

Lack of obligation
don't have to and *don't need to*
Why _____n't Alan _____ _____ explain the procedure?
You _____n't _____ _____ worry about me.

Past forms: *didn't have to* and *didn't need to*
Alan didn't have/need to collect snake venom last week.

▶ Answers and Practice
Language File page 116

5.3 EXTRAORDINARY PEOPLE
What could have happened to them?

Making deductions and speculating about the past
must have and *can't have*
could/may/might have

1 OPENER

Look at the photo and the map. You are going to read about a brave female pilot. What do you think she did?

2 READING

2.08 Read the text. Why didn't Earhart and Noonan complete the flight around the world?

3 AFTER READING

True, false, or no information? Correct the false sentences.

1. Amelia Earhart was the first person to fly solo across the Atlantic.
2. She flew from Newfoundland to Ireland in under 14 hours.
3. She beat the previous transatlantic record by three hours.
4. Her flight from Hawaii to California took longer than her transatlantic flight.
5. Earhart and Noonan disappeared over the Atlantic Ocean.
6. Earhart had reported over the radio that they were short of fuel.
7. Although there was a major search for their plane, it was never found.
8. The plane could have blown up in mid-air.
9. Earhart and Noonan were probably U.S. spies.
10. Earhart wanted to die in her plane.

Your response What were the difficulties and dangers in long solo flights in the 1930s? In what ways is flying a different experience today?

Amelia Earhart
Pioneer in the Sky

Born in 1897, Amelia Earhart was a record-breaking American pilot, who in 1932 became the first woman to make a solo flight across the Atlantic. The flight was difficult and dangerous. She flew through strong winds and a lightning storm, and once almost crashed into the ocean. It took her 13½ hours to make the trip from Newfoundland to Ireland, where she had to make an emergency landing in a field. But she had completed the crossing—and set a new world record. Earhart was also the first person to fly solo across the Pacific Ocean, when she flew from Hawaii to California in 1935. Every previous attempt had failed, not least because the distance is greater than a transatlantic crossing.

Her most daring journey was in 1937, when she attempted to fly around the world with navigator Frederick Noonan. But after they had completed three-quarters of the trip, their plane disappeared during the flight from New Guinea to tiny Howland Island in the Pacific. No trace of the aircraft or Earhart and Noonan was ever found.

What could have happened to them? There has been a great deal of speculation. Many believe the plane must have run out of fuel and crashed into the Pacific Ocean—Earhart had reported over the radio that they were short of fuel. But there was a massive search operation, so why wasn't the plane found? It can't have blown up in mid-air because it had used up most of its fuel. Some people think that Earhart and Noonan may have been U.S. spies on a secret mission, and the Japanese might have shot down their plane. Others think that they could have ended up on a desert island, or even that aliens might have abducted them. Or did Earhart and Noonan simply get lost? Neither of them knew much about using the radio equipment on the aircraft.

Whatever happened, Earhart may have died as she had wished. "When I go," she often said, "I'd like best to go in my plane."

4 WRITING

Rewrite the sentences using the verb in parentheses and *have*.

1 She must have been very brave.

1. She was certainly very brave. (must)
2. I'm sure she didn't sleep during her solo flight. (can't)
3. It's possible that they survived. (might)
4. Maybe they landed on a desert island. (could)
5. I'm sure aliens didn't abduct them. (can't)
6. Maybe the plane went down in the ocean. (could)
5. It's possible that they got lost. (may)
8. I'm sure she loved flying. (must)

> **Extension** What do you think happened to Earhart and Noonan? Write at least two possible explanations.

5 PRONUNCIATION

🔴 **2.09** Listen and check your answers to exercise 4. Repeat the sentences and mark the stressed words. What happens to *have* in these sentences?

6 VOCABULARY

Complete with the correct form of these verbs.

> **Word Bank** Phrasal verbs with *up*
>
> blow end grow look make
> sum take use wake

1. We've run out of milk—we've _____ it all up.
2. My little sister wants to be a pilot when she _____ up.
3. Maybe the plane _____ up in mid-air.
4. I don't believe his story—I think he _____ it up.
5. After traveling around the world, he _____ up in Brazil.
6. Now I'd like to _____ up what I've just said.
7. A loud noise _____ me up in the middle of the night.
8. Earhart _____ up flying when she was a young woman.
9. I didn't understand the word, so I _____ it up in the dictionary.

Which of these phrasal verbs with *up* can you find in the text in exercise 2?

7 SPEAKING

Discuss the stories in *Unexplained Mysteries* and say what you think happened in each case.

Carolyn must/can't have …
She could/may/might have …

8 WRITING

Write about another unexplained mystery that interests you—or make one up!

Describe the event and say what you think happened, giving your reasons.

UNIT **5**

Unexplained Mysteries

Mystery island
In June 1974, pilot Carolyn Cascio was flying to Grand Turk Island in the Bahamas. When she flew over Grand Turk, people on the island could see her plane, but she sent a radio message: "There is nothing down there!" Then Cascio's plane suddenly disappeared and she was never seen again.

Tunnel vision
In the winter of 1975, Mr. and Mrs. Wright were driving to New York City in a snowstorm. When they reached the Lincoln Tunnel, they stopped to clean snow off the car windows. Mrs. Wright went to clean the back window—and she disappeared forever.

Foreign visitor
In 1905, a man was arrested in Paris because he was a pickpocket. He spoke a completely unknown language, but finally he found a way to communicate with people. He said he came from a city called Lisbian—which doesn't exist.

Time travel
A National Airlines 727 plane was flying to Miami in 1969 when it suddenly lost contact with air traffic control. Ten minutes later, it reappeared on the radar screen. No one on the plane had noticed anything unusual, but when the plane landed on time, the watches of all the passengers and crew were ten minutes slow.

> ### LANGUAGE WORKOUT
>
> Complete.
>
> **Deduction**
> *must have* and *can't have* + past participle
> The plane _____ _____ run out of fuel.
> It _____ _____ blown up in mid-air.
>
> **Speculation**
> *could/may/might have* + past participle
> What could _____ happened to them?
> They could _____ _____ up on a desert island.
> Earhart and Noonan may _____ _____ U.S. spies.
> Aliens _____ _____ abducted them.
>
> We use _____ _____ when we are sure something happened.
> We use _____ _____ when we are sure something didn't happen.
> We use *could/may/might have* to talk about what possibly happened.
>
> ▶ Answers and Practice
> Language File page 117

5.4 EXTRAORDINARY PEOPLE

Integrated Skills
Contrasting facts and ideas

1 OPENER

Look at the photo. How popular is women's soccer in your country? Are there other sports that more men than women play? Are there sports that more women than men play?

"IS IT A MAN'S GAME?" ASKS MARIGOL

1. Mexico's star woman soccer player, Maribel Dominguez, is known as "Marigol" because she scores so often—46 goals in 49 international games. But life isn't, and hasn't been, easy for her in a man's world—soccer.

2. Maribel started to play when she was nine years old on **wasteland** near her new home in Mexico City. But she played with boys. The short-haired new arrival was soon accepted into the group of boys. They called her Mario.

3. "I tricked them for years," Maribel **confesses**. "They only found out I wasn't a boy when they saw my picture in the paper. I'd gotten into a junior national team. They went to my house and asked if I was a girl. They were pretty shocked."

4. Maribel was 20 when she joined the Mexican national team and played in the Women's World Cup in the U.S. in 1999. The team lost all their games, but Maribel was soon playing for a professional women's team in Atlanta in the U.S. Then came the 2004 Athens Olympics and the Mexican women's team reached the **quarter-finals**, while the men's team was **knocked out** in the first **round**. By now Maribel was famous and also lucky that she had escaped serious injuries.

5. "Maribel really is very, very good," says Nora Herrera, one of a few women soccer journalists in Mexico. "She has an incredible nose for a goal, she can smell it, and she's fast and **courageous**, and surprisingly strong too."

6. In 2004, Maribel shocked the Mexican soccer world by joining a second-**division** club called Celaya, which was looking for a center forward. It was a men's club. The Mexican Soccer Association said it had no problem with her playing on a **male** team, but they had to ask FIFA, the world soccer organization. Just before Christmas 2004, FIFA announced its decision: "There must be a clear separation between men's and women's soccer." In other words, no!

7. "I just wanted to be given the chance to try," said Maribel. "If I had failed, I would have been the first to say that I couldn't do it. But at least I would have tried." So Maribel moved to Europe to play professional women's soccer for Barcelona.

8. Maribel scored the goal that qualified Mexico for the 2011 World Cup, and she hopes to continue playing. When she retires, she wants to start a soccer school for girls. She is saving money for it, but women soccer players are paid much much less than men. In Mexico Maribel got $1,000 a month, whereas a top male player got $100,000. "To play in one of those competitions feels fabulous. It is the best thing for a woman. The very best. Well, for a **female** soccer player, it's the best thing that can happen. For a man, maybe earning a million dollars a month is better. I don't know."

READING

2 Read *"Is it a man's game?" asks Marigol* and match these topics with the paragraphs.

> A discovery   A review   The future   A surprise decision   Her career
> Introducing Marigol   A new continent   Early days

3 Find the highlighted words in the text to match these definitions. The parts of speech in *italics* refer to the highlighted words in the text.

1 woman *adj*
2 says that he/she has done something wrong *v*
3 series of games in a competition *n*
4 man *adj*
5 unused open ground *n*
6 last four games between eight players or teams in a competition *n*
7 put out of a competition after losing a game *v*
8 brave *adj*
9 group of teams that play against each other *n*

4 **Linking words:** *whereas* and *while*

We can use *whereas* or *while* to contrast two facts or ideas. Find an example of each in the text.

5 LISTENING

🔊 2.10 Read and complete as much of the text as you can for Maribel. Then listen and take notes so you can complete the text for Hanna as well.

> Both Maribel Dominguez and Hanna Ljungberg are well-known international __1__ players. Maribel has scored __2__ goals in __3__ internationals, whereas Hanna has scored __4__ goals in __5__ internationals. Maribel started playing when she was __6__, while Hanna started when she was __7__. Maribel joined the Mexican team when she was __8__, whereas Hanna joined the Swedish team when she was __9__. Maribel played in the __10__ World Cup in the U.S., but Hanna __11__. Both women are __12__ soccer players, and both were asked to play for __13__ teams. Neither did. Hanna retired in __14__, whereas Maribel continues to play in Spain.

Hanna Ljungberg, Sweden

Now listen and check your answers.

6 SPEAKING

FIFA says that boys and girls can play soccer together until they are 13, but after that, there must be separate male and female teams. Do you agree? And why are male soccer players paid so much more than female players?

In what other areas of life do men and women have different opportunities and pay? Think about sports, education, and jobs. Discuss your ideas with other students.

7 GUIDED WRITING

Write three paragraphs contrasting the situations of men and women in your country. Is it easier to be a man or a woman—what are the advantages and disadvantages?

UNIT 5

LEARNER INDEPENDENCE

8 Thinking skills: Reviewing groups of words or phrases

- Make a word map on a big piece of paper. Use words and phrases you want to review, e.g., words that have to do with sports.
- Hang the piece of paper on your door and look at it every time you leave your room.
- After a week take the paper down, and make a new word map for another topic.
- You can save the papers for last-minute review.

9 Word creation: Make adjectives ending in *-ous* from these nouns and complete the sentences.

> courage   danger   infection
> luxury   nerve   poison
> space   superstition

1 She's very _____—she's not afraid of anything.
2 The hotel was really _____—I've never stayed anywhere as nice.
3 It's not safe—in fact it's quite _____.
4 People who believe in magic are often _____.
5 My cold's getting better—I don't think I'm _____ now.
6 All soccer players get _____ before a game.
7 The room is very _____—it can hold up to fifty people.
8 Those mushrooms are _____, so you can't eat them.

10 🔊 2.11 **Phrasebook:** Find these useful expressions in Unit 5. Then listen and repeat.

> I don't know why.
> And that's it.
> Once is enough!
> You don't need to worry.
> What could have happened?
> In other words …
> I just wanted to be given the chance.

Now write a six-line dialogue using at least three of these expressions.

69

5 EXTRAORDINARY PEOPLE
Inspired EXTRA!

LANGUAGE LINKS

Read *Language and the mind*. Which part of the brain is normally used to produce speech? Which part is used to understand what we hear?

Language and the mind

Humans are cousins of the apes, and modern humans evolved around 200,000 years ago. We probably started to develop language 100,000 years ago, and the first humans walked out of Africa into Asia about 75,000 years ago. As humans spread around the world (arriving on the American continent possibly as late as 30,000 years ago), different languages developed.

Humans have extra-large brains, and in most cases it is the left hemisphere of the brain that deals with language. The front part of the left hemisphere produces what we say, while the back part understands what we hear. When we learn a new language, the brain operates in the same way.

Children are born with the ability to speak, and start to say their first words by the age of one. But reading and writing are not natural abilities—they are skills that children have to learn, and they involve making new connections in the brain. So learning to read is literally a mind-changing experience.

We write and read English from left to right. Do you know of any languages which are written and read from right to left?

SKIT *The Break-in*

🎧 2.12 Read and listen.

A couple have just walked into their apartment after a vacation.

WOMAN Oh, no—what a terrible mess!
MAN There must have been a break-in! Burglars!
WOMAN They could have gotten in through the window—look, it's broken.
MAN They can't have come in through the window. We're on the 15th floor!
WOMAN Then they must have come through the door.
MAN They can't have—the door was locked.
WOMAN They might have had a key. Maybe it was someone we know.
MAN I can't believe that. But what's missing? What have they taken?
WOMAN They haven't taken the computer. What about the TV?
MAN Let's check the living room.
WOMAN Oh, heavens—it's total chaos in here.
MAN Look! There's a body under a blanket on the sofa!
WOMAN Is it alive?
MAN I don't know. We'd better call the police.

The person on the sofa throws off the blanket.

SAM Oh, hi, Mom, hi, Dad.
WOMAN Sam!!! Are you all right?
SAM Yes, of course I'm all right. I'm just tired, that's all.
MAN But there's been a break-in, hasn't there? What on earth happened?
SAM Ah, sorry about the mess. A few friends came over last night. If I'd known you were coming home today, I'd have cleaned the place up.

Now act out the skit in groups of three.

Game Link-up

- Form two teams.
- One team chooses a letter square from the game board. The teacher asks a question about a word beginning with the letter. If the team guesses the word, they win the square.
- Then the other team chooses a letter square …
- The first team to win a line of *linked* squares, from top to bottom or from left to right, is the winner. You can go in any direction, but all your squares must touch!

C	A	M	R
B	J	Q	F
W	T	P	Y
D	G	S	E

UNIT 5

CONSOLIDATION

LESSON 1 Write sentences using *wish/if only* and the past perfect.

1 He failed his exams and can't go to college (If only)
2 She got the message and it was bad news. (wish)
3 There wasn't much food and I wanted more. (wish)
4 I took your advice and everything went wrong. (If only)
5 She didn't back up her computer and it crashed. (wish)
6 He stayed in his job and hated it. (If only)

1 If only he hadn't failed his exams.

LESSON 2 Look at exercise 5 on page 65 and write about the qualifications needed for the job you didn't write about in exercise 6.

LESSON 3 The famous soccer player Terry Wayne has disappeared. Rewrite the sentences using the verb in parentheses.

1 What do you think has happened to him? (can)
2 I'm sure he was tired of the publicity. (must)
3 Perhaps he's gone to stay with friends. (may)
4 It's possible that he's had an accident. (might)
5 Maybe he wanted a vacation. (could)
6 I'm sure he hasn't decided to give up soccer. (can't)

EXTENSION

LESSON 1 Look at exercise 7 on page 63. Think of an event that changed your life or the life of someone you know. Write a paragraph saying what would/wouldn't have happened if things had been different.

My mother met my father when she was a nurse. He was brought to the hospital after breaking his leg in a soccer game. If he hadn't ...

LESSON 2 Look at the text on page 64. Write a conversation between Jo Kinsey and Jeanette Ewart in which they compare their jobs.

LESSON 3 Read about the mystery voyage of the *Mary Celeste*. Then write sentences making deductions and speculating about what happened to the people on the ship.

On November 7, 1872, the *Mary Celeste* set out from New York to sail to Italy with a cargo of wine. On December 4, the *Mary Celeste* was found sailing off the coast of Portugal. There was no one on board and the lifeboat was missing. The captain and crew had apparently left in a hurry, and they were never seen again. But everything on the ship was in order, and there was plenty of food and water.

YOUR CHOICE!

CONSTRUCTION *must*, *can't*, or *don't need to*?

Complete with *must*, *can't*, or *don't need to*.

A You __1__ miss your train. Let me drive you to the station.
B Thanks, but you __2__ bother. There's plenty of time and I __3__ catch this train. And you __4__ finish your work.
A You __5__ worry about me—I can finish my work tomorrow. I __6__ finish it today.
B Well, I __7__ get some fresh air and exercise, so I'm happy to walk. Anyway, you __8__ park at the station. There are *No Parking* signs everywhere.
A I __9__ park the car—you just have to jump out!

ACTION Picture flash

- You need a number of pictures of people, places, or objects taken from magazines.
- Student A holds a picture upside down with its back to the other students. Holding the picture at the sides with both hands, he/she flashes it so that the other students see it for less than a second.
- The other students say what they think the picture *must/may/could/might/can't have been*.
- Student A flashes the picture again until one student guesses correctly.
- That student flashes the next picture.

REFLECTION Modal verbs

Match the examples a–i with language functions 1–4.

1 Obligation   2 Lack of obligation   3 Deduction
4 Speculation

a You can't use your cell phone in class.
b It might have been your boyfriend on the phone.
c You have to wear a seat belt in the car.
d It can't have been my boyfriend—he's lost his phone!
e She could have gotten lost—she doesn't know the city well.
f You must turn off your phone in the theater.
g You don't have to pay to get into the museum.
h I may have been wrong—I don't know.
i You don't have to thank me—I was happy to help.

INTERACTION My favorite English words

- Work in a small group.
- On your own, think of five English words that you like for a special reason—it could be the sound of the word, or something it makes you think of, for example.
- Share your words with the rest of the group, saying why each word is special to you.
- Listen and ask questions as other students tell you about their favorite English words.

5 Culture

SAYING THE RIGHT THING

1 READING

Read and answer the *Shopping Skills* questionnaire.

SHOPPING SKILLS

Brush up your shopping skills! Choose the best answers.

1 You're in a store but you're not planning to buy anything. A salesperson asks if you want any help. What do you say?
- **A** I don't want to buy anything.
- **B** No, thanks. You can't help me.
- **C** No, thank you, I'm just looking.

2 You find a pair of jeans, and want to see if they fit. What do you say to the salesperson?
- **A** Excuse me, can I wear them?
- **B** Excuse me, could I try these on, please?
- **C** Do you mind if I put them on?

3 The jeans are too tight. What do you say?
- **A** Do you have them in a larger size?
- **B** Do you have a larger one?
- **C** Do you have a smaller pair?

4 The salesperson shows you a lime green jacket, saying "This is the latest color." It makes you look sick. What do you say?
- **A** It doesn't really look good on me.
- **B** I don't think it fits properly.
- **C** It doesn't match very well.

5 The salesperson shows you a jacket that you can't afford. What do you say?
- **A** I'm afraid that's more expensive.
- **B** Sorry, that's too expensive for me.
- **C** I wonder if you could knock $20 off.

6 You don't have enough money to buy something. You politely ask a friend to lend you $10. What do you say?
- **A** Give me ten bucks, will you?
- **B** Could you possibly borrow $10?
- **C** Would you mind lending me $10?

🔴 2.13 Now listen and check. Then turn to page 120 and read the explanations.

Culture

2 VOCABULARY

Complete the sentences with verbs from the questionnaire.

1 It's very cold today—_____ on a coat before you go out.
2 It's important to buy shoes that _____ properly.
3 The shirt is a nice color, but it doesn't _____ my pants.
4 I need some new clothes—I don't have a thing to _____!
5 Black doesn't really _____ good on you—it makes you look pale.
6 It's a good idea to _____ on clothes before you buy them.

3 SPEAKING

Make and respond to requests using expressions from the box. Remember: the bigger the request, the more important it is to ask your partner politely!

> Can I borrow a pen, please?

1 Ask to borrow a pen.
2 Ask to borrow his/her MP3 player.
3 Ask him/her to open the window.
4 Ask him/her to help with your homework.
5 Ask to share his/her book.
6 Ask if you can use his/her cell phone.
7 Ask if you can use his/her cell to call New York.
8 Ask him/her to take care of your dog while you're on vacation.
9 Ask him/her to help you paint your room.

Making requests	Responding to requests
Will you …?	Yes, sure. ☺
Would you …?	I'd rather not. ☹
Can I/you …?	No problem. ☺
Could I/you …?	I'm afraid not. ☹
More polite	
Would you mind _____ing …?	No, of course not. ☺
Do you mind if I …?	Not at all. Go ahead. ☺
I wonder if I/you could …	Yes, certainly. ☺
Could I possibly …?	I'd rather you didn't. ☹

4 LISTENING

You are going to hear a tourist in three different situations. First, try to match the sentences below with these places.

A Bank
B Train station 
C Youth hostel 

1 Could I change 1,000 pesos into dollars?
2 I'd like a room for tonight, please.
3 How would you like the money?
4 One way or round trip?
5 Have you made a reservation?
6 Single or double?
7 Tens and twenties, please.
8 A round trip, please.
9 Single, please, with a shower, if possible.
10 Here's your change.
11 There's one in five minutes.
12 Here's your receipt for the exchange.
13 Which platform does it leave from?
14 Would you mind filling out this form, please?
15 Do I have to change?

Now decide which sentences the tourist says, and which sentences the tourist hears.

🔴 2.14 Listen and check.

5 ROLE-PLAY

Choose one of the situations in this lesson: shopping for clothes, changing money, buying a train ticket, or reserving a room. Act out a similar conversation between a tourist and a salesperson, a bank clerk, a railroad ticket agent, or a front desk clerk.

Now change roles and situations.

6 MINI-PROJECT *Advertising*

Work with another student and write about how advertising makes us want to buy things. Think about:

- Different kinds of advertising, e.g., posters, TV commercials, Web pop-ups, junk mail
- Your favorite and least favorite ads
- How ads get their message across

Collect examples of ads (in English or your own language). Choose three and write a paragraph about each one, describing how they work and your reaction to them.

6 ON THE MOVE

1 I promised I wouldn't forget!

Reporting what people said
Reported speech with various reporting verbs

1 OPENER

Look at the photos of Kerala in India. What advice would you give to someone traveling there?

2 READING

🔘 2.15 Laura is 16 and lives in Miami. Read her e-mail to a friend. Do her parents agree to her vacation in India?

3 AFTER READING

Match these sentences in direct speech with the reported speech in Laura's e-mail. Then number sentences a–m of the dialogue in the right order.

a   I've changed my mind, I love Indian food. Please let me go.
b   We won't be by ourselves—Nisha's parents are going too.
c   I promise I won't forget.
d   Would you like to go to India with me in the summer?
e   But you don't like Indian food. Last time we had an Indian meal, you complained it was too spicy.
f   Why don't we invite Nisha and her parents for dinner? Then we can talk it over with them.
g   No, you can't go to India.
h   Remember, you must have vaccinations before you leave. And you need to take malaria pills.
i   Oh, all right—you can go. But you must keep in touch.
j   Oh, wow! I'll have to ask my parents—I hope they'll say yes.
k   Yes, you could get malaria if you forget to take them regularly.
l   It's out of the question—two young girls traveling halfway around the world by themselves.
m   Of course, I'll send lots of e-mails.

🔘 2.16 Now listen and check.

Your response If a friend of yours invited you to go on vacation, what issues would you discuss with your parents?

From: Laura
To: Susanna
Subject: Kerala
Attachments: Kerala1.jpg Kerala2.jpg

Hi, Susanna

You'll never guess what!

Nisha—she's my best friend at school—is going to visit her grandparents in India in the summer, and yesterday she invited me to go with her! I replied that I'd have to ask my parents, and I hoped they'd say yes. At first, they refused to let me go—Dad said it was out of the question. I explained that we wouldn't be by ourselves because Nisha's parents were coming too. Then Mom pointed out that I didn't like Indian food, but I told her I'd changed my mind, and I loved it. In the end, they agreed to let me go! 😊😊😊

Dad told me to keep in touch and I promised to send lots of e-mails. Mom reminded me that I had to have vaccinations before I left, and that I needed to take malaria pills. Dad warned me that I could get malaria if I forgot to take them regularly. I promised I wouldn't forget! Then Mom suggested inviting Nisha and her parents for dinner to talk it over—they're coming over tonight.

I'm so excited!

Laura xxxx

P.S. I'm attaching two photos of Kerala, where Nisha's grandparents live—doesn't it look amazing?!

4 PRONUNCIATION

Mark the stress on these two-syllable reporting verbs. Which two verbs are different?

> advise   agree   complain   explain   invite   offer
> promise   refuse   remind   reply   suggest

🔘 **2.17** Now listen and check. Repeat the words.

5 SPEAKING

Laura asked for travel tips on a website forum. Read the replies and tell another student the answers to these questions.

1. What did Jackie tell Laura to do?
2. What did Kim explain?
3. What did Sandy warn Laura not to do?
4. What did Roger advise her to do?
5. What did Sara suggest?
6. What did Peter remind her to do?

> Take more money and fewer clothes than you think you'll need. — **Jackie**
>
> It's best to request an aisle seat on the plane, so you can easily get up and walk around. — **Kim**
>
> You shouldn't take more luggage than you can run with! — **Sandy**
>
> Carry a local newspaper under your arm so you don't look like a tourist. — **Roger**
>
> If I were you, I'd buy a cotton sarong in India. You can wear it as a skirt, and you can also use it as a towel, a sheet, or a bag. — **Sara**
>
> Don't forget to take some insect spray to keep the mosquitoes away! — **Peter**

Extension Write five more sentences giving travel tips. Exchange sentences with another student and write what your partner advised you to do.

6 SPEAKING

Interview two other students. Ask them about the situations in the *What do you say?* questionnaire and write down their answers.

Questionnaire What do you say?

1. You're playing music in your room and your parents complain that it's too loud.
2. You order a meal in a restaurant but when the waiter brings your food, it's cold.
3. A friend tells you he's very nervous about an exam tomorrow.
4. Your teacher asks you why you were late for school this morning.
5. A friend of yours has a very bad toothache.
6. You see a woman on the bus with her bag open.
7. A friend tells you she's going on a snowboarding vacation.
8. You're going to a party and your parents tell you to be home by 11 p.m.
9. A friend is miserable because her boyfriend is dating another girl.

7 WRITING

Use your notes from the questionnaire to report the answers of the two students you interviewed. Use as many reporting verbs as possible.

Pedro agreed that the music was too loud and said he would turn it down, but Ana refused to turn it down!

LANGUAGE WORKOUT

Complete.

Reported speech with various reporting verbs
Verb + infinitive
agree   ask   hope   offer   promise   refuse
They agreed _____ _____ me go.
I promised _____ _____ lots of e-mails.

Verb + object + infinitive
advise   ask   invite   promise   tell   warn
She invited _____ _____ _____ with her.
Dad told _____ _____ _____ in touch.

Verb + (*that*) clause
agree   complain   explain   hope   point out   promise
reply   say   suggest   warn
Mom pointed out that I _____ n't like Indian food.
You complained it _____ too spicy.

Verb + object + (*that*) clause
promise   remind   tell   warn
Mom reminded _____ that I _____ to have vaccinations.

suggest* + -*ing
Mom suggested _____ Nisha and her parents for dinner.

▶ Answers and Practice
Language File page 117

UNIT 6

6 ON THE MOVE

2 The waitress wanted to know if …

Reporting what people asked
Reported questions

1 OPENER

How much do you know about your own country? What would be the best way to find out more?

2 READING

Read *You're welcome*. What couldn't the writer stop doing?

You're welcome

Bill Bryson, an American writer who had lived in Britain for ten years, returned to the U.S. to rediscover his homeland. He borrowed his mother's old Chevrolet and drove 13,978 miles through 38 states, keeping mainly to side roads and small towns. This is Bryson's description of a meal in a town named Littleton in New Hampshire.

It was the friendliest little place I had ever seen. I went into the Topic of the Town restaurant. The other customers smiled at me, the lady at the cash register showed me where to put my jacket, and the waitress couldn't do enough for me.

She brought me a menu and I made the mistake of saying thank you. "You're welcome," she said. Once you start this, there's no stopping. She came and wiped the table with a damp cloth. "Thank you," I said. "You're welcome," she said. She brought me some cutlery wrapped in a paper napkin. I hesitated but I couldn't stop myself. "Thank you," I said. "You're welcome," she said.

I ordered the fried chicken special. As I waited, I became uncomfortably aware that the people at the next table were watching me and smiling at me in a slightly crazy way. The waitress was watching me too. Every few minutes she came over and asked if everything was all right. Then she filled my glass with ice water and told me my food would only be a minute. "Thank you," I said. "You're welcome," she said.

Finally, the waitress came out of the kitchen with a tray the size of a tabletop and started putting plates of food in front of me—soup, a salad, a plate of chicken, a basket of hot rolls. It all looked delicious. Suddenly I realized I was starving.

The waitress wanted to know if she could get me anything else.

"No, this is just fine, thank you," I answered with my knife and fork ready to attack the food.

"Would you like some ketchup?"

"No, thank you."

"Would you like some more dressing for your salad?"

"No, thank you."

"Do you have enough gravy?"

There was enough gravy to drown a horse. "Yes, plenty of gravy, thank you."

"How about a cup of coffee?"

"Really, I'm fine."

"You're sure there's nothing I can do for you?"

"Well, you might just go away and let me eat my dinner," I wanted to say, but I didn't, of course. I just smiled sweetly and said, "No, thank you."

3 AFTER READING

Match the beginnings with the endings. There are two extra endings.

1. After living abroad for a long time, Bryson wanted to
2. He feels that once you've started saying thank you, you
3. He was uncomfortable about the way people
4. When the food came, he wanted to
5. The waitress asked if he would
6. She wanted to know if he
7. She asked if he had
8. She wondered if she could
9. Bryson was sure there was nothing the waitress
10. He didn't really tell the waitress to

a. bring him some coffee.
b. looked at him.
c. like some ketchup.
d. enough gravy.
e. ask for some more.
f. could do for him.
g. go away.
h. have to continue.
i. eat, not talk.
j. like some more chicken.
k. get to know the U.S. again.
l. would like some more dressing.

Your response What would you have done in Bryson's situation?

76

4 VOCABULARY

Find these words and phrases in the text, and match them with their definitions.

Word Bank Restaurant

cash register   dressing *n*   gravy
ketchup   napkin   roll   special *n*   tray

1 dish of the day
2 individual portion of bread, like a very small loaf
3 tomato sauce
4 kind of sauce for salad
5 machine where you pay in a store or restaurant
6 juice of cooked meat
7 you use it to carry plates of food, glasses, etc.
8 you use it to protect your clothes when eating

5 PRONUNCIATION

🔴 **2.18** Listen and underline the most important word in each sentence.

1 Would you like some more chicken?
   No, thank you, but I'd like some more fries.
2 Do you have enough gravy?
   Yes, thanks, but I'd like some more bread.
3 Would you like some ketchup?
   No, thank you, but I'd like some dressing.
4 How about some coffee?
   Yes, please, and some cake.

Now listen again and repeat. What part of speech are the stressed words?

6 LISTENING

🔴 **2.19** Listen to an interview with Lizzie about her last vacation and decide: true or false? Correct the false sentences.

1 The interviewer asked when Lizzie had first gone on vacation.
2 Lizzie told him she had gone on vacation in January this year.
3 She said she had been to Aspen, Colorado, for two weeks.
4 She added that it was a school trip, so she went with her family.
5 The interviewer wondered if Lizzie had done any water sports there.
6 Lizzie replied that she had done a lot of snowboarding.
7 She explained that they had taken packed lunches with sandwiches, fruit, and potato chips.
8 The interviewer wanted to know what Lizzie had enjoyed most and least.
9 She remarked that doing jumps on the snowboard was really difficult.
10 The interviewer agreed that falling over in the snow was fun.

7 SPEAKING

Interview another student about their last vacation and write down the answers. Ask about:

Time	When did you ...?
Place	Where did you ...?
People	Who did you ...?
Activities	What did you ...?
	Did you ...?
Food	What did you ...?
	Did you ...?
Enjoyment	What did you ... most/least?

8 WRITING

Use your notes from exercise 7 to write sentences reporting the questions and answers.

I asked Sara when she had last been on vacation. She told me that she had had a vacation in July.

Extension Write a report of an imaginary interview on the same topic with a famous person (e.g., pop star, movie star, sports personality). Make up all the answers.

LANGUAGE WORKOUT

Complete.

Reported questions

Direct speech	Reported speech
"Is everything all right?"	➝ She asked _____ everything _____ all right.
"Can I get you anything else?"	➝ She wanted to know _____ she _____ get him anything else.
"Would you like some ketchup?"	➝ She wondered _____ he _____ like some ketchup.

In reported questions, the word order is the same as in statements. We _____ use a question mark after reported questions. Modal verbs *could*, *should*, _____, *might* do not change.

▶ Answers and Practice
Language File page 117

6 ON THE MOVE

3 You'd like to stay there, wouldn't you?

Asking for agreement and checking information
Tag questions

1 OPENER

Match these buildings with the photos.

> exhibition pavilion   hotel
> igloo   museum   skyscraper

LISTENING

2 🔊 2.20 Sophie is looking at a website about unusual buildings with her boyfriend, Zak. Listen and number the photos in the order you hear about them.

A

B

C

D

E

78

UNIT 6

3 🔊 2.21 Listen again to the descriptions of the photos and choose the correct answer.

1 The modern art museum is in Athens/Vienna.
2 The skyscraper is in Dubai/Shanghai and is 828/1,828 meters high.
3 The exhibition pavilion changed color/shape when people moved around inside it.
4 The hotel suite is in Greece/Italy. It's called the Governor Villa, and costs $2,700/$7,200 a night.
5 The world's biggest igloo is 14/40 meters around, 12 meters across, and five meters high. It's in Puvirnituq in northern/southern Canada.

Your response Which of the places in the photos would you like to visit and why? What's your favorite building in your city/country?

4 PRONUNCIATION

🔊 2.22 Complete with these tag questions, and then listen and check your answers. Repeat the sentences.

can it	did she	didn't he
do you	doesn't he	isn't it
weren't they	would he	

1 The hotel is in Athens, _____?
2 You don't know what that is, _____?
3 Zak and Sophie were talking about buildings, _____?
4 Zak asked Sophie about the photos, _____?
5 Sophie didn't expect Zak to know about the tallest skyscraper, _____?
6 Zak wouldn't like to stay in the Governor Villa, _____?
7 Zak likes the modern art museum, _____?
8 The igloo can't hold 500 people, _____?

We use tag questions with falling intonation to ask for agreement, and with rising intonation to check information. Which of the sentences have falling intonation and which have rising intonation?

5 SPEAKING

Take the quiz and discuss your answers with another student using tag questions.

Around the World Quiz

1 Which is the highest mountain in the southern hemisphere?
2 Where is the island of Honshu?
3 Which is the largest country in the world?
4 Where are the Galápagos Islands?
5 What is the capital of Alaska?
6 Where did the Aztec people live?
7 Where is Lake Titicaca?
8 What is the capital of South Africa?
9 Where do the Maori people live?
10 What are the names of the five Great Lakes?
11 Which three countries share borders with Chile?
12 Where is the Aswan Dam?
13 Where is the Golden Gate Bridge?
14 Who was America named after?
15 Where are the Angel Falls?

A It's in the Andes, isn't it?
B It begins with A, doesn't it?

Extension Write your own five-question quiz and ask another student to take it.

6 WRITING

Write descriptions of three different places. Then read your descriptions aloud, but don't say the names of the places. Can other students guess what they are?

It's a city in the U.S. and it has a famous red bridge.

LANGUAGE WORKOUT

Complete.

Tag questions
They looked at the website, **didn't they?**
Zak doesn't want to stay in the hotel, **does he?**
You can see that, _____ you?
You'd like to stay there, _____ you?
It's been in the news, _____ it?
You didn't expect me to know that, _____?

Affirmative statement → negative tag
Negative statement → affirmative tag

▶Answers and Practice
Language File page 118

6 ON THE MOVE

4 Integrated Skills
Reporting and summarizing what people said

1 OPENER

In this lesson, two teenagers talk about vacations with their parents. What are the advantages and disadvantages of vacations with parents?

READING

2 Read *Family Vacations* and match these questions with Isabel's answers.

a What do you enjoy doing most on vacation?
b Do you have any advice for people going on vacation with their parents?
c What's the best vacation you've ever had?
d Where are you going next?
e Do you help decide where you go?
f What's your favorite way of traveling?

Family Vacations

Isabel Martin, 18, lives in Toronto

1 It was a trip to Argentina with my parents six months ago. "What? You're going on vacation with your parents?" My friends were amazed. "But you're 18—you can go on vacation by yourself!" Well, that's true. But this was a special vacation, and I've never had a better time. Let me explain. My dad's parents were originally from Argentina, where he still has family, and for years, he'd been talking about going there to see them.

2 Yes, we always discuss things. Dad's family live in Mendoza—that's in the northwest of Argentina at the foot of the Andes—but I wanted a beach vacation. So we agreed to go to Mar del Plata on the east coast and invite Dad's relatives to come and stay with us. In the end, they turned out to be pretty well off, so we shared the cost of the villa.

3 I'm not a great one for museums and sightseeing. My ideal vacation is lots of time on the beach, just lazing around. I love sunbathing and swimming. We did a lot of that in Mar del Plata. I also like playing on my game console. We used the cooking facilities at the villa, so we had to go shopping for groceries and do the cooking. But we shared that with our relatives, and I learned how to make *locro*—a traditional Andean stew with meat, beans, and other vegetables.

4 I enjoy going by train, but I don't think you can get to Argentina that way! First, we flew from Toronto to Buenos Aires—it took 13 hours and the plane was packed, but I didn't mind because I love flying. Then we took another flight down to Mar del Plata. We rented bikes there, and we rode our bikes everywhere.

5 My first rule about vacations with parents is: don't always believe what they tell you. My father claimed to speak some Spanish and told us that our relatives didn't speak much English. In fact, it was the opposite—they spoke excellent English, and Dad couldn't remember a word of Spanish. I learned to say "Lo siento, no entiendo.", which means, "Sorry. I don't understand." and I said it a lot! My second rule is obvious: let your parents pay for everything!

6 Back to Argentina! I got along really well with one of my cousins named Mariela, and she's invited me to go and stay with her in Mendoza. I've been working to save up for the vacation because—guess what!—this time I'm going on my own! I've also been trying to learn more Spanish—I can't just say "No entiendo" all the time.

3 Find words or phrases in the text to match these definitions. The parts of speech in *italics* refer to the words in the text.

1 members of a family, e.g., cousins *n*
2 rich, or having enough money to live well *adj*
3 relaxing *v*
4 electronic equipment for playing computer games *n*
5 food and other household goods *n*
6 extremely crowded *adj*
7 paid to use something for a short time *v*
8 very clear, easy to see, or understand *adj*

4 What do the words in *italics* refer to?

Paragraph
1 … for years he'd been talking about going *there* to *see them*.
2 … invite Dad's relatives to come and stay with *us*.
3 We did a lot of *that* in Mar del Plata.
4 … I don't think you can get to Argentina *that* way!
5 … I said *it* a lot!
6 … invited me to go and stay with *her* …

5 LISTENING

You are going to hear an interview with Ben Mackenzie, who lives in New York. First, look at the photos and try to predict some of his answers to the questions in exercise 2.

🔴 2.23 Now listen and see if you were right. Write down Ben's answers to the questions.

6 SPEAKING

Use your notes to tell each other what Ben said in the interview.

A He said his best vacation had been in Canada …
B … and they'd seen whales and dolphins.

Now ask another student the six questions from exercise 2 (in the right order). Write down the answers.

7 GUIDED WRITING

Write a report of your interview with the student in exercise 6. You can summarize the information—you don't need to include all the details. Use various reporting verbs, e.g., *ask, want to know, reply, tell, explain, complain, point out*.

I asked Rafael where his best vacation had been, and he told me …

LEARNER INDEPENDENCE

8 Thinking skills: Listening and note taking

- Before you listen, try to predict some of the words and information you are going to hear. Think about the topic, look at pictures or charts, and read through comprehension questions.
- While listening, focus on key words— they're usually stressed—and don't try to understand every word.
- When taking notes, only write down the most important words and phrases. Ben gave examples of water sports he enjoyed—surfing, snorkeling, swimming, sailing—but the most important phrase was *water sports*.
- Remember that people often say the same thing twice in different ways, e.g., "Parents are far too bossy on vacation— they don't need to tell us what to do all the time."

9 Word creation: Complete the sentences with these words to make compound adjectives: *well* + past participle.

balanced   behaved   done
dressed   known   off   paid

1 She wears stylish clothes and always looks well _____.
2 He doesn't have a well-_____ job, so he can't afford to take a vacation.
3 If you want to be healthy, it's important to eat a well-_____ diet.
4 "How would you like your steak cooked?" "Well _____, please."
5 The children are usually polite and well _____.
6 Unfortunately, a lot of people aren't _____ when they retire.
7 Bill Bryson is a well-_____ author of books about travel.

10 🔴 2.24 **Phrasebook:** Find these useful expressions in Unit 6. Then listen and repeat.

You'll never guess what!
I've changed my mind.
It's out of the question.
You're welcome.
Let me explain.
I'm not a great one for …
In fact, it was the opposite.

Now write a five-line dialogue using three of the expressions.

6 ON THE MOVE
Inspired EXTRA!

PROJECT
Ideal vacation

1. Work in a group and make a list of different kinds of vacations, for example, beach vacations, hiking vacations, adventure vacations, sailing vacations. Then choose one kind of vacation to write about.

2. Research: Find out as much as you can about your ideal kind of vacation from newspapers and magazines, travel brochures, and the Internet, and make notes.

   - Where can you have this vacation?
   - What time of the year is best for the vacation?
   - Do you need any special skills, preparation, or equipment?
   - What can you do to be a "good" tourist?
   - Are there any disadvantages, e.g., cost, location, timing?
   - Is there anyone you can interview who has been on this vacation?

3. Work together and use your notes to write about your ideal vacation. Read your work carefully and correct any mistakes. Find photos from travel brochures, magazines, or the Web for your project. Show your work to the other groups.

Antarctic Dream

Our ideal kind of vacation is one where you can see unusual birds and wildlife. It's something you can do anywhere in the world, but the place we'd like to go to is Antarctica. The best time of the year to see wildlife there is from mid-November to mid-February. Wind is the main weather enemy there, so you need to take windproof and waterproof jackets and pants and lots of warm "layers" of clothes. Good boots are essential and take the best camera you can get. The photo opportunities are amazing. Antarctica is a protected area, and there are strict rules about what you can do when you are ashore. The main problem, of course, is that it is a long way away. Flights are expensive and so is the vacation itself, on board a special ship. But it's a once-in-a-lifetime opportunity!

Game — Question games

1 Questions and answers

- Form two teams. One student is the question master.
- The question master writes the answer to an imaginary question on the board. For example, *150* or *At home*.
- The teams have five minutes to write as many questions as possible that can go with the answer on the board. For example:

  How old are you? What's 3 times 50?
  What's your house number?
  or *Where's your book? Where did you sleep last night?*

- The winner is the team with the most questions.

2 Only questions

- Play in pairs. The object is to have a conversation asking only questions.
- Student A asks a question, Student B replies with a question, Student A replies with another question, and so on, until one student makes a statement or repeats a question.
- Students lose a point if they make a statement or repeat a question. A student wins when the other student has lost three points.

UNIT 6

CONSOLIDATION

LESSON 1 Look at Laura's e-mail on page 74. Write questions beginning with *Who ...?* using these reporting verbs, and answer the questions.

> invite   reply   hope   refuse   explain   point out
> agree   promise   remind   warn   suggest

Who invited Laura to go to India with her?
Nisha did.

LESSON 2 Look at exercise 4 on page 77. Write five sentences, each using at least one of the words in the Word Bank.

The waitress brought me a napkin and some rolls.

LESSON 3 Write a paragraph about a famous person. Then read your paragraph aloud, but don't say the person's name. Can the other students guess who it is?

EXTENSION

LESSON 1 Look at the *What do you say?* questionnaire on page 75. Write a similar questionnaire about five situations. Ask two other students the questions and write a paragraph reporting the answers using as many reporting verbs as possible.

LESSON 2 Look at exercise 7 on page 77. Write a report of the questions another student asked you and your answers.

Bianca asked me when I went on vacation last year.
I replied that I had been on vacation in July.

LESSON 3 Look at exercise 2 on page 78. Use the Internet or your library to find information about other buildings around the world. Write a five-question *True-False* quiz about the buildings, and ask another student to take your quiz.

This tall building in New York opened in May 1931, and many tourists still visit it and go to the top.

YOUR CHOICE!

CONSTRUCTION Reported speech

Complete with the correct form of these reporting verbs.

ask   offer   refuse   remind   reply   suggest   warn   wonder

1. Laura _____ Nisha what the weather in Kerala would be like.
2. Laura's mother _____ her to take a guidebook.
3. Laura's father _____ that she took a camera with her.
4. Laura's mother _____ her not to forget her passport.
5. Nisha's parents _____ if Laura's parents had any questions.
6. Nisha's parents _____ to take any money for Laura's stay in Kerala.
7. Nisha _____ to teach Laura some words of Malayalam, the language of Kerala.
8. When Laura asked how many people spoke Malayalam, Nisha _____ that 38 million did.

ACTION Sense mimes

- Work in a small group.
- Each student acts out eating something, e.g., spaghetti, a boiled egg, a hot Mexican dish, a melon, fish with lots of bones. The other students try to guess what it is.
- You can also act out listening to something, e.g., rock music, a boring lesson, someone using a cell phone on a train, instructions on how to do something, a phone call with bad news.

REFLECTION Reported speech

Match the examples a–j with language functions 1–8.

1 Advice   2 Command   3 Invitation   4 Offer
5 Question   6 Statement   7 Suggestion   8 Warning

a They wondered if there was anything they could do to help.
b Her father warned her not to eat unwashed salad.
c She suggested taking a big backpack.
d The police officer told him to get out of the car.
e She invited her to stay the night.
f He explained that it was a 12-hour flight.
g She asked what the time difference was between Miami and Kerala.
h He replied that he didn't know.
i She wanted to know if it was safe to drink tap water.
j He advised her to look in the guidebook.

INTERACTION A collage of myself

- Work individually and then in a small group. A collage is a big piece of paper with cut-out pictures, drawings, and words stuck to it.
- Make a collage that shows the person you are, but don't put your name on it. You can use magazine pictures, your own photos of things that mean a lot to you, and words that are important to you.
- Show your collage to your group and answer questions about it.
- Show your group's collages to other students and see if they can identify whose they are.

REVIEW
UNITS 5–6

1 Read and complete. For each number 1–10, choose word or phrase A, B, or C.

Reindeer Man

Researcher Piers Vitebsky spends part of each year with the Eveny people. They live in the Verhoyansk Mountains of northeast Siberia, where winter temperatures fall to −71 °C.

"I communicate mostly in Russian, but if I hadn't learned Eveny, I __1__ have been able to understand everything. The Eveny language has about 1,500 words to describe the appearance and behavior of reindeer. I learned Eveny because otherwise I __2__ have misunderstood exactly what people meant.

The Eveny move camp every few days. We're moving camp today, and I wake in a tent full of the smells of reindeer fur and wood smoke. One of us makes sweet tea. Another has already used his dog to help bring the herd of 2,000 reindeer back to the camp. Then we catch the reindeer. We __3__ catch all 2,000, just the ones we'll ride and use to carry our things.

Now we need __4__ our tents. I've calculated that the old lady in the family I'm with __5__ have packed and unpacked 1,500 times. When the Eveny leave a camp, they believe they __6__ look back or they will never return to the place. And they always leave wood and stones behind for the next year. Other people can use these, but they __7__ always replace them.

On the first morning in a new camp it's important to tell each other what you dreamed about in the night. These dreams show how successful the new camp will be. Last time we moved I told the herders that I __8__ about mountains, animals, and running water. They asked me __9__ I dreamed about these things when I was back home. I replied that I only dreamed about reindeer when I was in the Verhoyansk Mountains.

I explained that I would have to return to Britain. As always, I wished that I __10__ more time with the Eveny. There is never enough time to get everything done."

1 A can't	B won't	C wouldn't
2 A can	B will	C might
3 A must	B don't need to	C didn't have to
4 A packed	B to pack	C are packing
5 A had to	B must	C will
6 A don't have to	B can't	C don't need to
7 A must	B need	C had to
8 A am dreaming	B dream	C had dreamed
9 A if	B when	C where
10 A did have	B have had	C had had

2 Write sentences saying what would and wouldn't have happened if things had been different.

The ship hit an iceberg. It sank.
If the ship hadn't hit an iceberg, it wouldn't have sunk.

1 Amelia Earhart was daring. She tried to fly around the world.
2 Something strange happened. The plane didn't reach the island.
3 The boys didn't realize Maribel was a girl. They called her "Mario."
4 Maribel was an excellent soccer player. She played for Mexico.
5 FIFA said Maribel couldn't play for a men's club. She didn't play for Celaya.
6 Nisha invited her. Laura went to India.
7 The restaurant looked friendly. Bill Bryson decided to have dinner there.
8 Isabel didn't speak Spanish. She was worried about meeting her relatives.

3 Nick planned to fly to Brazil for a vacation, but everything went wrong. What does he regret? Write sentences beginning with *I wish …* and *If only …*.

He decided to drive to the airport.
"I wish I hadn't decided to drive to the airport."

1 He didn't take the train.
2 The traffic was heavy.
3 He didn't stop for gas.
4 The car ran out of gas.
5 He didn't get to the airport in time.
6 He missed his flight.
7 He didn't have a vacation.

4 Complete with *can't*, *need(s) to*, or *don't need to* and these verbs.

| forget | go | have | look | reserve | start | stay | stop |

1 He _____ his eyes tested because he often gets headaches.
2 We _____ a table—the restaurant is never full.
3 I _____ up too late—I've got an exam tomorrow.
4 She _____ taking malaria pills before she goes to India.
5 There's plenty of food in the refrigerator, so you _____ to the supermarket.
6 I _____ at the road map because I know the way.
7 You _____ to lock the door when you leave.
8 We _____ at a gas station before we run out of gas.

5 You're waiting for a friend to join you at a concert, but she's very late. Talk about what could/might have happened to her.

get the date wrong
A She could have gotten the date wrong.
B Yes, she might have gotten the date wrong.

1 lose the address
2 forget about it
3 feel too tired
4 go to another concert
5 miss the bus
6 decide not to come

REVIEW

6 Write the sentences in reported speech using the correct form of these verbs.

> complain explain invite offer
> refuse remind suggest warn

1. Paul: "Sue, don't forget to call me tonight."
2. Sally: "Tom, would you like to go to the movies?"
3. Robert: "You press the red button to turn on the DVD player."
4. Marta: "I'm not going to clean up my room."
5. Dan: "Emma, don't drive too fast."
6. Doctor: "Why don't you take a vacation, Mr. Evans?"
7. Jenny: "I can't concentrate with all this noise."
8. Bill: "I'll carry your suitcase, Mom."

7 Marion is a tourist in the U.S. Report her questions using the words in parentheses.

1. "When does the next train leave?" (want to know)
2. "Do I have to change trains?" (wonder)
3. "How long does the trip take?" (ask)
4. "Is the hotel near the train station?" (want to know)
5. "How much does a single room cost?" (wonder)
6. "Can I pay by credit card?" (ask)

8 Complete with tag questions.

1. Laura and Nisha went to India, _____?
2. Laura didn't forget her passport, _____?
3. You'd like to go to the party, _____?
4. You don't want to be late, _____?
5. It hasn't rained for ages, _____?
6. We waste a lot of water, _____?
7. Isabel likes flying, _____?
8. She can't speak fluent Spanish, _____?

VOCABULARY

9 Complete with correct form of these verbs.

> advise change collect complain confess
> fit point out score supervise warn

1. The burglar _____ that he had stolen money.
2. She _____ him that the dog was dangerous, but he didn't listen.
3. She's happy because she _____ the winning goal.
4. I don't know what you want—you keep _____ your mind.
5. I searched the Internet to _____ information for my project.
6. An experienced diver _____ us when we made our first dives.
7. These shoes are too tight—they don't _____.
8. Her father _____ that the flight would be very expensive.
9. If your room isn't clean, you should _____ to the hotel manager.
10. If you have a toothache, I _____ you to see a dentist.

10 Match these words with their definitions.

> abduct aisle blow up hemisphere
> massive previous qualification trace *n*

1. enormous
2. ability or quality needed for a particular job
3. kidnap
4. happening before, earlier
5. explode
6. sign
7. where you can walk between lines of seats
8. half of the Earth

11 Match the verbs in list A with the words and phrases in list B.

	A	B
1	change	a pill
2	fly	a goal
3	give	a club
4	score	solo
5	join	someone a chance
6	take	course

LEARNER INDEPENDENCE SELF ASSESSMENT

Look back at Lessons 1–3 in Units 5 and 6.

How good are you at …?	✓ Fine	? Not sure
1 Talking about unreal or imaginary past events Workbook pp50–51 exercises 1–3	☐	☐
2 Expressing regret about the past Workbook p50 exercise 4	☐	☐
3 Expressing obligation and lack of obligation Workbook pp52–53 exercises 2–4	☐	☐
4 Making deductions and speculating about the past Workbook pp54–55 exercises 1–4	☐	☐
5 Reporting what people said Workbook pp62–63 exercises 1–4	☐	☐
6 Reporting what people asked Workbook pp64–65 exercises 1–4	☐	☐
7 Asking for agreement and checking information Workbook pp66–67 exercises 1–3	☐	☐

Not sure? Take a look at Language File pages 116–118 and do the Workbook exercise(s) again.

Now write an example for 1–7.

1. *More people would have survived if the lifeboats had been full.*

PREVIEW

UNITS 7–8

COMMUNICATIVE AIMS
LEARNING HOW TO ...

1. Describe changes and experiences
2. Talk about what's right
3. Use the phone
4. Talk about past ability
5. Express purpose
6. Express obligation and ability
7. Talk about obligation, permission, and prohibition

TOPICS AND VOCABULARY

Idioms
Furniture, fixtures, and fittings
Science
Cell phones
Telephone language
Phrasal verbs
Languages
Achievements
Education
Family rules
Volunteering

A

I wasn't allowed to go to any of her concerts.

B

While he was in prison, he decided to become a poet and was able to educate himself.

1. Match five of the communicative aims (1–7) with the pictures (A–E).

2. Complete the words on the right and put them into categories.

   Education   Music
   Furniture, fixtures, and fittings

b_nd   c_llege   comp_ser
c_pboard   c_rriculum
ex_mination   g_itar   op_ra
sch_dule   sh_lf   s_nger   s_nk
st_ve   t_ble   tuit_on   t_ne
un_form   w_ndow

86

PREVIEW

C

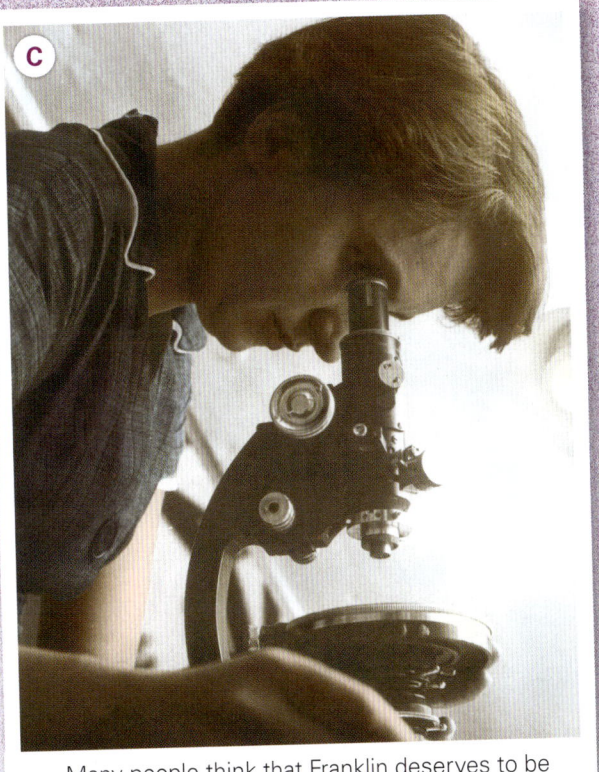

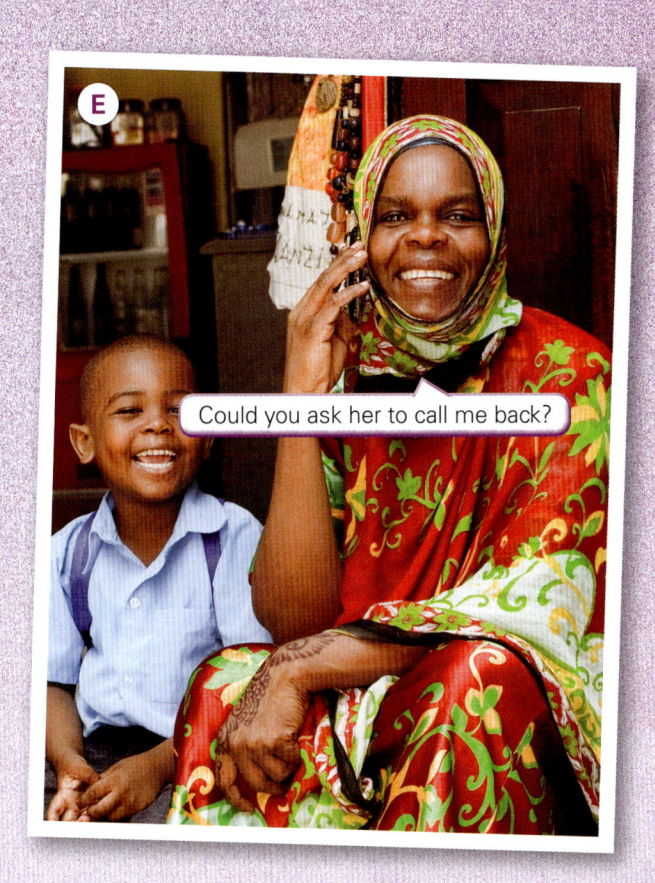

Many people think that Franklin deserves to be awarded a Nobel Prize now.

E

Could you ask her to call me back?

D

She moved to Edinburgh in order to be near her sister.

3 🔊 2.25 Listen to extracts 1–3 from Units 7 and 8. Match them with three of the text types A–D.

- A An interview with a singer/songwriter
- B A biography of a composer
- C A poem about school
- D A conversation about a kitchen

4 Play *Backward* and *Forward* with another student.

- Turn to the Word List on page 121 and choose two of the categories. Choose six words from each category and write them down.
- Tell your partner the name of the first category. Then spell the words out one by one backward. Your partner tries to figure out what the words are.
- Tell your partner the name of the second category. Then spell the words out one by one leaving out the first two letters. Your partner tries to figure out what the words are.

Believe it or not! The first text message was sent on December 3, 1992 and said "Happy Christmas!" 95% of text messages are delivered within 10 seconds.

87

7
1 GETTING THE MESSAGE ACROSS

Good job—keep it up!

Describing changes and experiences
Passive tenses

1 OPENER

An idiom is an expression whose meaning isn't obvious from the words. For example, "out of the question" means "definitely not a possibility." Do you remember these English idioms?

> believe it or not
> down to earth
> Good job!
> face to face
> knock on wood
> learn by heart

2 READING

Read *What does it mean?* Which of these idioms are new to you?

Why do people say, "I've been **fired**" when they've lost their job? It's thought that the expression comes from the days when a person used illegal ways to get rid of an unpleasant neighbor. The neighbor came home to find his house destroyed—by fire!

If someone is doing well, for example at school or in a sport, we can say "Good job—**keep it up**!" to encourage the person to continue to do well. The phrase comes from the game of badminton or shuttlecock, where the shuttlecock is kept up in the air for as long as possible.

What does it mean?

Thousands of idioms have entered the English language throughout its history. Here are some common idiomatic words and phrases.

When you're **under the weather**, you don't feel very well. This expression also has nautical roots. In the past, when a sailor was sick, he was sent down below the deck of the ship, away from the weather, to help him recover.

If you **know the ropes**, you understand how a system works. This expression comes from the days of sailing ships, when sailors had to learn what to do with hundreds of different ropes. So when you start a new job or activity, someone with experience will explain what to do: you will be shown the ropes.

The word **jumbo**—meaning *very large*—came into English thanks to a very large elephant. The elephant was named Jumbo when he arrived at the London Zoo in 1865. Jumbo became extremely popular and since then, unusually big things have been called *jumbo-sized* or *jumbo*, for example, the Boeing 747 jumbo jet.

The English language is constantly changing, and new words and expressions are being added to dictionaries all the time. Meanings of words are being changed too. The adjective **wicked** means *very bad* or *evil*. But now *wicked* is being used by some people as slang for *very good* or *fantastic*: "We had a wicked time!" Similarly, *cool* means the opposite of *warm*, but it is now being used, mainly by young people, to describe something very good—or wicked!

88

3 AFTER READING

Answer the questions.

1. What does "He's been fired" mean? Why?
2. Which two expressions are connected with sailing?
3. How can you describe a very large bag of potato chips? Where does this word come from?
4. What can you say to encourage someone to continue working hard? Where does the expression come from?
5. What can you say if you're not feeling very well?
6. Which two words are slang for "very good"?
7. How can you describe a person with a lot of experience in his/her job? Where does this expression come from?

Your response Are any of these idioms the same in your language? If not, do you have idiomatic expressions with the same meanings?

4 LISTENING

🔊 2.26 *Changing Places* is a TV show where a room is improved in three days. Look at the kitchen plan and listen to a phone conversation between the producer and kitchen designer on Day 2. For each item on the kitchen plan, write Y (yesterday), N (now), or T (tomorrow).

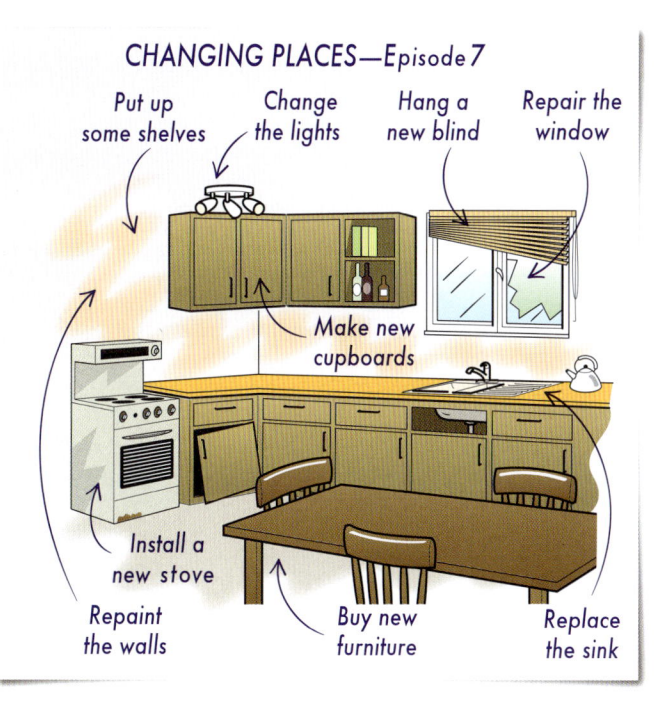

CHANGING PLACES—Episode 7

- Put up some shelves
- Change the lights
- Hang a new blind
- Repair the window
- Make new cupboards
- Install a new stove
- Repaint the walls
- Buy new furniture
- Replace the sink

Now tell each other what was done yesterday, what is being done now, and what will be done tomorrow.

5 PRONUNCIATION

🔊 2.27 Listen and repeat.

A	B
They've been made.	They're being made.
It's been bought.	It's being bought.
He's been asked.	He's being asked.
She's been called.	She's being called.

Now listen and decide: A or B?

6 SPEAKING

Ask two students the questions in the *What about you?* questionnaire and write down their answers. If they answer yes, ask for more information.

A Have you ever been injured playing a sport?
B Yes, I have.
A What happened?
B I was injured playing basketball last year—I twisted my ankle. What about you?

Questionnaire What about you?

1. Have you ever been injured playing a sport?
2. Have you ever been involved in a demonstration?
3. Are you given an allowance or paid for household tasks?
4. Have you ever been sent a chain e-mail?
5. Are you allowed to wear whatever you like?
6. Have you ever been taken to the hospital in an ambulance?
7. Have you ever been given a prize or an award?
8. Are you often asked to do things you don't want to do?
9. Will you be taken on vacation this year?
10. Are you being taught to do something new?

Extension Write three more questions beginning *Have you ever been …?* in the passive and interview two more students.

7 WRITING

Use your notes from the questionnaire to write a paragraph comparing the two students.

Sara hasn't been injured playing a sport, but Stefan has. He was injured playing basketball last year, and he twisted his ankle.

LANGUAGE WORKOUT

Complete.

Passive tenses

Simple past	The elephant _____ _____ (name) Jumbo.
Present perfect	I _____ _____ _____ (fire).
Simple present	The shuttlecock _____ _____ (keep) up in the air.
Present progressive	New expressions _____ _____ _____ (add) all the time.
Simple future	You _____ _____ _____ (show) the ropes.

We form the different passive tenses with the appropriate tense of _____ + past participle.

▶ Answers and Practice
Language File page 118

7.2 GETTING THE MESSAGE ACROSS

She deserves to be awarded a prize

Talking about what's right
Passive infinitive
either … or   both … and

1 OPENER

Look at the photo on the left. What structure does it show?

2 READING

🔴 2.28 Read the text. What was Rosalind Franklin's great achievement?

They Cracked the Code—Or Did They?

Francis Crick and James Watson solved the mystery of human DNA in 1953 and shared the Nobel Prize for Medicine in 1962. But was it all their own work, or did they steal someone else's?

Many believe that Crick and Watson's discovery was largely based on X-ray pictures of atoms taken by a female scientist, Rosalind Franklin. In 1950, Franklin started taking photos of atoms at King's College London, believing that the structure of DNA could be discovered from them. In the race to describe DNA, either Franklin or Crick and Watson could have been the first to publish their results. But did the men win by cheating?

Franklin was accustomed to male prejudice against female scientists. Her father had initially refused to pay for her to study at Cambridge University, but he was persuaded to change his mind. And when she passed her exams, the university did not give her a full degree—only men could be given full degrees. At King's College, women couldn't be served in the same dining room as male scientists. What's more, her male colleague, Maurice Wilkins, treated her like an assistant; according to Watson, he believed that Franklin "had to go or be put in her place."

But it was Franklin's pictures, described as "the most beautiful X-ray photographs of any substance ever taken," which provided the clue to the mystery of DNA. In 1953, Maurice Wilkins showed one of Franklin's X-rays (Photo 51) to Watson without telling her. Wilkins explained to Watson how the picture could be used to figure out the structure of DNA. Both Crick and Watson clearly benefited from Franklin's work, but didn't acknowledge it at the time. Ironically, the cancer from which Franklin died five years later, at the age of 37, was probably caused by X-rays.

Many people think that Franklin deserves to be awarded a Nobel Prize now. However, Nobel Prizes may only be given to the living, so Franklin can't be honored in this way. But her life shouldn't be seen as a failure. She is beginning to be recognized as a brilliant scientist, and in 2002, the British government created the Franklin prize, worth £30,000, to be given each year to a female scientist.

3 AFTER READING

Complete the questions with *How, What, When, Who,* or *Why.* Then match the questions with the answers.

1 _____ were both Crick and Watson given the Nobel Prize?
2 _____ was Crick and Watson's work largely based on?
3 _____ did Franklin start taking X-ray photos of atoms?
4 _____ could have been the first to publish a description of DNA?
5 _____ was Franklin not given a degree by Cambridge University?
6 _____ did Wilkins treat Franklin?
7 _____ was Watson shown Photo 51 by Wilkins?
8 _____ could Photo 51 be used to do?
9 _____ did Franklin die?
10 _____ can't Franklin be given a Nobel Prize?

a In 1950.
b Figure out the structure of DNA.
c In 1958.
d Only men could be given them.
e In 1953.
f X-ray pictures of atoms.
g It can't be given to dead people.
h Like an assistant.
i In 1962.
j Crick and Watson, or Franklin.

Your response What's your opinion? Did Crick and Watson steal Franklin's work? Why didn't they acknowledge her work at the time?

4 VOCABULARY

Complete the sentences with these words.

> acknowledge benefit colleague deserve
> honor persuade prejudice recognize

1 Franklin finally _____ her father to pay for her studies.
2 I'm out of the office tomorrow, but my _____ will be able to help you.
3 They used Franklin's work, but they didn't _____ it.
4 Unfortunately there's still a lot of _____ against people with disabilities.
5 Franklin didn't immediately _____ the importance of her X-ray photos.
6 The students will _____ if the school has more teachers.
7 You _____ a medal for all your hard work!
8 The award was created to _____ the memory of a brilliant scientist.

> **Extension** Which words in the box can be both nouns and verbs?

5 PRONUNCIATION

Mark the stress on the words in the Vocabulary box in exercise 4. Which words are stressed on the first syllable?

🔊 2.29 Now listen and check. Repeat the words.

6 WRITING

Complete the text with the passive infinitive form of the verb.

WOMEN SCIENTISTS WHO SHOULD __1__ (NOT FORGET)
In 1786, Caroline Herschel became the first woman to discover a comet. Her brother was the king's astronomer and she worked as his assistant. But scientists now think what she did deserves __2__ (give) more recognition.
  Lise Meitner, who was described by Einstein as "Germany's Marie Curie" for her work on nuclear fission, is someone else who people think should __3__ (award) a Nobel Prize now. However, like Franklin, she can't __4__ (honor) in this way because she died in 1968. The Nobel Prize for Chemistry was given to her male colleague Otto Hahn instead.
  Jocelyn Bell Burnell was a Cambridge University research student who discovered tiny stars called pulsars, and also deserved __5__ (give) an award. Her discovery led to a Nobel Prize in 1974—for her male teacher.
  Many people think the Nobel rules should __6__ (change) to allow prizes __7__ (award) after someone's death. The worth of some people's work may not __8__ (recognize) while they are alive. Or is the reason why scientists like Meitner, Franklin, and Burnell don't get Nobel Prizes really because of prejudice against women?

Your response What's your answer to the final question in the text?

7 SPEAKING

Write notes under these headings and discuss them with another student.

How teenagers want to be treated

Three things that teenagers should be encouraged to do:

think for themselves

> We should be encouraged to think for ourselves.

Three things that teenagers deserve:

to be listened to

> We deserve to be listened to.

> **Extension** Role-play a discussion between a teenager and a parent about how teenagers should be treated.

8 WRITING

Write an article for the school magazine explaining how teenagers want to be treated, using the ideas you discussed in exercise 7.

We deserve to be listened to and we should be encouraged to think for ourselves.

LANGUAGE WORKOUT

Complete.

Passive infinitive
Many people think that Franklin deserves _____ _____ _____ a Nobel Prize.
She is beginning _____ _____ _____ as a brilliant scientist.

After modal verbs
The picture could _____ _____ to figure out the structure of DNA.
Women couldn't _____ _____ in the same dining room.
Nobel Prizes may only _____ _____ to the living.
Her life shouldn't _____ _____ as a failure.

either ... or, both ... and
_____ Crick _____ Watson clearly benefited from Franklin's work.
_____ Franklin _____ Crick and Watson could have been the first.

▶ Answers and Practice
Language File page 118

7 GETTING THE MESSAGE ACROSS

3 They couldn't call up a doctor

Using the phone
Phrasal verbs

1 OPENER

You are going to read about cell phones in Africa. Which of these words and phrases do you expect to find in the text?

> bus conductor   business
> colleague   contact
> driver's license   ladder
> landline   lifeboat   passport
> signal   subscribers

2 READING

🔴 2.30 Read *It's Good to Talk*. What do you think is the most surprising information in the article?

3 AFTER READING

True, false, or no information? Correct the false sentences.

1 Africa has more cell phone users than the U.S.
2 Very few Africans had phones at the beginning of the 21st century.
3 Nearly half the population of South Africa had cell phones in 2010.
4 The Japanese spend more time talking on their cell phones than the French.
5 People in Nigeria use cell phones more than people in South Africa.
6 Entrepreneurs in Ghana charge people to make calls from phone towers.
7 Only rich Africans can afford to buy cell phones.
8 Cell phones have made a huge difference to the lives of people in Africa.

Your response What do you use your phone most for? Texting, surfing the Web, or talking?

It's Good to Talk

The cell phone explosion is transforming Africa. It has already become the first continent to have more cell phone users than landline subscribers. The International Telecommunications Union (ITU) says Africa is the world's fastest-growing cell phone market. Cell phone subscriptions there went up from 54 million to almost 350 million between 2003 and 2008.

In 2001, only three percent of Africans had telephones of any kind. Countless thousands of people died because they couldn't call up a doctor. "Now every bus conductor and street vendor has a cell phone," said Anthony Zwane, a sociologist at the University of Swaziland. "They've become the people's way of communicating." It's estimated that cell phone ownership neared 100% in South Africa by the time the first match in the 2010 soccer World Cup kicked off. That's one phone for every person within a decade!

Traditional African culture, with its emphasis on oral story telling, encourages phone use as a means of social and family contact. The average Nigerian uses his or her cell for 200 minutes a week, compared to 154 minutes per week in France, 149 minutes in Japan, 120 in Britain, and 88 in Germany.

Cell phone transmission signals can be cut off by hills, but smart entrepreneurs in Ghana have found out how to solve this problem. They have put up tall towers with a platform on top where you can pick up a cell phone signal. People pay a small amount, climb up a ladder, and make a call. It's much easier than taking a bus to a place where there's a signal.

Phone companies had thought that only very rich Africans would buy cell phones. But it turned out that it was ordinary people who needed them most. People with cell phones no longer have to walk miles to talk to a friend or make a business deal. In countries like Kenya and Uganda, cell phones are used to transfer money. The pace of life in Africa is speeding up. And Africa's cell phone revolution is likely to go on for many years.

4 VOCABULARY

Rewrite the sentences replacing the words in *italics* with the correct form of these phrasal verbs.

> **Word Bank** Phrasal verbs
>
> call up   come down   cut off   find out
> go on   go up   kick off   pick up   put up

1. They plan to *build* a cell phone tower near our school.
2. Could you *telephone* the restaurant and reserve a table?
3. While we were talking on the phone, we were *disconnected*.
4. I *continued* speaking, but he couldn't hear me.
5. You can't *receive* a signal on your cell phone in a tunnel.
6. The cost of cell phone calls is *falling*.
7. Have you *discovered* what time the soccer game *starts*?
8. The use of cell phones in Africa has *increased* dramatically.

Extension Write nine more sentences using the phrasal verbs in the Word Bank.

The price of computers is coming down.
All the lights went out because the electricity was ...

5 LISTENING

You are going to hear a phone conversation between a caller (C) and a company receptionist (R). Before you listen, look at sentences 1–8 and decide who says what.

1. Good morning, can I help you?
2. May I speak to Carol Evans, please?
3. Hold on, I'll put you through.
4. Oh, sorry, the line's busy.
5. Can I take a message?
6. Could you ask her to call me back?
7. Can I take your name and number?
8. I'll give her your message as soon as possible.

🔘 2.31 Now listen and check. Then listen again and write down the message.

6 PRONUNCIATION

🔘 2.32 Listen and repeat the sentences in exercise 5.

7 ROLE-PLAY

A group of American students are visiting your school.

Student A answers the school phone and writes down messages. Student B plays the roles of American callers who want to contact the visitors. He/She invents the callers' names and messages, or can use some of these ideas:

> call home tonight
> send the e-mail address of the host family
> send a text with the host family's phone number
> invite the host family to come and stay in the U.S.
> take pictures of the host family
> remember to buy the host family a gift
> remember to bring home some souvenirs

A

- Say hello and the name of your school.
- Say that the group is out on a trip. Offer to take a message.
- Ask for the caller's phone number. Promise to pass on the message.

B

- Say hello and ask to speak to X.
- Say who you are and leave a message.
- Reply.

Now change roles.

8 WRITING

Write out three of the messages from the phone conversations in exercise 7.

Message for Peter Preston: Your father called at 11:20 a.m. Your sister has had a baby girl. Both mother and child are fine. Can you call him back as soon as possible?

LANGUAGE WORKOUT

Complete.

Phrasal verbs
Verb + adverb
The pace of life in Africa is speeding _____.
It is likely to go _____ for many years.

Verb + adverb with direct object
They have put _____ tall towers.
OR They have put tall towers _____.
The noun object can go before or after the adverb.

They have put them _____.
The pronoun object must go between the verb and the adverb.

Verb + preposition with direct object
People climb _____ a ladder.
People climb _____ it.
Noun and pronoun objects go at the end of the phrase.

Words like *up* and *on* can be either adverbs or prepositions. They are usually stressed as adverbs, but not as prepositions.

▶ Answers and Practice
Language File pages 118-119

7 GETTING THE MESSAGE ACROSS

4 Integrated Skills
Discussing languages

1 OPENER

How many languages are spoken in your country and by whom? Which languages are taught in school?

READING

2 Read and complete the text with phrases a–h.

a what they have left behind
b like Chinese
c The answer is yes
d on radio and television
e or a plant species
f a bigger, more powerful language
g and can't be re-created
h that's 3,000 languages in 1,200 months

Which words in the phrases helped you to complete the text?

3 Find words or phrases in the text to match these definitions. The parts of speech in *italics* refer to the words in the text.

1 people who study languages *n*
2 in danger of something bad happening to it *v*
3 events that cause a lot of damage, or kill or injure a lot of people *n*
4 small number of people *n*
5 varieties of a language that are only spoken by particular groups of people *n*
6 recognized position *n*
7 able to speak a language well *adj*

4 What do the words in *italics* refer to?

Paragraph
1 Of *these*, there are 51 languages …
2 Should we be worried about *this*?
3 … or man-made *ones* like war …
4 linguists say there are at least half a dozen *more*.
5 Romansch Grishum, as *it* is now called …

Language Death or Language Murder?

Linguists tell us that there are about 6,000 languages in the world. Of these, there are 51 languages with just one speaker left, nearly 500 languages with less than 100 speakers, and 1,500 languages with less than 1,000 speakers. About half the world's languages are going to die out during the next century: __1__.

Should we be worried about this? Yes, in the same way that we ought to be concerned when an animal __2__ is threatened with extinction. When people die, archaeologists can investigate __3__. But when a spoken language dies, it leaves nothing behind it __4__.

Why are languages dying? Language death may be caused not only by natural disasters like earthquakes, or man-made ones like war, but also by "language murder." This term is used to explain what happens when speakers of a minority language stop using it in favor of a "killer language," __5__.

English is often called the world's most dangerous killer language, but linguists say there are at least a half a dozen more. These killers are not only European languages, like French, but also Asian ones, __6__.

Can anything be done? __7__. Take the case of Romansch, which is spoken in Switzerland. In the 1980s, Romansch, whose five very different dialects were used by fewer and fewer people, was facing a difficult situation. The solution was the creation of a written language for all these dialects. Romansch Grishum, as it is now called, has official status in parts of Switzerland and is increasingly used in its spoken form __8__.

The Maori language has been kept alive in New Zealand through lessons, where under-five-year-olds are taught the language. And in Japan, new government policies brought the Ainu language, which only had eight fluent speakers left, back from the edge of extinction.

Ainu speakers

5 The article says that there are at least half a dozen killer languages, apart from English. Which do you think they are?

6 **Linking words:** *not only ... but also*

We can use *not only ... but also* instead of *and* to add emphasis. Find two examples in the text.

7 Non-defining relative clauses

Non-defining relative clauses begin with *which*, *who*, or *whose*. They give us more information about a noun and are separated from it by a comma. For example, *Take the case of Romansch, which is spoken in Switzerland*. Find two more examples in the text.

8 LISTENING

🔊 2.33 Listen to a debate about learning foreign languages. What is the result? Then listen again and complete the speakers' notes and the details of the voting.

Introduction

CHAIR Hello, my name's Anna and I'm chairing this debate. The motion today is: "The growth of English is killing other languages. Other foreign languages should be studied at school instead." Susy is proposing the motion and Peter is opposing it. Susy, would you like to start?

Susy's notes for the start of her speech

What I'm going to argue is that we need to be able to speak lots of languages. First, because knowing a language helps us __1__ the people who speak it better. Second, because the growth of English all around the world makes everywhere seem __2__. And third, because people like to buy and sell in their own language. Being able to speak some else's language is good for __3__.

Peter's notes for the end of his speech

What I've argued is this. First, the world has a __4__ language already—and that's English. Second, it's better to be able to speak one language really __5__ than lots of languages badly. And third, who is going to __6__ which languages are taught?

Conclusion

CHAIR Thank you both very much. Now you have one sentence each to sum up your argument before we have a vote.
SUSY The more languages the better—not just one.
PETER We can't survive without English.
CHAIR And now raise your hands to vote. Those in favor of the motion? Thank you. And those against? Thank you. The result is __7__ votes for the motion and __8__ votes against.

9 SPEAKING

Have a class or group debate. Choose a chair and two speakers. Use the structure for a debate in exercise 7 on page 55.

Choose your own topic or one of these:
- What's the point of saving disappearing languages? Hardly anyone speaks them.
- English isn't a killer language—it's what the world communicates in.
- Why should we learn other languages? Everyone speaks English.

10 GUIDED WRITING

Write two paragraphs giving the arguments for and against the topics of your debate.

LEARNER INDEPENDENCE

11 Thinking skills: A study diary

Reflecting on the way you study can make you a better learner.

- Keep a diary showing your study plan and details of what you've studied each week.
- Say how you feel about different study techniques. Which ones work best for you?
- Review your plan and set a new target for this week.

12 Word creation: Add the prefix *re-* to these verbs and complete the sentences.

> appear build create discover
> paint place play tell write

1 The students _____ the text after they had corrected the mistakes.
2 After the earthquake, everyone worked to _____ the houses.
3 Please _____ the books on the table after you have looked at them.
4 A "lost" Picasso was _____ in a house near Miami last week.
5 When she _____, she had changed into dry clothes.
6 I don't like the color of the door, so I'm going to _____ it.
7 You can't _____ a spoken language when it is dead.
8 He _____ the recording several times but still couldn't hear the message.
9 When she _____ the story to the police, some of the details had changed.

13 🔊 2.34 **Phrasebook:** Find these useful expressions in Unit 7. Then listen and repeat.

> Keep it up.
> know the ropes
> under the weather
> I'll put you through.
> Can I take a message?
> Can anything be done?
> The more ... the better.

Which expression means ...?
a I'll connect you.
b not feeling very well
c Continue to do it.
d understand how a system works

7 GETTING THE MESSAGE ACROSS
Inspired EXTRA!

LANGUAGE LINKS

Read *False friends*. Which of the six English words are false friends in your language? What is the accurate translation of these words in your language?

False friends

"False friends" are English words that look similar to words in other languages but that have a different meaning.

actually is used to emphasize what is really true or what really happened: *We've spoken on the phone, but we've never actually met.* But to speakers of Dutch, French, German, Italian, Portuguese, Russian, and Spanish, it looks like a word that means "now, at present, currently."

demand in English expresses a strong statement of what you want: *He demanded a pay increase.* However, to speakers of French and Italian, it sounds more like their word for "ask for."

eventually means "at the end of a long process or period of time": *Eventually, we became good friends.* But in Dutch, French, German, Italian, and Spanish, a similar word means "possibly."

library means a place where you can borrow books. But in French, Italian, Portuguese, and Spanish, a similar word means "bookstore."

sensible in English means reasonable and practical: *This seems to be a sensible way of dealing with the problem.* However, it is easy for speakers of French, German, Italian, and Spanish to think it means "sensitive."

sympathetic means "willing to understand someone's problems and help them": *Jill was a sympathetic listener.* But Dutch, French, German, Italian, Portuguese, Russian, and Spanish speakers think of a word in their own language that means "nice, pleasant."

What other English false friends can you think of?

SKIT Find a Friend

🔴 2.35 Read and listen.

SARAH Find-a-Friend, Sarah speaking. Can I help you?
KEVIN Yes, I hope so. I'm looking for a friend.
SARAH OK, let me take down your personal details. May I have your name?
KEVIN My name is Kevin Morgan.
SARAH How old are you, Kevin?
KEVIN I'm 24.
SARAH Right, and what color are your hair and eyes?
KEVIN I have dark hair and blue eyes. But …
SARAH And what are your hobbies?
KEVIN I don't understand—why are you asking me all these questions?
SARAH I need to find out your personal details.
KEVIN But don't you want to know about my friend?
SARAH We'll talk about the kind of person we're looking for in a minute.
KEVIN Can we talk about her now, please? Her name is Maggie and she's 22.
SARAH How do you know?
KEVIN Well, we've been dating for three months!
SARAH I'm sorry, Kevin. I'm afraid you have the wrong end of the stick.
KEVIN Stick, what stick? What do you mean?
SARAH You've misunderstood—we find girlfriends or boyfriends for people.
KEVIN That's fine—Maggie is my girlfriend. But she didn't show up for our date last night. And her cell phone is turned off.
SARAH I'm sorry, but we don't look for missing people.
KEVIN You don't?
SARAH No—this is a dating agency. If you think your girlfriend is missing, you should call the police.
KEVIN Well, actually, I think she's found another boyfriend. So I'd like you to find me another girlfriend, please!

Now act out the skit in pairs.

Game Call my bluff

- Work in groups of three, each group with a dictionary.
- Each group chooses a word from the dictionary which they think the other students don't know. They write out the definition of the word and then make up two more wrong definitions.
- When all groups have chosen a word and have three definitions of it, only one of which is correct, the game begins.
- Each group reads out their word and the three definitions. Without using the dictionary, the other students decide which is the correct definition. If they are right, they get a point; if they are wrong, the group giving the definitions gets a point.

UNIT 7

CONSOLIDATION

LESSON 1 Look at exercise 4 on page 89. Write sentences saying what has been done, what is being done, and what will be done.

The window has been repaired. The new cupboards are being ....

LESSON 2 Look at exercise 3 on page 90. Write five more questions beginning with *How, What, When, Who,* or *Why* and answer them.

When did Crick and Watson solve the mystery of human DNA? In 1953.

LESSON 3 Look at exercise 5 on page 93. Write a phone conversation between a receptionist and a caller who wants to speak to someone who is not there.

EXTENSION

LESSON 1 Look at the questionnaire in exercise 6 on page 89. Write answers to the questions for yourself.

LESSON 2 Look at *They Cracked the Code—Or Did They?* on page 90. Write a conversation between someone who believes Crick and Watson cheated and someone who doesn't.

LESSON 3 Look at exercise 7 on page 93 and write out the role-play conversation for one of the ideas in the box.

YOUR CHOICE!

CONSTRUCTION The passive

Complete with the correct form of the verbs: simple past or simple future.

"English is not enough" is true not only for native speakers but also for second language speakers of English. A language other than English __1__ (speak) at home in 14 million U.S. households. But foreign languages __2__ (study) by only 44% of U.S. high school students. Foreign language classes in the U.S. __3__ (take) by almost 7 million students in grades 7–12. The most popular language that __4__ (teach) in public school to native English speakers is Spanish. French, the next most popular language, __5__ (take) by over one million students. A recent report estimates that 160,000 speakers of foreign languages other than English __6__ (need) in the next five years in India, but that only 40,000 __7__ (produce) by the educational system.

REFLECTION The passive

Match the beginnings with the endings.

1 The simple present passive is formed with the simple present of *be*
2 We can use the passive with a modal verb. The form is: modal verb
3 The present perfect passive is formed with
4 Negatives and questions in the passive are formed
5 The passive is often used
6 When we want to focus on the "doer" of the action we use

a in writing to describe processes.
b *by* + agent.
c + *be* + past participle.
d in the same way as in active sentences.
e the present perfect of *be* + past participle.
f + past participle.

ACTION It could be used for ...

- Work in groups of four. Each group is given a small everyday object, e.g., a hat, a pen, a paper clip, a fork, a coat hanger, a rubber band, a plastic bag, a sock.
- Groups work together for five minutes to think of as many uses as possible for their object.
- One student from each group takes the object to another group and acts out the uses that have been thought of. The group tries to guess what the uses are.
- Then a different student takes the object to another group.

INTERACTION The other me

- Work in a small group.
- Imagine you are another person: the person you have always wanted to be, the person of your dreams.
- Take turns interviewing each other: you are the "other you" and the rest of the group are reporters. The reporters ask questions:
Tell us a few things about yourself now and in the past.
What are you most proud of now?
What was your greatest success?
What do you do best?
What do you think the future will bring?
... and follow-up questions:
Really? For example? Why is that?
Can you say some more about ...?

7 Culture

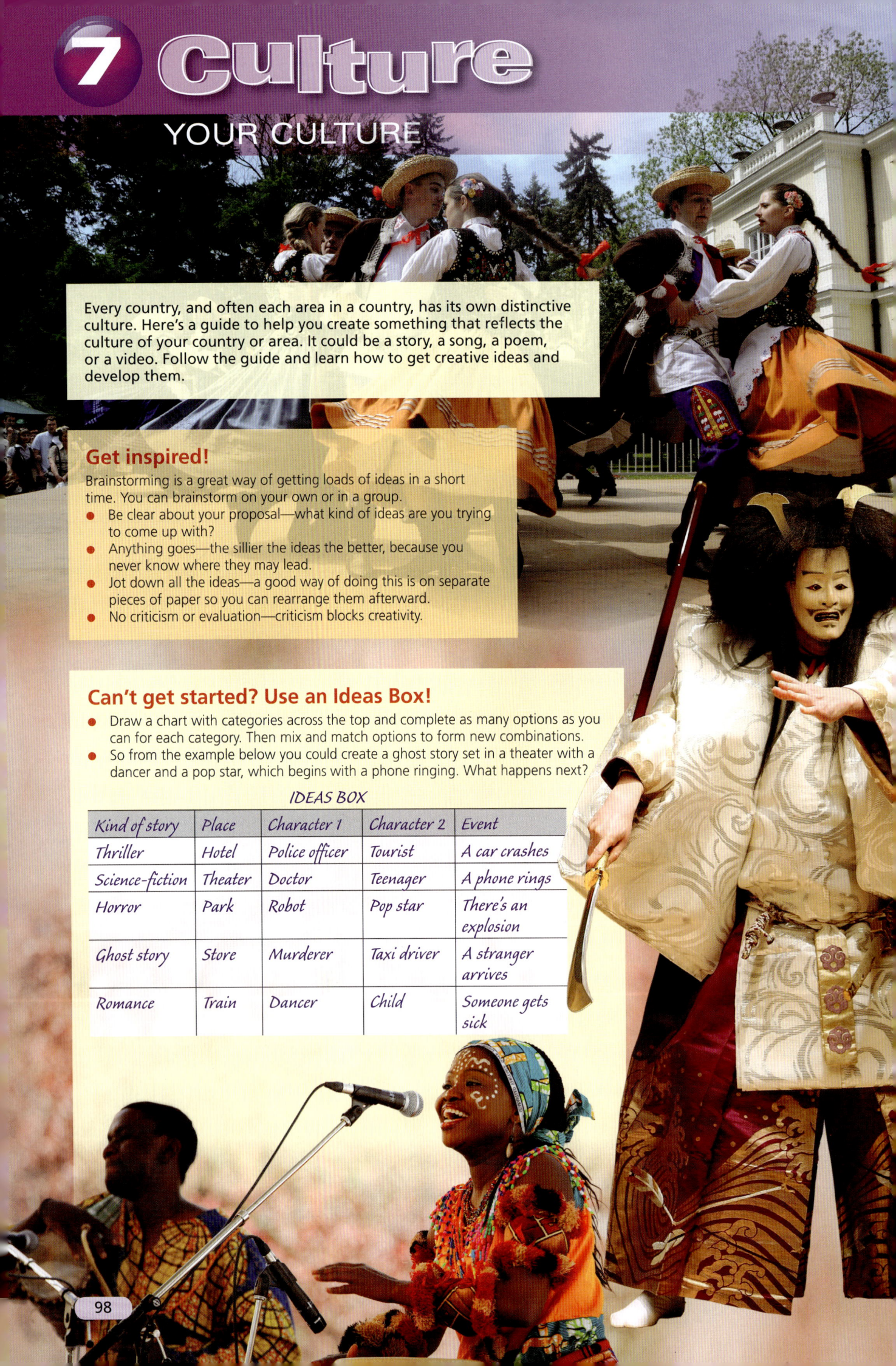

YOUR CULTURE

Every country, and often each area in a country, has its own distinctive culture. Here's a guide to help you create something that reflects the culture of your country or area. It could be a story, a song, a poem, or a video. Follow the guide and learn how to get creative ideas and develop them.

Get inspired!

Brainstorming is a great way of getting loads of ideas in a short time. You can brainstorm on your own or in a group.
- Be clear about your proposal—what kind of ideas are you trying to come up with?
- Anything goes—the sillier the ideas the better, because you never know where they may lead.
- Jot down all the ideas—a good way of doing this is on separate pieces of paper so you can rearrange them afterward.
- No criticism or evaluation—criticism blocks creativity.

Can't get started? Use an Ideas Box!

- Draw a chart with categories across the top and complete as many options as you can for each category. Then mix and match options to form new combinations.
- So from the example below you could create a ghost story set in a theater with a dancer and a pop star, which begins with a phone ringing. What happens next?

IDEAS BOX

Kind of story	Place	Character 1	Character 2	Event
Thriller	Hotel	Police officer	Tourist	A car crashes
Science-fiction	Theater	Doctor	Teenager	A phone rings
Horror	Park	Robot	Pop star	There's an explosion
Ghost story	Store	Murderer	Taxi driver	A stranger arrives
Romance	Train	Dancer	Child	Someone gets sick

Culture

1 READING

Read the guide and answer the questions.

1. What should you do before you start brainstorming?
2. Why are silly ideas good when brainstorming?
3. What shouldn't you do when brainstorming?
4. In what situation is it a good idea to use the Ideas Box?
5. What should you always keep with you?
6. What technique helps you to continue writing a story?
7. What's the first thing to do when you've finished writing?
8. What should you do after you've shown people your work and listened to any criticisms?

Use a creativity notebook to plan and develop your ideas

- Always have it with you—you never know when inspiration will arrive!
- Use drawings as well as words to explain your ideas.
- You can write anything in your notebook: thoughts, feelings, or things you see or hear.
- Your mind is very creative while you're asleep, so keep your notebook by the bed. Write down your dreams and how you feel about them.
- When you're stuck for an idea, look through your notebook for inspiration.

Action! Start writing

- To plan a video, create a storyboard with drawings of the scenes and the dialogue underneath.
- When writing a song or poem, say the words aloud as you write them.
- In a story, always stop before the end of a paragraph. Then when you start again it's much easier to continue.
- Don't be afraid to show friends or family what you've written. Let them ask you questions about it. Don't be defensive in your answers.

Presentation

- Take care with the appearance of your work and check it carefully.
- Show or read what you've written to someone whose opinion you value.
- You may want to post your work on a website or message board.
- Listen to any criticism and take notes.
- Don't take criticism personally—it's your work that's under discussion, not you!
- Finally, reflect on what you've done. Were there problems? Did you find solutions? What did you learn? How will you do better next time?

2 VOCABULARY

Match the words and phrases with their definitions.

1. anything goes
2. jot down
3. block v
4. mix and match
5. stuck
6. be defensive
7. take care
8. post on a website
9. reflect on

a. react badly to criticism
b. think carefully about
c. everything is possible
d. put on the Internet
e. prevent
f. write a quick note
g. put different things together
h. unable to do something
i. be careful

3 LISTENING

2.36 Your creative space is where you generate ideas, put them together, and make them into something real. Look at the list below and listen to artist Andy March. For each item on the list, choose which alternative he prefers.

Your creative space
Think about where you work best. What helps you to be creative?

- well lit or softly lit?
- noisy or quiet?
- cool or warm?
- alone or with others?
- space to move around or not?
- neat or messy?
- morning, afternoon, evening, or night?
- music or silence?

How about you? Where do you work best? Compare your views with other students.

4 MINI-PROJECT
Creative writing

Work with another student. Use the guide to help you create a story, a song, a poem, or a plan for a video.

- Choose your format: story/song/poem/video.
- Brainstorm your ideas.
- Use an Ideas Box.
- Start writing your first draft.
- Check your draft and get feedback.
- Rewrite your draft.

Read your work carefully and correct any mistakes. Then show it to other students.

8.1 MAKING THE GRADE

He wasn't able to get a job

Talking about past ability
Expressing purpose
could(n't), was(n't) able to, managed to
in order to   so that

1 OPENER

Look at the photos of four famous people. What do you know about them? What are they famous for?

2 READING

🔘 2.37 Read *Success Stories*. Which of the four people was not criticized by their teacher?

3 AFTER READING

Choose the best answer.

1. Beethoven's music teacher thought he
   A could compose music.
   B was no good at composing.
   C hoped to be a composer.

2. Toward the end of his life, Beethoven couldn't
   A hear.
   B see.
   C work.

3. Zephaniah was taken out of school because he
   A asked too many questions.
   B couldn't read or write.
   C was a problem student.

4. J.K. Rowling began writing the first Harry Potter book
   A on a train to Manchester.
   B while she was living in Portugal.
   C over 20 years ago.

5. She moved to Edinburgh so that she could
   A finish the first Harry Potter book.
   B live near her sister.
   C teach English.

6. Einstein wasn't able to
   A read when he was seven.
   B study in Switzerland.
   C work at a Swiss university.

Your response What can you learn from *Success Stories*? Do you know people who have done well in life after a difficult start?

Success Stories

Ludwig van Beethoven's music teacher once said that he was hopeless as a composer. But Beethoven became one of the most important classical composers of all time. Although he was often sick, and finally became totally deaf, he managed to produce an extraordinary quantity of work, including concertos, symphonies, and operas. It has often been said: "Although Beethoven wasn't able to hear, he was able to listen."

Ludwig van Beethoven 1770–1827

Millions of people around the world have heard the voice of Benjamin Zephaniah, Britain's best-known rap poet. But Zephaniah was told by his teacher that he was "a born failure," and he was taken out of school at the age of 12 because he couldn't behave. "I was one of those kids that kept asking 'Why?'" He was sent to an approved school (a kind of youth prison) and then twice to prison. But while in prison, he decided to become a poet and was able to educate himself. "I wasn't really able to read and write until I was in my 20s," Zephaniah says. He started performing with bands so that his poems could reach people who didn't read books. Today, his books of poetry are bestsellers and one of his most famous fans is Nelson Mandela.

Benjamin Zephaniah 1958–

J.K. Rowling started writing the Harry Potter series in 1990 on a train from Manchester to King's Cross station in London. In fact, it's from Platform 9¾ at King's Cross that Harry catches the train to Hogwarts. During the next five years, Rowling planned each book so that she knew what was going to happen before she began writing. In 1991, she went to Portugal, where she taught English and continued writing the first novel. In 1994, she moved to Edinburgh in order to be near her sister. There, she managed to complete *Harry Potter and the Sorcerer's Stone*. It was published in 1997 and became an instant bestseller. J.K. Rowling is now one of the most successful authors in the world.

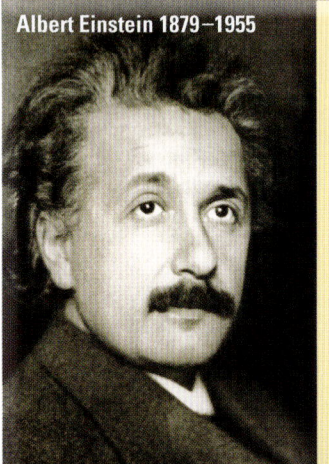

J.K. Rowling 1965–

Albert Einstein 1879–1955

Nobel Prize-winner Albert Einstein didn't speak until he was four, and couldn't read until he was seven. One of his teachers called him "mentally slow." After failing the entrance examination once, he managed to get a place at the Swiss Institute of Technology in Zurich in 1896. Although he did fairly well as a student in Zurich, he wasn't able to get a job at a Swiss university because he was thought to be extremely lazy. But in 1905, at the age of 26, Einstein published his *Special Theory of Relativity*, which led to the most famous equation in physics: $E=mc^2$.

UNIT 8

4 VOCABULARY

Find words in *Success Stories* to match these definitions. The parts of speech in *italics* refer to the words in the text.

1 completely *adv*
2 amount *n*
3 most famous *adj*
4 the opposite of success *n*
5 young people *n*
6 people who admire a famous person very much *n*
7 immediate *adj*
8 in the mind *adv*
9 not willing to work hard *adj*

5 PRONUNCIATION

Mark the stressed syllable.

> behave   classical
> educate   examination
> institute poetry
> relativity technology

🔊 2.38 Now listen and check. Repeat the words.

6 SPEAKING

🔊 2.39 Read and listen to the poem *Confessions of a Runner* by Benjamin Zephaniah.

Now discuss these questions with other students.

- Why is the poem called *Confessions of a Runner*?
- Which day at school did the child enjoy most/least?
- Zephaniah has invented the word "schoolology." What do you think it means?
- Which two words has he put together to make one word?
- What's your opinion of this poem?

> **Extension** Can you remember your first day at school? What were the most difficult and the most enjoyable moments?

7 WRITING

Work in groups of five if possible. Following the pattern of the poem, each group member writes a verse for a different day beginning: *On my ... day at school.*

Put your verses together to make your own group poem. Choose a title for your poem.

Confessions of a Runner

On my first day at school
　My sister cried and cried
On my first day at school
　I could have died and died
On my first day at school
　My twin embarrassed me
On my first day at school
　I learnt schoolology

On my second day at school
　My sister wouldn't come
On my second day at school
　She was dragged there by my Mom
On my second day at school
　I came dressed in pink
On my second day at school
　I was made to think

On my third day at school
　I explored everywhere
On my third day at school
　I fell offa my chair
On my third day at school
　We all went for a swim
On my third day at school
　I cried just like my twin

On my fourth day at school
　They made me run in shorts
On my fourth day at school
　I discovered sports
On my fourth day at school
　I ran fast and far
On my fourth day at school
　I earned myself a star

On my fifth day at school
　We had tomato crumble
On my fifth day at school
　I began to grumble
On my fifth day at school
　My teacher got stuck in red tape
On my fifth day at school
　Me and my twin escaped

LANGUAGE WORKOUT

Complete.

Past ability: could(n't), was(n't) able to, managed to

could and couldn't
He started performing with bands so that his poems _____ reach people who didn't read books.
Einstein _____ read until he was seven.

was/wasn't able to
Although Beethoven _____ _____ _____ hear, he _____ _____ _____ listen.
Einstein _____ _____ _____ get a job at a Swiss university.

We don't use *could* in the affirmative to talk about past ability on a particular occasion. Instead we use *was able to* or *managed to*.
Zephaniah was able to educate himself in prison.
Einstein managed to get a place at SIT.

Expressing purpose: in order to and so that
She moved to Edinburgh **in order to** be near her sister.
= She moved to Edinburgh **so that** she could be near her sister.

▶ Answers and Practice
Language File page 119

8 MAKING THE GRADE

2 They had to pay

Expressing obligation and ability
Modal expressions in the past and future

1 OPENER

Look at the pictures of schools in the past. What do you think school life was like then? What subjects did children study? What differences are there between school then and now?

2 READING

Read the text. When did it become compulsory for all American children to go to school?

School in the Past and in the Future

In the U.S. and Britain in the mid-nineteenth century, children didn't have to go to school at all. There were schools, of course, but you had to pay to go to them, and often parents couldn't afford the tuition costs. Many people also believed that girls didn't need to go to school because their future was to get married and have children. Although from 1870, the law in Britain said that all children aged 5 to 10 had to go to school, many poor families weren't able to pay. The children of these families needed to have a job in order to pay the tuition costs, and school schedules were organized to make this possible. In the U.S., by the end of the 1800s, free public education was available to children, but it wasn't until 1918 that children in every state had to go to school.

Schools 100 years ago were certainly very different from those today. But what about the future? A newspaper organized a competition for schools called *The School I'd Like*, asking students to describe their ideal school. "I'm concerned that the pressures of the curriculum will mean that there won't be time for a project like this," said a reporter. She needn't have worried, as there were over 15,000 entries full of ideas!

And what great ideas: a school in a giant submarine with waterproof maps of the underwater world, private planes to fly students to France for French lessons, and rockets to take children to distant planets to study the solar system. There are also some down-to-earth suggestions: clean toilets with locks that work so that students won't have to wait until they get home, no uniforms so that students will be able to choose what to wear, chill-out rooms to relax in, and enough computers so that students won't need to wait their turn for them. Safety and comfort are clearly important: one student suggests an anti-bullying alarm, and another writes: "We don't want interactive whiteboards—we want comfortable chairs!"

3 AFTER READING

Match the beginnings with the endings. There are two extra endings.

1 In the nineteenth century, parents often
2 A hundred years ago many people thought that girls
3 In Britain, until 1870, children
4 Children of poor families needed to work so that they
5 From 1918, children all over the U.S.
6 There were 15,000 competition entries, so the reporter
7 One idea is for schools to have rockets so that students
8 Another idea is a school without uniforms where students
9 More computers are recommended so that students
10 An anti-bullying alarm is also suggested so that students and teachers

a won't all have to wear the same clothes.
b were able to pay the tuition costs.
c didn't have to go to school.
d will be able to study the stars and planets.
e didn't have to school until they were ten years old.
f had to go to school.
g won't need to wait to use one.
h will need to study more and more subjects.
i needn't have worried.
j will be able to take action before it starts.
k weren't able to pay the tuition costs.
l didn't need to be educated.

Your response What do you think of the ideas for schools in the future?

4 VOCABULARY

Complete the phrases below with words from the Word Bank to make ten compound nouns. You can use one word several times!

Word Bank Education

board   college   class   curriculum   degree
elementary   exam(ination)   rules   schedule
school   subject   tuition costs   uniform

1 _____ degree
2 elementary _____
3 entrance _____
4 high _____
5 _____ room
6 _____ rules
7 _____ schedule
8 _____ subject
9 _____ uniform
10 white _____

5 PRONUNCIATION

2.40 Listen and decide if the speaker is stating a fact (F) or is very surprised (S).

1 Students will have to stay at school until they're 21.
2 They'll also need to study more subjects.
3 They'll be able to do all their classwork on computers.

Now say these sentences. Then listen and check.

4 They won't need to go to school every day. (F)
5 They'll be able to study online at home. (S)
6 They won't have to take any exams. (S)

LISTENING

6 **2.41** Read the questionnaire. Then listen to Mary's answers and decide: true or false? Correct the false answers.

THEN AND NOW QUESTIONNAIRE

Tell me about something that you:
1 can do now which you weren't able to do a year ago.
2 had to do in the past, but don't have to do now.
3 didn't have to do in the past which you have to do now.
4 didn't need to worry about.
5 need to do now, but hope you won't need to do in the future.
6 can't do now, but will be able to do.
7 don't have to do now, but will have to do.
8 can do now, but won't be able to do in the future.

Mary
1 Swim on my back.
2 Get help with spreadsheets.
3 Work hard in science class.
4 Making friends.
5 Go to bed really early.
6 Drive a car.
7 Iron.
8 Beat my sister at tennis.

7 **2.42** Listen to Matt's answers and correct the false ones.

Matt
1 Fix a flat tire.
2 Pick my brother up from school.
3 Work in a bookstore on Saturdays.
4 Exams.
5 Think before I speak in Spanish.
6 Vote.
7 Clean my own room.
8 Get into this shirt.

Extension Write sentences comparing Mary's and Matt's answers.
Mary wasn't able to ... and Matt wasn't able to ... a year ago, but they both can now.

8 SPEAKING

Do the *Then and Now* questionnaire with two other students and write down their answers.

9 WRITING

Write two paragraphs comparing the students' answers to the questionnaire.

Alicia and Maria weren't able to use PowerPoint® a year ago, but they can now.

LANGUAGE WORKOUT

Complete.

Modal expressions in the past: had to, didn't have to, was(n't) able to, were(n't) able to, needed to/ didn't need to, needn't have

You _____ _____ pay to go to them.
Children _____ _____ _____ go to school at all.
Many poor families _____ _____ _____ pay.
People believed that girls _____ _____ _____ go to school.
She _____ _____ worried.

didn't need to refers to something that wasn't done because it wasn't necessary.
needn't have refers to something that was done but was unnecessary.

Modal expressions in the future: will/won't have to, will/won't be able to, will/won't need to

Students _____ _____ _____ wait until they get home.
Students _____ _____ _____ _____ choose what to wear.
Students _____ _____ _____ wait their turn.

▶ Answers and Practice
Language File pages 119–120

8 MAKING THE GRADE

3 It made me feel great

Talking about obligation, permission, and prohibition
make and *let*
be allowed to

1 OPENER

Which of these words do you expect to find in an interview with a singer/songwriter?

> band chords equation
> gigs hum influence
> inspired inventor lyrics
> perform tune uniform

2 READING

🔊 2.43 Read *KEZZA—girl in a million!* and match questions a–f with Kezza's answers. Then listen and check.

a Who are your strongest musical influences?
b When did you start performing?
c What advice do you have for young musicians?
d What was the first song you wrote?
e How easy do you find songwriting?
f When did you get your first guitar?

3 AFTER READING

True, false, or no information? Correct the false sentences.

1 Kezza knew what she wanted to be when she was in her mid-teens.
2 She heard someone singing *Inspired!* and wrote down the words.
3 She chose the title of her first song because it reminded her of a friend.
4 Kezza has had three top ten hits.
5 She usually starts writing a song with a tune and fits the words to it.
6 She bought her first guitar with her own money.
7 Adele doesn't do any silly things to get people to buy her songs.
8 Kezza doesn't think young musicians should listen to advice.
9 She makes a lot of money from her songs.

Your response Would you like to be a singer/songwriter? Why/Why not?

KEZZA—girl in a million!

1 It was at a friend's party when I was 15. I knew one of the guys in the band, and he let me sing a couple of songs with them. It made me feel great. I knew then what I wanted to do in life.

2 After that party, I started singing at gigs, but it was always other people's songs. Then, one day, when I was out walking, a tune came into my head. I hummed it and tried to fit some words to it. I called the song *Inspired* because it inspired me to start songwriting.

3 It's not always easy. *Inspired* just came to me, but generally you have to work hard at songwriting. I keep a notebook by my bed and write down things I remember from my dreams. Sometimes the lyrics come first, sometimes the music. You can't make a song happen—you just have to let it take shape.

4 Let me think—it was when I was 14. I asked my parents to give it to me as a birthday gift, but they didn't like the idea. So I was made to save up enough money to buy it myself. Then I practiced around the clock, playing chords and finger picking—well, practice makes perfect, as they say.

5 When I was younger, it was Beyoncé, but I wasn't allowed to go to any of her concerts. My parents were really strict—it drove me mad sometimes! Alicia Keys is another big influence, and someone I admire a lot is Adele. Her music is so good that she doesn't need any gimmicks to sell it.

6 Don't let other people tell you what to do! Sure, you should listen to other people, but in the end, it's up to you. Be true to yourself—that's all that matters, as far as I'm concerned. Writing and singing songs is such a personal thing—I'm really lucky I can do it for a living.

4 PRONUNCIATION

Write the words in the correct column.

> finger hungry singer single song strong
> strongest thing young younger wrong

/ŋ/ long	/ŋg/ longer

🔊 2.44 Now listen and check. Repeat the words.

5 VOCABULARY

Make a word map for music. Use words from this lesson, and add other words you know.

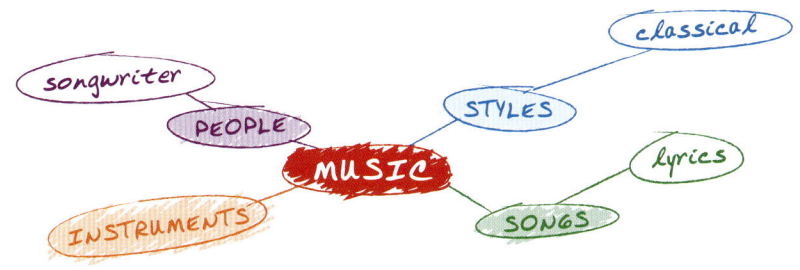

MUSIC — PEOPLE (songwriter), STYLES (classical), SONGS (lyrics), INSTRUMENTS

6 LISTENING

🔊 2.45 You are going to hear Luke, who is 16, talking about his parents. First look at the list below and guess what his parents make him do and what they let or don't let him do. Then listen and write M (make), L (let), or X (don't let).

- turn his music down
- stay up late to watch TV
- watch too much TV
- go to bed at 10:30 on school days
- stay up later on weekends and during vacation
- set the table for meals
- clean his room
- go out by himself at night
- say where he is going when he goes out
- stay out late

7 SPEAKING

Tell another student what Luke's parents make him do and what they let or don't let him do.

A They make him turn his music down.
B They let him …
A They don't let him …

Now tell each other what Luke is made to do and what he is/isn't allowed to do.

> He's made to turn his music down.
> He isn't allowed to …

Now ask two students these questions and write down their answers.

- What do your parents make you do?
- What do they let you do?
- What don't they let you do?

> Ricardo's parents make him take the dog for a walk every day.

Extension Do you think your parents are strict or not? How does your situation compare with Luke's?

8 WRITING

Use your notes from exercise 7 and write two paragraphs comparing the students' answers.

LANGUAGE WORKOUT

Complete.

make and *let*
You can't _____ a song happen.
He _____ me sing a couple of songs.

Active: *make* and *let* are both followed by object + infinitive without *to*.

Passive: *make* is followed by object + infinitive with *to*.
I was _____ to save up enough money.
The verb *let* has no passive form. Instead we use *be allowed to*.
I wasn't _____ _____ go to any of her concerts.

▶Answers and Practice
Language File page 120

8 MAKING THE GRADE

4 Integrated Skills
Making an application

1 OPENER

Have you ever thought about doing volunteer work, or do you know someone who has done it? What kinds of volunteer work can people do?

READING

2 Read Tiffany's letter and match these topics with sections of the letter 1–10.

> **Topics**
> Her personal reasons for choosing a particular expedition
> Ending the letter   Her address
> Personal details   Date
> Why she is writing   Money
> Address of the person she is writing to
> Why she would be a successful volunteer
> Starting the letter

REEF AID
VOLUNTEER WITH US AND HELP SAVE THE PLANET
- Expeditions to endangered coral reefs.
- Work with local people to protect the environment.

NO MONEY? We'll show you how to fund-raise to pay for your trip.
NO TIME? You can join our expeditions for only four weeks.
NO SKILLS? We'll teach you what you need, including scuba diving.

CLICK HERE TO FIND OUT MORE

(1) 53 Mill Lane
Cincinnati, OH 45202
(2) May 26

(3) Janet Rawlings
ReefAid
3345 Broadway
New York, NY 16024

(4) Dear Ms. Rawlings:

(5) I have read about ReefAid on your website, and I would like to apply to join a coral reef expedition.

(6) I am 17, and I am still in high school. I am taking the SAT in about a month. I want to major in art history in college. My native language is English, and I also speak good Spanish. I like to exercise, and I go dancing a lot. I am very interested in politics, but not in politicians! One of my main interests is conservation.

(7) I believe that I would be a good team member because I enjoy working as a volunteer at our local nature reserve. I get along well with most people and enjoy making new friends.

(8) I would like to join an expedition to Honduras because I speak Spanish, and also because I have always wanted to go to Central America. I am a good swimmer, and the chance to learn scuba diving is a great opportunity for me.

(9) I understand that I will have to pay for my airfare and living expenses, and make a contribution to the cost of the conservation project. I am confident that I will be able to raise the money.

(10) I look forward to getting more information from you, and to hearing if my application has been successful.

Sincerely,

Tiffany Bello

Tiffany Bello

3 ReefAid asked Tiffany to fill out a form. Complete it using the information in her letter.

APPLICATION FORM **REEF AID**
(please complete in black ink)

Last name: _____
Other names: _____
Age: ____ Male/female Married/(single)
Nationality: American
Address: _____
(Block capitals)
Telephone no: (212) 555-6557
Cell phone: (212) 555-6699
E-mail address: tiffany4@iweb-net.com
Occupation: Student
Languages: (fluent/good/basic) _____
Interests: _____

Give two reasons why we should select you as a volunteer.
_____

Circle the expedition you would you like to join and say why.
    Fiji   Honduras   Indonesia   Malaysia

NOW PLEASE TURN OVER AND COMPLETE THE MEDICAL DETAILS.

4 LISTENING

2.46 Listen to four extracts from telephone interviews with Janet Rawlings of ReefAid and match the applicants with four of the problems 1–8.

Ann Jake Carol Steve

1. Sent in the application too late.
2. Wants to be with a boy/girlfriend.
3. Not free at the time of the expedition.
4. Didn't give reasons for wanting to join.
5. Has already been on an expedition.
6. Has the wrong scuba diving certificate.
7. Didn't complete the whole form.
8. Not old enough.

One of the applicants calls back and is offered a place on an expedition. Discuss which applicant you think it will be and why. Then listen and check.

5 SPEAKING

Complete the ReefAid application form for yourself or an imaginary person. Use the completed form to role-play a telephone interview between an applicant (A) and a worker at ReefAid (B).

6 GUIDED WRITING

Write a letter of application to one of these volunteer organizations. Structure your letter like the one in exercise 2. You can write as yourself or an imaginary person.

MAKE A DIFFERENCE
Short-term aid projects on South Pacific islands
Contact: VolAid

WATER IS LIFE
Help bring clean water to sub-Saharan Africa
Write to us at WatAid

THINK GLOBAL VOLUNTEER LOCAL
Volunteer work in your local environment: nature reserves, protecting wildlife, and much more.
Contact EcolVol

LEARNER INDEPENDENCE

7 Thinking skills: Visualizing exam success

- Top athletes always visualize before a competition, closing their eyes and going through the event in their minds until they win. You can do the same when studying for exams.
- Look at or smell something that you are going to take into the exam with you, like a pencil case, or perfume/aftershave on a tissue. Close your eyes and imagine the exam itself. Think about yourself doing really well and getting good grades.
- When you go into the exam, look at the pencil case, or smell the tissue, and you will get the feeling of success that you visualized and be really confident.

8 Word creation: Add the suffix *-ness* to these adjectives to make nouns and complete the sentences.

> careless   happy   ill   polite   sad
> thoughtful   useful   weightless

1. He was famous for his _____—he always said "please" and "thank you."
2. We share your _____ at the loss of your pet.
3. _____ is always a problem for astronauts.
4. Oh, no! You've broken another glass! I'm fed up with your _____.
5. It's terrible. He's never well and gets one _____ after another.
6. Many thanks for your _____—you always think about other people.
7. I'm not complaining about the new computer's _____, just about its cost.
8. _____ is the one thing money can't buy.

9 **2.47** Phrasebook: Find these useful expressions in Unit 8. Then listen and repeat.

> around the clock
> Practice makes perfect.
> It drove me mad.
> It's up to you.
> That's all that matters.
> as far as I'm concerned

Which expression means …?

a That's the most important thing.
b You're the one who must decide.
c in my view
d all day and night
e It made me angry.

8 MAKING THE GRADE
Inspired EXTRA!

PROJECT Ideal school

1. Work in a group and look back at Lesson 2. Then discuss your ideal school in general terms, e.g., Where will it be? How big will it be? Will it be strict or liberal?

2. Research: Use the Internet or your library to find out about different schools around the world and to get ideas.

3. Make notes to answer these questions about your ideal school:
   - What will the buildings and the classrooms be like?
   - What subjects will students be able to study? What sports will be offered?
   - How much homework will students have to do? What about exams?
   - How long will the school terms be? What about vacations?
   - What school rules will there be? Will students have to wear uniforms?
   - What will the teachers be like?

4. Work together and write about your ideal school. Read your work carefully and correct any mistakes. Draw pictures or use photos from magazines to illustrate your school. Show your work to the other groups. Finally, have a class vote on the best ideal school.

Our Ideal School

Our ideal school will be run by the students. It will be very big so it can have lots of facilities and will look more like a hotel than a school. The classrooms will be small and comfortable with armchairs and laptops for all the students. The students will be able to choose what subjects they study and which classes they go to. The school won't offer any sports at all—students can use the city sports facilities. Homework will be done online and so will exams. Our ideal school will only have lessons in the morning, and there'll be just two short winter and summer vacations. The students will decide on the school rules, so they will obey them! And they won't have to wear uniforms. The teachers will be chosen by the students—they'll be a mixture of male and female, young and old, from our country and from abroad.

Game Puzzle words

- Work in pairs.
- Each of the boxes contains a nine-letter word. All the consecutive letters of the words touch each another. Find the three words as quickly as possible.

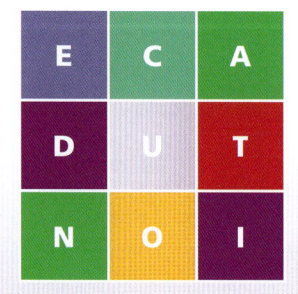

T	N	W		E	C	A		E	T	N
E	I	E		D	U	T		E	L	U
R	V	I		N	O	I		R	O	V

- Now make your own puzzle word: copy the grid, choose a nine-letter word from *Inspired 4* and arrange it in the squares so that all the letters touch.
- Exchange your puzzle with another pair and try to find their puzzle word.

UNIT 8

CONSOLIDATION

LESSON 1 Look at the text on page 100. Write five questions beginning with *What, When, Where, Who,* and *Why,* and answer them.

What kind of music did Beethoven compose?

Classical music, including concertos, symphonies, and operas.

LESSON 2 Look at the *Then and now* questionnaire on page 103. Write your answers to the questions.

LESSON 3 Look at exercise 7 on page 105. Write about two things your parents make you do, two things they let you do, and two things they don't let you do.

My parents make me take a shower every day.

EXTENSION

LESSON 1 Think about situations in the past when you finally managed to do something that you couldn't do before. Think about sports, music, school subjects, life skills, etc. Write about three situations.

I learned to swim when I was seven, but I couldn't dive. I kept trying, and I finally managed to dive into the swimming pool when I was ten.

LESSON 2 Look at the Language Workout on page 103 again and write two paragraphs using some of the modal expressions.

Paragraph 1: Write about your time at elementary school.
Paragraph 2: Write about will happen after you finish school.

LESSON 3 Think about the rules of soccer or another sport. Write sentences saying what you are and are not allowed to do.

YOUR CHOICE!

CONSTRUCTION Modal expressions

Rewrite the sentences using the correct form of the verb in parentheses.

1 Thank you! But it wasn't necessary to buy me a gift. (need)
2 He got up early because he needed to finish his homework. (have)
3 Are you allowed to wear what you like at school? (let)
4 We have to take a math test every week. (make)
5 It's OK—you won't have to pay for your ticket. (need)
6 I wasn't able to figure out the answer. (could)
7 Will you manage to attend an interview next week? (be able)
8 They don't let us wear jewelry at school. (allow)

REFLECTION Modal expressions

Match the examples a–h with language functions 1–6.

1 Ability   2 Obligation   3 Permission   4 Possibility
5 Prohibition   6 Request

a The students were made to learn 50 words a week.
b Could you write down your phone number, please?
c You aren't allowed to send text messages during class.
d I don't know how old he is—he could be 21.
e Could you read when you were five years old?
f Our teacher said we could go home early.
g My parents let me stay up late on weekends.
h He'd lost his key, but he managed to get in through a window.

ACTION Hot-air balloon

- Work in a small group. Imagine you are in a hot-air balloon.
- Each group member chooses a different role, e.g., doctor, teacher, engineer, musician, single parent with four children. Alternatively, you can choose to be famous people.
- The balloon is losing height, and one person will have to jump out. Take turns explaining to the rest of the group why you should stay in the balloon.
  Parent: My children won't be able to manage without me…
- Finally everyone votes for the person they think should jump.

INTERACTION Farewell gifts

- Look at the list of personality adjectives below. Can you think of positive words to add to the list?
- Imagine that you are going to give one of the words to another student as a farewell gift. Which word would you like to give? Which word would you like to receive and why?
- Write a short note to the student to whom you are giving the word explaining why you have chosen it.

Personality adjectives
enthusiastic friendly funny happy helpful
imaginative inspiring intelligent kind polite
popular reliable responsible strong successful

REVIEW
UNITS 7–8

1 Read and complete. For each number 1–15, choose word or phrase A, B, or C.

The medium and the message

People have always been able to send messages over short distances. Before message-sending machines __1__, information __2__ transmitted in all kinds of ways, for example, by drums, fires, bells, or flashing mirrors. But with the invention of __3__ the electric telegraph and Morse code in the 19th century, people __4__ to send messages over much greater distances. (The word *telegraph* comes from Greek words for *distant* and *write*.)

It wasn't long before people who were far apart __5__ actually speak to each other on the telephone (*distant + sound*). But until recently, long-distance phone calls were extremely expensive and callers usually __6__ speak very loudly __7__ be heard. Sometimes they __8__ hear each other at all. Nowadays, international calls __9__ transmitted via satellites in space __10__ messages can travel much farther and more clearly. Communication has __11__ even easier by the development of cell phones, which __12__ people contact each other almost anywhere.

And in the future? Some people think that one day we __13__ use phones at all—messages __14__ via telepathy (*distant + feeling*), so we __15__ to communicate directly with each other's minds!

	A	B	C
1	are invented	were invented	had invented
2	has	was	were
3	each	either	both
4	were able	were allowed	could
5	were able	managed	could
6	have to	had to	needed
7	in order to	so that	to make
8	can't	couldn't	weren't able
9	are	have	have been
10	because	in order to	so that
11	made	been made	been making
12	let	make	allow
13	needn't	won't need to	needn't have
14	are sent	are being sent	will be sent
15	can	could	will be able

2 Complete with the correct passive form of the verbs: simple past, present perfect, simple present, present progressive, or simple future.

A 44-year-old man __1__ (send) to prison after walking in the Scottish Highlands wearing only a hat, socks, and walking boots.

Stephen Gough __2__ (arrest) several times over the last six months. He is coming to the end of a 1,500-kilometer trek from Land's End in southwest England to John O'Groats in Scotland. On November 29, the police __3__ (call) by someone who had seen Gough walking through a village. Eventually he __4__ (find) and __5__ (take) to a police station.

Gough argues that not wearing clothes __6__ (permit) by the Human Rights Act as freedom of expression, and it is wrong that he __7__ (treat) like a criminal. Since he started his trek, he __8__ (ask) by dozens of people to have their pictures taken with him.

Now Gough __9__ (hold) in a local prison, but it is likely that he __10__ (release) in a few days. He has 160 kilometers to go to complete his journey.

3 Complete with the passive infinitive of these verbs.

allow	encourage	give	hear	pay	see	tell	treat

1 Women deserve _____ the same as men for doing the same job.
2 If you don't speak up, your voice won't _____.
3 Do you think people should _____ to smoke in public places?
4 We don't have _____ what to do all the time.
5 Students need _____ the chance to express themselves.
6 Young people must _____ to get more exercise.
7 Teenagers want their ideas _____ with respect.
8 People no longer believe that "children should _____ and not heard."

4 Complete the sentences with these phrasal verbs.

cut off	figure out	fill out	make up
put up	take in	turn off	turn up

1 Would you _____ *the sound on the radio* so I can hear the news?
2 Tiffany was asked to _____ *an application form*.
3 It's hard to _____ *difficult mathematical equations*.
4 Don't forget to _____ *the lights* when you leave.
5 She looks very different—she's _____ *all her hair*!
6 Could you help me _____ *some shelves*?
7 It's hard to _____ *so much new information*.
8 I didn't _____ *the story*—it's all true.

Now rewrite the sentences replacing the words in *italics* with pronouns. Remember that the pronoun goes between the verb and the adverb.

1 *Would you turn it up so I can hear the news?*

110

5 Complete with *could(n't)*, *was(n't) able*, or *managed to*.

When Thomas Edison was a boy, his teacher told him he ___1___ learn anything because he was too stupid. He once said: "I ___2___ to do well at school—I was always at the bottom of my class." But Edison ___3___ become one of the most famous inventors in history. One of his first inventions was the phonograph (1877), a machine that ___4___ record sounds and play them back. Later, Edison and other inventors improved its design so that it ___5___ to record music. Edison also ___6___ invent a practical light bulb. He didn't invent the first light bulb, but after eighteen months of hard work, he ___7___ to produce a reliable, long-lasting bulb in 1879. He said: "Genius is one percent inspiration and 99 percent perspiration."

6 Complete with *didn't need to* or *needn't have* and the correct form of the verb.

1 I knew we had plenty of time, so we _____ (hurry).
2 You _____ (cook) all this food—there's only two of us.
3 He _____ (worry) about his exam results—he got good grades.
4 They _____ (buy) tickets in advance—they paid at the door.
5 I _____ (wait) long for a train—one came almost immediately.
6 She _____ (be) so upset about losing her watch—it wasn't valuable.

7 Rewrite the sentences using the correct form of the verbs in parentheses.

1 You can't park your car here during the day. (allow)
2 The thief forced me to give him my cell phone. (make)
3 Did your teacher allow you to go home early? (let)
4 The hot sun caused the ice to melt. (make)
5 I won't allow you to talk like that. (let)
6 We had to work 12 hours a day. (make)
7 They don't let you carry weapons on planes. (allow)
8 I know a joke that will cause everyone to laugh. (make)

VOCABULARY

8 Complete with ten of these words.

composer   cupboard   dialect   earthquake
expedition   fan   platform   prejudice   quantity
submarine   tuition   uniform   volunteer   waterproof

1 The train to Chicago will depart from _____ two.
2 "Hip-hop English" is a kind of _____ spoken by young people.
3 She's a big _____ of Johnny Depp and has seen all his movies.
4 Do you have to wear a school _____?
5 There's still a lot of _____ against women in politics.
6 Most people have to pay _____ costs to study at college.
7 The _____ crossed the ocean underwater.
8 You don't earn money if you work as a _____.
9 The plates are on the bottom shelf of the _____.
10 Many houses had to be rebuilt after the _____.

9 Match these words with their definitions.

admire   chord   colleague   decade   emphasis
entrepreneur   lyrics   nautical   solar   transfer

1 words of a song
2 period of ten years
3 to do with the sun
4 person who works with you in an organization
5 to do with ships and sailing
6 move from one place or situation to another
7 special importance given to a particular thing
8 person who uses money to start a business
9 have great respect for someone/thing
10 two or more musical notes played together

10 Match the verbs in list A with the phrases in list B. Then write eight sentences using the expressions.

A	B
1 award	a stove
2 change	a problem
3 climb	a table
4 fail	an examination
5 install	a prize
6 repaint	the walls
7 reserve	up a ladder
8 solve	your mind

LEARNER INDEPENDENCE
SELF ASSESSMENT

Look back at Lessons 1–3 in Units 7 and 8.

How good are you at …?	✓ Fine	? Not sure
1 Describing changes and experiences Workbook pp74–75 exercises 2–4	☐	☐
2 Talking about what's right Workbook pp76–77 exercises 1–3	☐	☐
3 Using the phone Workbook pp78–79 exercises 3, 5, and 6	☐	☐
4 Talking about past ability Workbook pp86–87 exercises 1 and 2	☐	☐
5 Expressing purpose Workbook p87 exercise 3	☐	☐
6 Expressing obligation and ability Workbook pp88–89 exercises 1–4	☐	☐
7 Talking about obligation, permission, and prohibition Workbook pp90–91 exercises 2 and 3	☐	☐

Not sure? Take a look at Language File pages 118–120 and do the Workbook exercise(s) again.

Now write an example for 1–7.

1   *He's been fired.*

LANGUAGE FILE

Verbs not usually used in progressive forms
UNIT 1 LESSON 1

- The following verbs are not usually used in progressive forms. Many of these verbs refer to states (including mental states, e.g., *think*) rather than actions, or to the senses (e.g., *taste*):
  agree/disagree appear believe consist contain depend feel hear include know lack like/dislike love matter mean need prefer promise realize recognize remember see seem smell sound suppose taste think understand want
  > *Fruit juice contains sugar.*
  > *It often seems that this is true.*
  > *It doesn't matter whether they are fresh, frozen, ...*
  > *People suppose that they are OK.*
  > *They think that bottled water tastes better.*
- Modal verbs (e.g., *can*) do not have progressive forms.

> **PRACTICE: Simple present and present progressive**
>
> **1** Complete with the correct form of the verb.
> 1. Many people _____ (believe) that margarine _____ (contain) less fat than butter.
> 2. I _____ (see) that you _____ (make) a Chinese meal today.
> 3. She _____ (realize) salad is good for her, but she _____ (not like) eating it.
> 4. Mm, that _____ (smell) good. What _____ you _____ (cook)?
> 5. Why _____ you _____ (eat) cookies? You _____ (know) that dinner is ready!
> 6. I _____ (read) a new cookbook—it _____ (include) lots of vegetarian dishes.

Gerund
UNIT 1 LESSON 2

- A gerund (*-ing* form) is a noun formed from a verb. It can be the subject of a sentence:
  > *Going to sleep is easy.*
  > *Playing soccer is great fun.*
- We can also use a gerund after prepositions.
- We can use *by* + gerund to say how to do something:
  > *You can get to sleep by wearing this watch-like gadget.*
- We can use *for* + gerund to describe the function or purpose of something:
  > *It's a clever gadget for opening bottles.*

after/before + participle clause
UNIT 1 LESSON 2

- We can use the present participle (*-ing* form) in time clauses introduced by the conjunctions *after* and *before*:
  > *She came up with the idea after struggling to get up in the morning.*
  > *You are fully awake before turning it off.*
- We can also use *when, while,* and *since* to introduce participle time clauses:
  > *The media often exaggerate when reporting scientific research.*

Spelling: *-ing* form
UNIT 1 LESSON 2

- Most verbs add *ing*:
  play—play**ing**   wear—wear**ing**
- Verbs ending in *e* drop the *e* and add *ing*:
  hide—hid**ing**   make—mak**ing**
  But we don't make a change after *be* or *ee*:
  be—be**ing**   see—see**ing**
- One-syllable verbs ending in a consonant after a single vowel double the last letter and add *ing*:
  chop—cho**pp**ing   get—ge**tt**ing   plug—plu**gg**ing   put—pu**tt**ing
  run—ru**nn**ing   swim—swi**mm**ing
  Other verbs:
  begin—begi**nn**ing   forget—forge**tt**ing

> **PRACTICE: Gerund and participle clauses**
>
> **2** Complete with the *-ing* form of the verb, and *after*, *before*, *by*, or *for* where necessary.
> 1. Alarm clocks are _____ _____ (wake) people up.
> 2. _____ _____ (go) to sleep, I set my alarm clock.
> 3. _____ (count) sheep can help you go to sleep.
> 4. You unlock the door _____ _____ (turn) the key clockwise.
> 5. _____ (cook) a meal is easy if you follow a recipe.
> 6. I often feel sleepy _____ _____ (eat) a big meal.
> 7. _____ (listen) to English radio shows is a good idea.
> 8. You can keep fit _____ _____ (get) regular exercise.

Verb + gerund or infinitive
UNIT 1 LESSON 3

- We can use the gerund after these verbs:
  avoid enjoy go (+ activity) hate can't help keep like love mind quit risk can't stand start stop suggest
  > *I didn't exactly enjoy having acupuncture.*
  > *Acupuncture keeps growing in popularity.*
  > *He tried to quit smoking last year.*
- We can use the infinitive after these verbs:
  agree appear ask choose continue dare decide expect hope learn manage prepare pretend promise refuse seem want
  > *When people expect to get better, they often do.*
  > *I pretended to be calm.*
- Some verbs can be followed by either the gerund or the infinitive.
- *try* + gerund = do something to see what happens:
  > *Patients who tried having acupuncture had fewer headaches.*
  try + infinitive = attempt something difficult:
  > *He tried to quit smoking last year.*
- *remember/forget* + gerund refers to an action in the past:
  > *I remember going to the doctor.*
  > *I'll never forget meeting Nelson Mandela.*
  remember/forget + infinitive refers to a necessary action—something that should be done—and looks ahead:
  > *He didn't remember to take it every day.*
  > *Don't forget to lock the door.*
- *stop* is usually followed by the gerund, but it can also be followed by the infinitive of purpose:
  > *The walkers stopped (walking) to have a rest.*

LANGUAGE FILE

> **PRACTICE: Verb + gerund or infinitive**
>
> **3** Complete with the correct form of the verb.
>
> **A doctor talks about alternative medicine**
>
> "My own interest in alternative medicine goes back to when I was a medical student on a visit to China. I really enjoyed __1__ (travel) around the country. I'll never forget __2__ (go) into the operating room of a hospital in a small town. A woman was on the operating table with three needles in her left ear. I tried __3__ (see) if she had any other anesthetic, but there didn't appear __4__ (be) any. I kept __5__ (think) "They certainly didn't tell us this in medical school." I had forgotten __16__ (take) my camera with me, so unfortunately I couldn't take a picture. When I returned to the U.S., I tried __7__ (find) out more about acupuncture. I remember __8__ (tell) my professor about it, but he didn't really want __9__ (discuss) it."

Present perfect progressive
UNIT 2 LESSON 1

- We can use the present perfect progressive with *for* and *since* to talk about a continuous or repeated activity that started in the past and continues up to now:
  Since 1992, I've been making a series of drawings and prints of birds.
  For many years, Chris Ofili has been using elephant dung in his paintings.
  How long has Antony Gormley been creating sculptures?
- We can also use this tense to talk about recently completed continuous actions that have present results:
  I can tell she's been crying. (Her eyes are red.)
- We form the present perfect progressive with *have/has been* + present participle.
- See also Unit 1 Lesson 1 and Unit 2 Lesson 2.

> **PRACTICE: Present perfect progressive**
>
> **4** Write questions beginning *How long ...?* with the present perfect progressive, and answer them using both *for* and *since*.
>
> 1 *How long has Steven Spielberg been directing feature films?*
>   *He has been directing feature films for ... years, since ... .*
>
> 1 Steven Spielberg directed his first feature film, *Duel*, in 1971.
> 2 Robbie Williams started performing pop songs in 1990.
> 3 J. K. Rowling wrote her first story in 1971 at the age of six.
> 4 Orlando Bloom started acting in 1993.
> 5 Beyoncé started singing in public in 1998, when she was seven.
> 6 Cristiano Ronaldo started playing professional soccer at the age of 17 in 2002.

Present perfect: simple and progressive
UNIT 2 LESSON 2

- We can use the simple present perfect to talk about a recent completed action or series of actions:
  Some of the work has been rather badly paid.
  I've only had two jobs so far.
- We can use the present perfect progressive to talk about a recent action or a repeated series of actions that continues up to now. The activity may still be continuing and is often temporary:
  I've been working on the new Bond movie.
  I've been calling the agency every morning.
  They've been trying to get the lighting right.
- We use the simple present perfect to focus on *how much/many*.
  How much work have you had this year?
  I've had plenty of job offers.
- We use the present perfect progressive to focus on *how long*:
  My phone has been ringing all week.
- See also Unit 1 Lesson 1 and Unit 2 Lesson 1.

> **PRACTICE: Present perfect: simple and progressive**
>
> **5** Complete with the correct form of the verb.
>
> **From ex-teacher to extra!**
>
> Ex-teacher, 34-year-old Adrian Jenkins __1__ (make) a successful career as an extra and __2__ (appear) in more than 40 feature films and TV shows. "I __3__ (work) as an extra for over five years now, and I __4__ (never be) bored. For the last two days, I __5__ (do) a commercial for a bank—that finishes tomorrow. After that, I don't know—something will turn up. I __6__ (just change) my agency, and the new agency __7__ (work) really hard to find me jobs. They __8__ (show) my photo to lots of directors, and as a result, I __9__ (have) plenty of offers. So you can see that I __10__ (not sit) around at home watching daytime TV—even if I am in some of the shows!"

Past perfect: simple and progressive
UNIT 2 LESSON 3

Simple past perfect   Simple past   NOW

Past perfect progressive -------->

- We use the simple past perfect to describe the earlier of two past events, to make the order of events clear. We use the simple past for the more recent event:
  Frankenstein was horrified by the creature he had made.
  He realized that he hadn't made a man, he had produced a monster.
- If the order of events is clear, we don't need to use the past perfect for the earlier event:
  After he (had) left school in 1934, he started working for Shell.
  But compare these sentences:
  The train left when I reached the station.
  (I saw the train.)
  The train had left when I reached the station.
  (I didn't see the train.)
- We use the past perfect progressive to talk about a continuous or repeated earlier activity:
  She had been thinking about her story for some time, when she had a dream.
  Before Mary started writing Frankenstein, *she had been reading a book about chemistry.*
- We form the simple past perfect with *had* + past participle.
- We form the past perfect progressive with *had been* + present participle.
- See also Unit 1 Lesson 1.

LANGUAGE FILE

> **PRACTICE: Simple past and past perfect tenses**
>
> **6** Complete with simple past and past perfect tenses, using the past perfect progressive where possible.
> 1. The weather in 1816 ____ (be) bad because there ____ (be) a huge volcanic eruption in 1815.
> 2. Mary ____ (write) her story after she ____ (have) an extraordinary dream.
> 3. She ____ (read) a book about chemistry just before she ____ (start) writing.
> 4. After Frankenstein ____ (create) his monster, he ____ (abandon) him.
> 5. Frankenstein ____ (decide) to destroy his creation after the monster ____ (kill) three people.
> 6. Mary ____ (write) stories ever since she ____ (be) a child.

Comparison of adverbs
UNIT 3 LESSON 1

- Adverbs ending in *-ly* take *more/most*:
  Lightning travels more slowly than light.
  Where does the Earth rotate most quickly?
- Adverbs with the same form as adjectives add *-er/-est*:

fast	faster	(the) fastest
hard	harder	(the) hardest
high	higher	(the) highest
late	later	(the) latest
long	longer	(the) longest

  Which travels faster?
  Which began later: life in the ocean or on land?
  Russian astronauts have been in space longest.
- Irregular forms:

well	better	(the) best
badly	worse	(the) worst
far	farther	(the) farthest

- We often use *the* before superlative adverbs when making comparisons with other things:
  Of all the planets, Jupiter rotates the most quickly.
  BUT The Earth rotates most quickly at the Equator.
  (The Earth isn't compared with anything else.)

Adverbs of degree
UNIT 3 LESSON 1

- These adverbs are followed by another adverb or by an adjective:
  extremely   incredibly   pretty   really   very
  The universe has been expanding extremely rapidly.
  Our universe is incredibly large.
  Lightning also travels really quickly.

> **PRACTICE: Adverbs**
>
> **7** Complete with the correct form of the adverbs.
> 1. After the Big Bang, the universe expanded ____ ____. (incredible, quick)
> 2. Light travels ____ than lightning. (fast)
> 3. The Earth rotates ____ at the Equator. (rapid)
> 4. The Earth turns _____ as you move _____ away from the Equator. (slow, far)
> 5. Tomatoes are almost ____ made up of water. (complete)

Position and order of adverbial phrases
UNIT 3 LESSON 1

- Adverbial phrases usually follow the verb in this order:
  Manner → Place → Time
  Life began suddenly in the sea after that.
  Apes started to walk on two feet millions of years ago.
  The Earth rotates most quickly at the Equator.

> **PRACTICE: Order of adverbial phrases**
>
> **8** Put the adverbial phrases in the correct order.
> 1. The Big Bang happened …
>   (over 13 million years ago/suddenly)
> 2. Life developed …
>   (in the ocean/for billions of years/slowly)
> 3. Organisms started to breathe oxygen …
>   (400,000,000 years ago/on land)
> 4. Apes walked …
>   (over 3,000,000 years ago/on two feet)
> 5. The Earth rotates …
>   (in both London and Paris/at roughly the same speed)

Making exclamations
UNIT 3 LESSON 2

- We can use *What (a/an)* + (adjective) + noun to express surprise and make exclamations:
  What fun!   What a discovery!   What a fantastic sight!
- We can also use *so* + (adjective/adverb) and *such (a/an)* + (adjective) + noun to make exclamations:
  It's so unexpected!
  The three of us are having such an amazing time!

Result clauses: *so/such … that*
UNIT 3 LESSON 2

- We can use these structures to express consequence or result:
  so + (adjective/adverb) + *that*
  It was so deep that they didn't expect to see any life.
  such (a/an) + (adjective) + noun + *that*
  It's been such an exciting dive that I haven't noticed the time.
- We often leave out *that*, especially in spoken English:
  It was so dark (that) I couldn't see anything.

> **PRACTICE: Result clauses: *so/such … that***
>
> **9** Complete the sentences with *so* or *such (a/an)*.
> 1. It was ____ dark night that we couldn't see anything.
> 2. The winter was ____ cold that the ocean began to freeze.
> 3. It's ____ amazing experience to swim with dolphins.
> 4. We had ____ great time on our adventure vacation.
> 5. He was ____ happy that he couldn't stop smiling.
> 6. I'm ____ excited to hear ____ wonderful news.

Order of adjectives
UNIT 3 LESSON 2

- Adjectives usually precede the noun in this order:
  Opinion → Size → Age → Shape → Color → Origin
  I've just seen a beautiful, small, flat, blue fish.
  We're diving in a comfortable, spacious, modern, Russian submersible.

LANGUAGE FILE

The future
UNIT 3 LESSON 3 AND UNIT 4 LESSON 1

- We use the simple future (*will/won't*) to give information about future events and to make predictions:
  Every passenger will have a spectacular view.
  I'm sure the cost of space flights will come down.
  It won't be cheap.
  Will the dream ever become reality?
- We use the simple present to talk about schedules and timetables:
  The tour starts at 9:45 a.m.
- We use the present progressive to talk about fixed future arrangements:
  I'm visiting the Kennedy Space Center tomorrow.
- We use *going to* to talk about plans and intentions:
  Branson is going to travel on the first flight.
  I'm going to make a reservation!
- We use the future progressive to talk about events that will be in progress at a particular time in the future:
  In 2020 ...
  They'll be working longer.
  Doctors won't be treating diseases anymore.
  Will we all be living longer?
  We can also use the future progressive to talk about future arrangements:
  I'll be seeing Jenny later, so I can give her your message.
- We use the future perfect to talk about something that will/won't have finished by a certain time in the future:
  Scientists will have invented earrings that take our pulses.
  We won't have gotten rid of cars.
  Will we have created a bright new future?
- See also Unit 4 Lesson 2.

> **PRACTICE: The future**
>
> **10** Complete with the most suitable form of the verb: simple future, simple present, or present progressive.
>
> 1. Each Virgin Galactic spaceship _____ (carry) six passengers.
> 2. I'm scared of flying, so I definitely _____ (not be) a space tourist.
> 3. My friends _____ (fly) to Florida on the weekend.
> 4. Their flight _____ (depart) at 6 p.m. on Saturday.
> 5. They've made a reservation at a hotel in Orlando, and they _____ (stay) there for a week.
> 6. Do you think lots of people _____ (travel) in space?
> 7. Where _____ (you go) for your next vacation?
> 8. Can you tell me what time the tour _____ (end)?
>
> **11** Complete these predictions with the future progressive or future perfect of these verbs.
>
> | become   create   learn   live   retire   talk   wear |
>
> By 2020 ...
> 1. Scientists _____ the world's first designer dog.
> 2. People _____ to their cars.
> 3. Household equipment _____ intelligent.
> 4. People (not) _____ from work earlier.
> 5. We _____ multifunction gadgets on our wrists.
> 6. People _____ around 40 years longer than today.
> 7. _____ we _____ to live together more happily?

First conditional
UNIT 4 LESSON 2

- We use the first conditional to talk about the possible future when discussing the consequences of actions or events. First conditional sentences have this structure:
  if/unless + simple present, simple future
  If we don't fly so much, we'll reduce carbon emissions.
  Unless we take action now, we won't reduce the impact ...
- The conditional clause can follow the main clause:
  We'll reduce carbon emissions if we don't fly so much.
  The situation won't improve unless we all work together.
- *unless* = *if not*

Future time clauses
UNIT 4 LESSON 2

- *when/as soon as/until* + simple present, simple future:
  The future will look brighter when all governments agree to reduce carbon emissions.
  As soon as carbon emissions decrease, air pollution will decrease.
- The time clause can follow the main clause:
  We won't halt global warming until we stop flying.
- *as soon as* = immediately after something happens
  until = up to the time when something happens

> **PRACTICE: First conditional and future time clauses**
>
> **12** Complete with the simple present or simple future form of the verb.
>
> 1. If we _____ (continue) flying so much, global warming _____ (get) worse.
> 2. People _____ (not stop) flying until train travel _____ (become) cheaper.
> 3. When flights _____ (get) more expensive, people _____ (use) other means of transportation.
> 4. Governments _____ (have) to work together if they _____ (want) to reduce carbon emissions.
> 5. There _____ (be) serious climate change unless we _____ (take) action soon.
> 6. As soon as everyone _____ (take) global warming seriously, the situation _____ (improve).

Second conditional
UNIT 4 LESSON 3

- We use the second conditional to talk about imaginary present or unlikely future situations. Second conditional sentences have this structure:
  if + simple past, *would(n't)* ...
  If I had enough time, I'd travel overland.
  If I was/were in Nepal for a short time, I wouldn't leave Kathmandu.
  If you could choose, where would you stay?
- In the conditional clause with the verb *be*, we can use either *was* or *were* after *I/he/she/it*. *was* is informal.
- We can use *If I were you, I'd/I wouldn't ...* to give advice and warnings:
  If I were you, I'd stay in a guesthouse.
- The conditional clause can follow the main clause:
  I'd stay in a guesthouse if I were you.

LANGUAGE FILE

wish/if only
UNIT 4 LESSON 3 AND UNIT 5 LESSON 1

- We can use *if only* or *wish* + simple past to express a hope or desire for something in the present to be different:
    I wish I could take all my friends!
    He wishes he had more time.
    If only people were like that in New York!
    I wish I was/were in Kathmandu.
- We can use *if only* or *wish* + past perfect to express regret about the past:
    I wish we had had binoculars.
    Most of the survivors wished they had never set sail on the Titanic.
    If only they had filled all the lifeboats!

PRACTICE: wish/if only + simple past

13 Complete with the simple past of these verbs.

| be | can | have | know |

1. It's raining. I wish I _____ my umbrella.
2. She feels lonely and miserable. She wishes she _____ at home.
3. He doesn't speak French. He wishes he _____ what they were saying.
4. I want to buy that jacket so much. If only I _____ enough money!
5. What a car! I wish I _____ how to drive.
6. She has to log on to the website now. If only she _____ remember the password!
7. They love pets. They wish they _____ a dog.
8. I wish I _____ on a tropical beach right now.

14 Rewrite the sentences using the words in parentheses and the simple past perfect.

I'm sorry I forgot your birthday. (wish)

I wish I hadn't forgotten your birthday.

1. I'm really sorry he failed his exams. (If only)
2. She's sorry she didn't get the message in time. (wish)
3. I shouldn't have eaten so much! (wish)
4. You should have listened to me! (If only)
5. He regrets not learning to play an instrument. (wish)
6. What a shame he lost his job. (If only)

Third conditional
UNIT 5 LESSON 1

- We use the third conditional to talk about unreal or imaginary past events. Third conditional sentences have this structure:
    if + simple past, *would(n't) have* ...
    If the ship had slowed down, there would have been time to change course.
    If the ship hadn't hit an iceberg, it wouldn't have sunk.
- The conditional clause can follow the main clause:
    The ship wouldn't have sunk if it hadn't hit an iceberg.

PRACTICE: Third conditional

15 Complete with the correct form of the verb: simple past perfect or *would(n't) have*.

1. If she _____ (have) the right number, she _____ (win) the lottery.
2. If I _____ (charge) my cell phone, I _____ (not miss) your call.
3. They _____ (get) cheaper tickets if they _____ (buy) them earlier.
4. If you _____ (listen) more carefully, you _____ (not misunderstand) what I said.
5. He _____ (be) able to drive home if he _____ (not lose) his car keys.
6. The team _____ (not lose) the game if they _____ (play) better.

must, can't, have to, and need to
don't have to and don't need to
UNIT 5 LESSON 2

- We use *must*, *have to*, and *need to* to express present and future obligation:
    You must/You have to = It's obligatory.
    You need to = It's necessary.
        Why must Jo be very careful?
        You have to watch their swim patterns.
        The team needs to clean the tank walls regularly.
- We use *can't* to say that something is not allowed or that it is wrong:
    She can't use a very hot hairdryer.
- The past tense of both *must* and *have to* is *had to*:
    I had to tell myself to stay calm.
- The past tense of *need to* is *needed to*:
    We needed to be careful.
- Note that *need* can also be followed by an object:
    The elaborate hairstyles need work.
- We use *don't have to* and *don't need to* to express lack of obligation:
    Why doesn't Alan have to explain the procedure?
    You don't need to worry about me.
    The past forms are *didn't have to* and *didn't need to*.
    Alan didn't have/need to collect snake venom last week.
- See also Unit 8 Lesson 2.

PRACTICE: must, can't, have to, and need to; don't have to and don't need to

16 Complete the sayings with the correct form of the verb.

1. A popular saying is that if you want to eat the fruit, you _____ (must) first climb the tree.
2. You _____ (have to) pay for the most valuable things in life like love and friendship.
3. A bad dancer _____ (can) say it's the fault of the floor.
4. You can't stop trouble coming, but you _____ (need) give it a chair to sit on.
5. The sign on the office wall says "You _____ (have to) be crazy to work here, but it helps."
6. My father used to say that you _____ (have to) learn to walk before you could run.
7. In Japan, people used to say that if you wanted to catch a tiger, you _____ (need) go into the tiger's cave.
8. You _____ (need) be afraid of a noisy dog, but you should be afraid of a quiet one.

LANGUAGE FILE

must have and *can't have* *could/may/might have*
UNIT 5 LESSON 3

- We use *must have* and *can't have* + past participle to make deductions about the past. We use *must have* when we are sure something happened:
   The plane must have run out of fuel.
  We use *can't have* when we are sure something didn't happen:
   It can't have blown up in mid-air.
- We use *could/may/might have* + past participle to speculate about the past and to talk about what possibly happened:
   What could have happened to them?
   They could have ended up on a desert island.
   Earhart and Noonan may have been U.S. spies.
   Aliens might have abducted them. (Less likely)

> **PRACTICE:** *must have* and *can't have*; *could/may/might have*
>
> **17** At a party, a girl bumps into you and you drop your food. Rewrite the sentences using the verb in parentheses and *have*.
>
> 1. It was definitely a mistake. (must)
> 2. I'm sure she didn't see me. (can't)
> 3. It's possible that she looked the other way. (might)
> 4. Maybe she fell over something. (could)
> 5. It's possible that she wanted to talk to me. (may)

Reported speech
UNIT 6 LESSONS 1 AND 2

- **Reported speech with various reporting verbs**
- Verb + infinitive:
  agree ask hope offer promise refuse
   They agreed to let me go.
   I promised to send lots of e-mails.
- Verb + object + infinitive:
  advise ask invite promise tell warn
   She invited me to go with her.
   Dad told me to keep in touch.
- Verb + (*that*) clause:
  agree complain explain hope point out promise reply say suggest warn
   Mom pointed out that I didn't like Indian food.
   You complained it was too spicy.
- Verb + object + (*that*) clause:
  promise remind tell warn
   Mom reminded me that I had to have vaccinations.
- *suggest* + *-ing*:
   Mom suggested inviting Nisha and her parents for dinner.
- **Reported questions**
  Reported *Yes/No* questions: we use *if* before the reported question.
  Reported *Wh-* questions: we use the question word before the reported question.
   "Is everything all right?"
   → *She asked if everything was all right.*
   "Can I get you anything else?"
   → *She wanted to know if she could get him anything else.*
   "Would you like some ketchup?"
   → *She wondered if he would like some ketchup.*
   "What do you want to drink?"
   → *She asked what he wanted to drink.*
  In reported questions, the subject–verb order is the same as in statements. We don't use a question mark after reported questions.

- In reported speech, verbs in the present usually change to the past, and verbs in the past usually change to the past perfect:

Direct speech		Reported speech
Simple present	→	Simple past
Present progressive	→	Past progressive
Simple past	→	Past perfect
Present perfect	→	Past perfect
am/is/are going to	→	was/were going to
must	→	had to
can	→	could
will	→	would

  Note: Modal verbs *could, should, would, might* do not change.

- Time phrases and other reference words also usually change in reported speech:

Direct speech		Reported speech
today	→	that day
tonight	→	that night
tomorrow	→	the next/following day
yesterday	→	the day before
now	→	then
here	→	there
this	→	that/the

> **PRACTICE:** Reported speech
>
> **18** Write these sentences in reported speech using the verb in parentheses.
>
> 1 *Laura invited Nisha ...*
>
> 1. Laura: "Nisha, would you like to come to dinner?" (invite)
> 2. Father: "The plane ticket will be expensive." (point out)
> 3. Nisha: "Don't forget your passport, Laura." (remind)
> 4. Mother: "Laura, you can't get sunburned." (warn)
> 5. Laura: "I'll be very careful!" (promise)
> 6. Nisha: "Let's go to the travel agency tomorrow." (suggest)
> 7. Laura: "Kerala is in the southwest of India." (explain)
> 8. Father: "Laura is a very lucky girl!" (say)
> 9. Nisha: "Laura, can I lend you a book about India?" (offer)
> 10. Laura: "I don't have any nice clothes to wear!" (complain)
>
> **19** Match the direct questions (1–5) with the reported questions (a–e).
>
> 1. How much do you know about our country?
> 2. What parts of our country have you visited?
> 3. What places would you like to visit?
> 4. Have you traveled around by bus, train, car, or plane?
> 5. Have you stayed in a hotel or with friends or family when you've been away from home?
>
> a. I asked if he/she had stayed in a hotel or with friends or family when he/she had been away from home.
> b. I wanted to know what parts of our country he/she had visited.
> c. I asked if he/she had traveled around by bus, train, car, or plane.
> d. I wondered how much he/she knew about our country.
> e. I wanted to know what places he/she would like to visit.
>
> Now ask another student the questions and write sentences reporting the questions and answers.
>
> *I asked how much Carlos knew about our country. He said that he had visited the south and west, but didn't know the rest of it very well.*

LANGUAGE FILE

Tag questions
UNIT 6 LESSON 3

- We can use tag questions with **falling** intonation to ask for agreement when we are sure about something:
  They looked at the website, didn't they?
  Zak doesn't want to stay in the hotel, does he?
  You'd like to stay there, wouldn't you?
  You didn't expect me to know that, did you?
- We can use tag question with **rising** intonation to check if something is true.
  You can see that, can't you?
  It's been in the news, hasn't it?
- When the statement in the first part of the sentence is affirmative, the tag question is negative.
- When the statement in the first part of the sentence is negative, the tag question is affirmative.

PRACTICE: Tag questions

20 Complete with tag questions.
1. It was your birthday yesterday, _____?
2. You didn't have a party, _____?
3. He can't play the trumpet, _____?
4. You like reggae, _____?
5. She wants to go to college, _____?
6. She's passed all her exams, _____?
7. We aren't late, _____?
8. They'd like to win the game, _____?

The passive
UNIT 7 LESSONS 1 AND 2

- We form the different passive tenses with the appropriate tense of *be* + past participle:
  Simple past: *The elephant was named Jumbo.*
  Present perfect: *I have been fired.*
  Simple present: *The shuttlecock is kept up in the air.*
  Present progressive: *New expressions are being added all the time.*
  Future simple: *You will be shown the ropes.*
- We form the passive infinitive with *to be* + past participle:
  Many people think that Franklin deserves to be awarded a Nobel Prize.
  She is beginning to be recognized as a brilliant scientist.
- After modal verbs, we use the infinitive without *to*:
  The picture could be used to figure out the structure of DNA.
  Women couldn't be served in the same dining room.
  Nobel Prizes may only be given to the living.
  Her life shouldn't be seen as a failure.
- We use the passive to focus on the action rather than the agent (the person or thing that performs the action). When we want to refer to the agent, we use *by* + noun:
  Now wicked *is being used by some people as slang for* very good.

PRACTICE: The passive

21 Write sentences using the correct passive form of the verb.
1. Written messages (deliver) by mail for a long time. *Present perfect*
2. Now millions of messages (send) by e-mail. *Simple present*
3. How do you think messages (transmit) in 2050? *Simple future*
4. In the past, most vacations (arrange) by travel agents. *Simple past*
5. These days more and more tickets (buy) online. *Present progressive*
6. One day, vacations (take) in space. *Simple future*
7. Electrical appliances (use) for 100 years. *Present perfect*
8. More and more work (carry) out by machines. *Present progressive*
9. In the future, housework (do) by robots. *Simple future*

22 Complete with the passive infinitive of these verbs.

> allow   catch   do   forbid   grade   teach   use   write

Internet cheats

What's wrong with a little Internet help with homework? Should students __1__ to download essays from the Internet if they like? Or should they __2__ to copy from the Web? Teachers argue that essays must __3__ by the students themselves, or else they can't __4__ fairly. But students say that sometimes homework can't __5__ without a little help from the Web. Schools, on the other hand, believe that cheaters must __6__ a lesson. But how can Internet cheaters __7__? Anticheating software can __8__ to check essays, but in the end, schools may just have to trust their students to be honest. After all, you can't copy something from the Web during an exam!

either ... or and both ... and
UNIT 7 LESSON 2

- We can use *either ... or*, meaning *one or the other*, to talk about two alternative possibilities:
  Either Franklin or Crick and Watson could have been the first.
- We can use *both ... and*, meaning *the two together*, for emphasis:
  Both Crick and Watson clearly benefited from Franklin's work.

Phrasal verbs
UNIT 7 LESSON 3

- Phrasal verbs are very common in English, and there are three main structures:
- Verb + adverb with no object:
  The pace of life in Africa is speeding up.
  It is likely to go on for many years.
  Sometimes the meaning of a phrasal verb is clear, e.g., *speed up*, but phrasal verbs are idiomatic, and their meaning isn't always obvious.
- Verb + adverb with direct object:
  The noun object can go before or after the adverb:
  They have put up tall towers.
  OR *They have put tall towers up.*
  The pronoun object must go between the verb and the adverb:
  They have put them up.
- Verb + preposition with direct object:
  Noun and pronoun objects go at the end of the phrase:
  People climb up a ladder.
  People climb up it.

LANGUAGE FILE

- Words like *up* and *on* can be either adverbs or prepositions. They are usually stressed as adverbs, but not as prepositions.
- We often use phrasal verbs instead of single-word verbs:
  It is likely to go on (= continue) *for many years.*
  They have found out (= discovered) *how to solve this problem.*
- Phrasal verbs often have several different meanings:
  I'm looking for a job—I hope something will turn up (= happen, appear) *soon.*
  He turned up (= arrived) *with a couple of friends.*
  Could you turn up (= increase) *the heat?*

PRACTICE: Phrasal verbs

23 Rewrite the sentences replacing the words in *italics* with pronouns.

1. She looked up *the phone number* in the directory.
2. He wrote down *the number* in his address book.
3. I want to talk to *my sister*.
4. Please turn off *your cell phones*.
5. We're looking for *the Pizza Palace restaurant*.
6. Don't forget to call up *your parents*.
7. It took an hour to climb up *the hill*.
8. Can you figure out *the answer*?

could(n't), was(n't) able to, managed to
UNIT 8 LESSON 1

- We can use *could/couldn't* and *was/wasn't able to* to talk about ability in the past.
  could and *couldn't*:
    He started performing with bands so that his poems could reach people who didn't read books.
    Einstein couldn't read until he was seven.
  was/wasn't able to:
    Although Beethoven wasn't able to hear, he was able to listen.
    Einstein wasn't able to get a job at a Swiss university.
- BUT we don't use *could* in the affirmative to talk about achieving something on a particular occasion. Instead, we use *was able to* or *managed to*:
    He was able to educate himself in prison.
    NOT *He could educate himself in prison.*
    He managed to get a place at SIT.
    NOT *He could get a place at SIT.*
- See also Unit 5 Lesson 2 and Unit 8 Lesson 2.

PRACTICE: could(n't), was(n't) able to, managed to

24 Rewrite the sentences using the correct form of the verb in parentheses.

1. Steven Spielberg couldn't get into film school because his grades weren't good enough. (be able)
2. Maria Sharapova succeeded in winning Wimbledon at the age of 17. (manage)
3. Pope John Paul II could speak eight languages. (be able)
4. Olympic triathlete Michelle Dillon wasn't able to swim until she was 23. (could)
5. At first, Michael Jordan couldn't play for his school basketball team because he was too short. (be able)
6. Mozart was able to play the piano at the age of four. (could)
7. Ming Kipa Sherpa, a 15-year-old girl, managed to climb Mount Everest in 2003. (be able)
8. Harry Houdini was able to escape from a locked prison cell in two minutes in 1902. (manage)

in order to and so that
UNIT 8 LESSON 1

- We can use *in order to* and *so that* to express purpose.
- We can use either form when the subject is the same:
    She moved to Edinburgh in order to be near her sister.
    = *She moved to Edinburgh so that she could be near her sister.*
- When the subject is different, we use *so that*:
    He started performing with bands so that his poems could reach people who didn't read books.
- We often leave out *that*, especially in spoken English:
    She moved to Edinburgh so (that) she could be near her sister.

PRACTICE: in order to and so that

25 Join the sentences with *in order to* where possible. Otherwise use *so that*.

1. The students read through all their notes. They wanted to pass the exam.
2. My parents gave me a camera. I could take pictures at the party.
3. The police locked the cell. The thief couldn't escape.
4. They're visiting the U.S. They want to learn English.
5. We left home early. We wanted to get to the concert on time.
6. He gave me his number. I could call if I got lost.
7. Can you buy some eggs? I want to make a cake.
8. She goes to the gym every day. She wants to keep fit.

Modal expressions in the past and future
UNIT 8 LESSON 2

- Modal expressions for obligation, ability, and necessity in the past:
  had to, didn't have to, was(n't) able to, were(n't) able to, needed to/didn't need to, needn't have:
    You had to pay to go to them.
    Children didn't have to go to school at all.
    Many poor families weren't able to pay.
    People believed that girls didn't need to go to school.
    She needn't have worried.
  didn't need to refers to something that wasn't done because it wasn't necessary.
  needn't have refers to something that was done but was unnecessary.
- Modal expressions for obligation, ability, and necessity in the future:
  will/won't have to, will/won't be able to, will/won't need to:
    Students won't have to wait until they get home.
    Students will be able choose what to wear.
    Students won't need to wait their turn.
- See also Unit 5 Lesson 2 and Unit 8 Lesson 1.

LANGUAGE FILE

PRACTICE: Modal expressions in the past and future

26 Complete with the correct form of the verb.

In the nineteenth century, rich families __1__ (need) to worry about paying school tuition costs. In fact, many rich children __2__ (have) to go to school at all—they had teachers at home until they were seven or eight. Then the boys were sent away to schools where they __3__ (have) to study Latin and Greek. However, girls from rich families __4__ (be) able to stay at home and study subjects like French, music, and sewing. Rich or poor, nineteenth century schoolchildren __5__ (have) to obey their teachers and show respect for them at all times. The word "respect" was also used a lot in *The School I'd Like* competition. "Of course there __6__ (have) to be rules," someone wrote, "and students __7__ (be) able to do whatever they like. But in the future, teachers and students will respect each other, so teachers __8__ (need) to shout so much, and __9__ (be) able to concentrate on their teaching. And students __10__ (have) to respect their teachers too!" So people who were worried that students would want to get rid of teachers __11__ (need) to be concerned.

UNIT 5 — CULTURE

***Shopping Skills* questionnaire**
Key
1 **C** is the best answer. Both **A** and **B** sound rude.
2 **B** is the best answer. "try on" means "put them on to see if they fit and take them off again"; "wear" and "put on" mean "put them on and keep them on."
3 **A** is the best answer. **B** is wrong because "jeans" is a plural noun, and **C** is wrong because bigger jeans are needed, not smaller.
4 **A** is the best answer. "It doesn't really look good on me" means "I don't look good in it." **B** is wrong because "fit" is about size, and **C** is wrong because "match" is used to say how one color goes with another.
5 **B** is the best answer. **A** is wrong because "more" is used to compare two things. **C** is quite rude—"knock off" is slang and it isn't usual to bargain in stores in the U.S.
6 **C** is the best answer. **A** is too informal for a polite request, and "bucks" is slang. **B** is wrong because the speaker means "lend me" and not "borrow."

---

make and *let; be allowed to*
UNIT 8 LESSON 3

- Active: *make* and *let* are both followed by object + infinitive without *to*:
  You can't make a song happen.
  It made me feel great.
  You just have to let it take shape.
  He let me sing a couple of songs.
- Passive: *make* is followed by object + infinitive with *to*:
  I was made to save up enough money.
  The verb *let* has no passive form. Instead, we use *be allowed to*:
  I wasn't allowed to go to any of her concerts.

PRACTICE: *make* and *let; be allowed to*

27 Complete the sentences with the correct form of *make*, *let*, or *be allowed to*.

1 Steel bands _____ me think of carnival.
2 Can you _____ me know when the concert starts?
3 You (not) _____ talk during this exam.
4 Interviews _____ a lot of people feel nervous.
5 The students _____ stay late at school yesterday.
6 _____ you _____ use cell phones at school?
7 Do your parents _____ you wear torn jeans?
8 Professional soccer players _____ to train hard.

WORD LIST

★ = fairly common words ★★ = very common words ★★★ = the most common and basic words

UNIT 1

acid (n) ★★	/ˈæsɪd/
advertising (n) ★★	/ˈædvərˌtaɪzɪŋ/
astronaut (n) ★	/ˈæstrəˌnɔt/
basically (adv) ★★	/ˈbeɪsɪkli/
bedtime (n)	/ˈbedˌtaɪm/
belief (n) ★★★	/bɪˈlif/
brain scan (n)	/ˈbreɪn ˌskæn/
capitalism (n) ★★	/ˈkæpɪt(ə)lˌɪzəm/
chest (n) ★★★	/tʃest/
choice (n) ★★★	/tʃɔɪs/
critic (n) ★★★	/ˈkrɪtɪk/
decay (n) ★	/dɪˈkeɪ/
disability (n) ★★	/ˌdɪsəˈbɪləti/
doubt (n) ★★★	/daʊt/
drawer (n) ★★	/drɔr/
electricity (n) ★★★	/ɪˌlekˈtrɪsəti, ˌilekˈtrɪsəti/
equally (adv) ★★★	/ˈikwəli/
essentially (adv) ★★★	/ɪˈsenʃ(ə)li/
evidence (n) ★★★	/ˈevɪdəns/
experiment (n) ★★★	/ɪkˈsperɪmənt, ɪkˈsperɪment/
expert (n) ★★★	/ˈekˌspɜrt/
factor (n) ★★★	/ˈfæktər/
fault (n) ★★★	/fɔlt/
fiction (n) ★★	/ˈfɪkʃ(ə)n/
form (of transportation) (n) ★★★	/fɔrm/
friendship (n) ★★	/ˈfren(d)ʃɪp/
gadget (n)	/ˈgædʒət/
globalization (n)	/ˌgloʊbələˈzeɪʃ(ə)n/
happiness (n) ★★	/ˈhæpinəs/
health (n) ★★★	/helθ/
highway (n) ★★	/ˈhaɪˌweɪ/
hope (n) ★★★	/hoʊp/
human (n) ★★★	/ˈhjumən/
importance (n) ★★★	/ɪmˈpɔrt(ə)ns/
individual (n) ★★★	/ˌɪndɪˈvɪdʒuəl/
insomnia (n)	/ɪnˈsɑmniə/
issue (= topic) (n) ★★★	/ˈɪʃu/
key ring (n)	/ˈki ˌrɪŋ/
label (n) ★★	/ˈleɪb(ə)l/
landmark (n)	/ˈlændˌmɑrk/
lightning conductor (n)	/ˈlaɪtnɪŋ kənˌdʌktər/
loser (n) ★	/ˈluzər/
muscle (n) ★★★	/ˈmʌs(ə)l/
myth (n) ★★	/mɪθ/
nature (n) ★★★	/ˈneɪtʃər/
neither … nor (conj)	/ˌniðər … ˈnɔr, ˌnaɪðər … ˈnɔr/
network (n) ★★★	/ˈnetˌwɜrk/
nightmare (n) ★★	/ˈnaɪtˌmer/
obviously (adv) ★★★	/ˈɑbviəsli/
opportunity (n) ★★★	/ˌɑpərˈtunəti/
orbit (n) ★	/ˈɔrbɪt/
participant (n) ★★	/pɑrˈtɪsɪpənt/
particularly (adv) ★★★	/pərˈtɪkjələrli/
point (= position) (n) ★★★	/pɔɪnt/
positively (adv) ★★	/ˈpɑzətɪvli/
pressure (n) ★★★	/ˈpreʃər/
priority (n) ★★★	/praɪˈɔrəti/
proof (n) ★★	/pruf/
raindrop (n)	/ˈreɪnˌdrɑp/
reaction (n) ★★★	/riˈækʃ(ə)n/
reality (n) ★★★	/riˈæləti/
regularly (adv) ★★★	/ˈregjələrli/
research (n) ★★★	/rɪˈsɜrtʃ, ˈriˌsɜrtʃ/
sale (n) ★★★	/seɪl/
saying (n) ★★	/ˈseɪɪŋ/
simply (adv) ★★★	/ˈsɪmpli/
snooze button (n)	/ˈsnuz ˌbʌtn/
society (n) ★★★	/səˈsaɪəti/
source (n) ★★★	/sɔrs/
spectator (n) ★	/ˈspekˌteɪtər/
statistics (n pl)	/stəˈtɪstɪks/
strength (n) ★★★	/streŋθ/
stuff (n) ★★★	/stʌf/
supporter (n) ★★★	/səˈpɔrtər/
trial (n) ★★★	/ˈtraɪəl/
truth (n) ★★★	/truθ/
type (n) ★★★	/taɪp/
view (= opinion) (n) ★★★	/vju/
wealth (n) ★★	/welθ/
whether (conj) ★★★	/ˈweðər, ˈhweðər/
wrist (n) ★★	/rɪst/

ADJECTIVES

acidic (adj)	/əˈsɪdɪk/
bottled (adj)	/ˈbɑt(ə)ld/
calm (adj) ★★	/kɑm/
clever (adj) ★	/ˈklevər/
dangerous (adj) ★★★	/ˈdeɪndʒərəs/
delicious (adj) ★	/dɪˈlɪʃəs/
economic (adj) ★★★	/ˌikəˈnɑmɪk, ˌekəˈnɑmɪk/
estimated (adj)	/ˈestɪmeɪtəd/
fake (adj)	/feɪk/
female (adj) ★★★	/ˈfiˌmeɪl/
fine (= delicate) (adj) ★★★	/faɪn/
generous (adj) ★★	/ˈdʒen(ə)rəs/
harmless (adj) ★	/ˈhɑrmləs/
healthy (adj) ★★★	/ˈhelθi/
herbal (adj)	/ˈɜrb(ə)l/
independent (adj) ★★★	/ˌɪndɪˈpendənt/
latest (superl. adj) ★★★	/ˈleɪtəst/
material (adj) ★	/məˈtɪriəl/
materialistic (adj)	/məˌtɪriəˈlɪstɪk/
medium (adj) ★★	/ˈmidiəm/
positive (adj) ★★★	/ˈpɑzətɪv/
prepared (adj)	/prɪˈperd/
profitable (adj) ★★	/ˈprɑfɪtəb(ə)l/
pure (adj) ★★★	/pjʊr/
risky (adj) ★	/ˈrɪski/
scientific (adj) ★★★	/ˌsaɪənˈtɪfɪk/
selected (adj)	/sɪˈlektəd/
sensible (adj) ★	/ˈsensəb(ə)l/
sleepless (adj)	/ˈsliPləs/
so-called (adj) ★★	/ˈsoʊ ˌkɔld/
synthetic (adj)	/sɪnˈθetɪk/
thirsty (adj) ★	/ˈθɜrsti/
unhealthy (adj)	/ʌnˈhelθi/

FOOD AND DRINK

balanced diet (n)	/ˌbælənt ˈdaɪət/
canned food (n)	/ˌkænd ˈfud/
cookie (n) ★★	/ˈkʊki/
cream (n) ★	/krim/
dish (n) ★★	/dɪʃ/
dried fruit (n)	/ˌdraɪd ˈfrut/
fat (n) ★★	/fæt/
junk food (n)	/ˈdʒʌŋk ˌfud/
margarine (n)	/ˈmɑrdʒərɪn/
mineral (n) ★	/ˈmɪn(ə)rəl/
olive oil (n)	/ˈɑlɪv ˌɔɪl/
portion (n) ★★	/ˈpɔrʃ(ə)n/
protein (n) ★★	/ˈproʊtin/
tap water (n)	/ˈtæp ˌwɔtər/
toast (n) ★	/toʊst/
vitamin (n) ★★	/ˈvaɪtəmɪn/

FOOD PREPARATION

add (v) ★★★	/æd/
beat (v) ★★★	/bit/
boil (v) ★	/bɔɪl/
chop (v) ★★	/tʃɑp/
drain (v) ★★	/dreɪn/
fry (v) ★	/fraɪ/
grate (v)	/greɪt/
heat (v) ★★	/hit/
ingredient (n) ★★	/ɪnˈgridiənt/
mixture (n) ★★★	/ˈmɪkstʃər/
recipe (n) ★★	/ˈresəpi/
serve (v) ★★★	/sɜrv/
slice (v) ★	/slaɪs/
sprinkle (v) ★	/ˈsprɪŋk(ə)l/
stir (in) (v) ★★	/stɜr/

KITCHEN EQUIPMENT

bottle opener (n)	/ˈbɑtl ˌoʊp(ə)nər/
bowl (n) ★★	/boʊl/
bread knife (n)	/ˈbred ˌnaɪf/
can opener (n)	/ˈkæn ˌoʊp(ə)nər/
cheese grater (n)	/ˈtʃiz ˌgreɪtər/
coffee maker (n)	/ˈkɑfi ˌmeɪkər/
corkscrew (n)	/ˈkɔrkˌskru/
frying pan (n)	/ˈfraɪɪŋ ˌpæn/
sandwich toaster (n)	/ˈsæn(d)wɪʃ ˌtoʊstər/
saucepan (n) ★	/ˈsɔsˌpæn/
teakettle (n)	/ˈtiˌket(ə)l/
toaster (n)	/ˈtoʊstər/

MEDICINE

acupuncture (n)	/ˈækjuˌpʌŋktʃər/
alternative medicine (n)	/ɔlˌtɜrnətɪv ˈmedɪsɪn/
aspirin (n) ★	/ˈæsprɪn/
drug (n) ★★★	/drʌg/
general anesthetic (n)	/ˌdʒen(ə)rəl ænəsˈθetɪk/
herbalist (n)	/ˈɜrbəlɪst/
illness (n) ★★★	/ˈɪlnəs/
open-heart surgery (n)	/ˌoʊpən ˈhɑrt ˌsɜrdʒəri/
operation (n) ★★★	/ˌɑpəˈreɪʃ(ə)n/
pain (n) ★★★	/peɪn/
patient (n) ★★★	/ˈpeɪʃ(ə)nt/
pharmaceutical (adj)	/ˌfɑrməˈsutɪk(ə)l/
placebo effect (n)	/pləˈsiboʊ ɪˌfekt/
remedy (n) ★★	/ˈremədi/
surgeon (n) ★★	/ˈsɜrdʒən/
treatment (n) ★★★	/ˈtritmənt/

VERBS

achieve (v) ★★★	/əˈtʃiv/
break down (v)	/ˌbreɪk ˈdaʊn/
charge (a phone) (v) ★★★	/tʃɑrdʒ/
claim (n & v) ★★★	/kleɪm/
consist (v) ★★★	/kənˈsɪst/
count (as) (v) ★★★	/kaʊnt/
damage (v) ★★★	/ˈdæmɪdʒ/
discourage (v) ★	/dɪsˈkʌrɪdʒ/
digest (v) ★	/daɪˈdʒest/
emphasize (v) ★★	/ˈemfəˌsaɪz/
exaggerate (v) ★	/ɪgˈzædʒəˌreɪt/
generate (v) ★★★	/ˈdʒenəˌreɪt/
go off (alarm) (v)	/ˌgoʊ ˈɔf, ˌgoʊ ˈɑf/
indicate (v) ★★★	/ˈɪndɪˌkeɪt/

WORD LIST

influence (v) ★★★	/ˈɪnfluəns/
insert (v) ★★★	/ɪnˈsɜrt/
lack (v) ★★	/læk/
measure (v) ★★★	/ˈmeʒər/
overcome (v) ★★	/ˌoʊvərˈkʌm/
plug in (v)	/ˈplʌɡ ˌɪn/
power (v)	/ˈpaʊər/
question (v) ★★★	/ˈkwestʃ(ə)n/
quit (v) ★★	/kwɪt/
recognize (v) ★★★	/ˈrekəɡˌnaɪz/
recommend (v) ★★★	/ˌrekəˈmend/
risk (n & v) ★★★	/rɪsk/
store (v) ★★	/stɔr/
strike (v) ★★★	/straɪk/
struggle (v) ★★	/ˈstrʌɡ(ə)l/
suffer (from) (v) ★★★	/ˈsʌfər/
suppose (v) ★★★	/səˈpoʊz/
swallow (v) ★★	/ˈswɑloʊ/

EXPRESSIONS

at best	/ət ˈbest/
at least	/ət ˈlist/
at worst	/ət ˈwɜrst/
in reality	/ɪn riˈæləti/
in terms of	/ɪn ˈtɜrmz əv/
in tune with	/ɪn ˈtun wɪð/
make the most of	/ˌmeɪk ðə ˈmoʊst əv/
on the contrary	/ˌɑn ðə ˈkɑntreri/
on the other hand	/ˌɑn ði ˈʌðər hænd/
peace of mind	/ˌpis əv ˈmaɪnd/

UNIT 2

agency (n) ★★★	/ˈeɪdʒənsi/
cable car (n)	/ˈkeɪbl ˌkɑr/
chairlift (n)	/ˈtʃerˌlɪft/
chemistry (n) ★★	/ˈkemɪstri/
childhood (n) ★★	/ˈtʃaɪldˌhʊd/
countryside (n) ★	/ˈkʌntriˌsaɪd/
creation (n) ★★★	/kriˈeɪʃ(ə)n/
creature (n) ★★★	/ˈkritʃər/
cupboard (n)	/ˈkʌbərd/
directly (adv) ★★★	/dɪˈrek(t)li, daɪˈrek(t)li/
eruption (n)	/ɪˈrʌpʃ(ə)n/
ever since (adv)	/ˌevər ˈsɪns/
excuse (n) ★★	/ɪkˈskjus/
ferryman (n)	/ˈferimən/
fighter pilot (n)	/ˈfaɪtər ˌpaɪlət/
freedom (n) ★★★	/ˈfridəm/
gang (n) ★★	/ɡæŋ/
hardly (adv) ★★★	/ˈhɑrdli/
heritage (n) ★★	/ˈherɪtɪdʒ/
hut (n) ★★	/hʌt/
incredibly (adv) ★	/ɪnˈkredəbli/
inside (adv, n & prep) ★★★	/ɪnˈsaɪd/
item (n) ★★★	/ˈaɪtəm/
knowledge (n) ★★★	/ˈnɑlɪdʒ/
monster (n) ★★	/ˈmɑnstər/
offer (n) ★★★	/ˈɔfər, ˈɑfər/
pole (n) ★★	/poʊl/
print (n) ★★	/prɪnt/
sculpture (n) ★★	/ˈskʌlptʃər/
series (n) ★★★	/ˈsɪriz/
staircase (n) ★	/ˈsterˌkeɪs/
statue (n) ★★	/ˈstætʃu/
symbol (n) ★★	/ˈsɪmb(ə)l/
title (n) ★★★	/ˈtaɪt(ə)l/
townhouse (n)	/ˈtaʊnˌhaʊs/
tribute (n) ★★	/ˈtrɪbjut/

ADJECTIVES

artificial (adj) ★★	/ˌɑrtɪˈfɪʃ(ə)l/
award-winning (adj)	/əˈwɔrdˌwɪnɪŋ/
bestselling (adj)	/ˌbestˈselɪŋ/
domestic (adj) ★★★	/dəˈmestɪk/
everyday (adj) ★★	/ˈevriˌdeɪ/
horrified (adj)	/ˈhɔrɪˌfaɪd/
massive (adj) ★★★	/ˈmæsɪv/
odd (= strange) (adj) ★★★	/ɑd/
previous (adj) ★★★	/ˈpriviəs/
prize-winning (adj) ★	/ˈpraɪzˌwɪnɪŋ/
proud (of) (adj) ★★	/praʊd/
racist (adj)	/ˈreɪsɪst/
shiny (adj) ★	/ˈʃaɪni/
striking (adj) ★	/ˈstraɪkɪŋ/
temporary (adj) ★★★	/ˈtempəˌreri/
terrified (adj)	/ˈterəˌfaɪd/
unique (adj) ★★★	/juˈnik/
volcanic (adj)	/vɑlˈkænɪk/
well-dressed (adj)	/ˌwelˈdrest/
well-polished (adj)	/ˌwelˈpɑlɪʃt/
wise (adj) ★★	/waɪz/

FILM-MAKING

double (v) ★★	/ˈdʌb(ə)l/
extra (n) ★	/ˈekstrə/
feature film (n)	/ˈfitʃər ˌfɪlm/
on location	/ˌɑn loʊˈkeɪʃn/
on screen	/ˌɑn ˈskrin/
scene (n) ★★★	/sin/
set (n) ★★★	/set/
studio (n) ★★★	/ˈstudiˌoʊ/
take (n)	/teɪk/

MATERIALS

bronze (adj & n) ★	/brɑnz/
cardboard (adj & n)	/ˈkɑrdˌbɔrd/
concrete (adj & n) ★★	/ˈkɑnˌkrit/
dung (n)	/dʌŋ/
gold (adj & n) ★	/ɡoʊld/
iron (adj & n)	/ˈaɪrn/
plaster (adj & n) ★	/ˈplæstər/
plastic (adj & n) ★★★	/ˈplæstɪk/
rubber (adj & n) ★★	/ˈrʌbər/
sandstone (adj & n)	/ˈsæn(d)ˌstoʊn/
styrofoam (adj & n)	/ˈstaɪrəˌfoʊm/
wood (n) ★★★	/wʊd/

NOUN SUFFIXES -MENT

advertisement (n) ★★	/ˌædˈvɜrtɪsmənt, ˌædvərˈtaɪzmənt/
amazement (n)	/əˈmeɪzmənt/
argument (n) ★★★	/ˈɑrɡjəmənt/
arrangement (n) ★★★	/əˈreɪndʒmənt/
equipment (n) ★★★	/ɪˈkwɪpmənt/
movement (n) ★★★	/ˈmuvmənt/
payment (n) ★★★	/ˈpeɪmənt/
treatment (n) ★★★	/ˈtritmənt/

VERBS

abandon (v) ★★	/əˈbændən/
base (on) (v) ★★★	/beɪs/
cast (n & v) ★	/kæst/
charge (money) (v) ★★★	/tʃɑrdʒ/
construct (v) ★★★	/kənˈstrʌkt/
crash-land (v)	/ˌkræʃˈlænd/
create (v) ★★★	/kriˈeɪt/
define (v) ★★★	/dɪˈfaɪn/
display (v) ★★★	/dɪˈspleɪ/
entertain (v) ★★	/ˌentərˈteɪn/
grumble (v)	/ˈɡrʌmb(ə)l/
hang around (v)	/ˌhæŋ əˈraʊnd/
injure (v) ★★	/ˈɪndʒər/
inspire (v) ★★	/ɪnˈspaɪr/
interact (v) ★	/ˌɪntərˈækt/
investigate (v) ★★★	/ɪnˈvestɪˌɡeɪt/
murder (v) ★★	/ˈmɜrdər/
reappear (v)	/ˌriəˈpɪr/
represent (v) ★★★	/ˌrepriˈzent/
row (v) ★	/roʊ/
rush around (v)	/ˌrʌʃ əˈraʊnd/
step (v) ★★★	/step/
take over (v)	/ˌteɪk ˈoʊvər/
trap (v) ★★	/træp/
warn (v) ★★★	/wɔrn/

WRITING

author (n) ★★★	/ˈɔθər/
comic (n) ★	/ˈkɑmɪk/
folk tale (n)	/ˈfoʊk ˌteɪl/
horror story (n)	/ˈhɔrər ˌstɔri/
novel (n) ★★★	/ˈnɑv(ə)l/
play (n) ★★★	/pleɪ/
poet (n) ★★	/ˈpoʊət/
publish (v) ★★★	/ˈpʌblɪʃ/
science-fiction (n)	/ˌsaɪənsˈfɪkʃən/

EXPRESSIONS

catch sight of	/ˌkætʃ ˈsaɪt əv/
free of charge	/ˌfri əv ˈtʃɑrdʒ/
stand still	/ˌstænd ˈstɪl/

UNIT 3

achievement (n) ★★★	/əˈtʃivmənt/
against (prep) ★★★	/əˈɡenst/
aircraft (n) ★★	/ˈerˌkræft/
aluminum (n) ★	/əˈlumɪnəm/
among (prep) ★★★	/əˈmʌŋ/
attempt (n) ★★★	/əˈtempt/
base (n) ★★★	/beɪs/
being (n) ★★	/ˈbiɪŋ/
benefit (n) ★★★	/ˈbenəfɪt/
blog (n)	/blɑɡ/
bottom (n) ★★★	/ˈbɑtəm/
chain (of life) (n) ★★★	/tʃeɪn/
chemical (n) ★★★	/ˈkemɪk(ə)l/
chimney (n) ★	/ˈtʃɪmni/
component (n) ★★	/kəmˈpoʊnənt/
contact (n) ★★★	/ˈkɑnˌtækt/
crack (n) ★★	/kræk/
curve (n) ★★	/kɜrv/
development (n) ★★★	/dɪˈveləpmənt/
discovery (n) ★★★	/dɪˈskʌvəri/
electromagnet (n)	/ɪˌlektroʊˈmæɡnət/
elevator (n) ★	/ˈeləˌveɪtər/
fare (n) ★★	/fer/
flipper (n)	/ˈflɪpər/
grandchild (pl -children) (n)	/ˈɡræn(d)ˌtʃaɪld/
humpback whale (n)	/ˌhʌmpbæk ˈweɪl/
hydrophobic (n)	/ˌhaɪdrəˈfoʊbɪk/
impact (n) ★★★	/ˈɪmˌpækt/
jury (n) ★★	/ˈdʒʊri/
liquid (n) ★★	/ˈlɪkwɪd/
method (n) ★★★	/ˈmeθəd/
mining (n) ★	/ˈmaɪnɪŋ/
observer (n) ★★	/əbˈzɜrvər/
organism (n) ★★	/ˈɔrɡəˌnɪzəm/
origin (n) ★★★	/ˈɔrədʒɪn/
paintwork (n)	/ˈpeɪntˌwɜrk/
parliament (n) ★	/ˈpɑrləmənt/
performance (n) ★★★	/pərˈfɔrməns/
pesticide (n)	/ˈpestɪˌsaɪd/
protest (n) ★★★	/ˈproʊˌtest/
rainbow (n) ★	/ˈreɪnˌboʊ/
rumor (n) ★★	/ˈrumər/
sensor (n)	/ˈsensər/
similarity (n) ★★	/ˌsɪmɪˈlerəti/

WORD LIST

social science (n) /ˌsoʊʃl ˈsaɪəns/
software (n) ★★★ /ˈsɔf(t)ˌwer/
substance (n) ★★★ /ˈsʌbstəns/
surface (n) ★★★ /ˈsɜrfəs/
technique (n) ★★★ /tekˈnik/
theory (n) ★★★ /ˈθiəri/
trench (n) /trentʃ/
trillion (n) /ˈtrɪljən/
voyage (n) ★ /ˈvɔɪɪdʒ/
windshield (n) /ˈwɪn(d)ˌʃild/
wiper (n) /ˈwaɪpər/

ADJECTIVES

accessible (adj) /əkˈsesəb(ə)l/
annual (adj) ★★★ /ˈænjuəl/
astonishing (adj) ★ /əˈstɑnɪʃɪŋ/
controversial (adj) ★★ /ˌkɑntrəˈvɜrʃ(ə)l/
cultural (adj) ★★★ /ˈkʌltʃərəl/
destructive (adj) /dɪˈstrʌktɪv/
due (adj) ★★★ /du/
inaccurate (adj) /ɪnˈækjərət/
luxurious (adj) /lʌgˈʒʊriəs/
magnetic (adj) ★ /mægˈnetɪk/
manned (adj) /mænd/
molten (adj) /ˈmoʊlt(ə)n/
optical (adj) ★ /ˈɑptɪk(ə)l/
oral (adj) ★★ /ˈɔrəl/
pioneering (adj) /ˌpaɪəˈnɪrɪŋ/
sour (adj) ★ /saʊr/
spacious (adj) /ˈspeɪʃəs/
standard (adj) ★★★ /ˈstændərd/
steel (adj & n) ★★ /stil/
transatlantic (adj) /ˌtrænsətˈlæntɪk/
unexpected (adj) ★★ /ˌʌnɪkˈspektəd/
weak (adj) ★★★ /wik/

ADVERBS

accurately (adv) /ˈækjərətli/
approximately (adv) ★★ /əˈprɑksɪmətli/
consequently (adv) ★★ /ˈkɑnsəkwəntli/
far (adj & adv) ★★★ /fɑr/
farther (comp. adj & adv) ★ /ˈfɑrðər/
farthest (superl. adj & adv) /ˈfɑrðəst/
perfectly (= in a perfect way) ★★★ /ˈpɜrfɪk(t)li/
rapidly (adv) /ˈræpɪdli/
successfully (adv) /səkˈsesfəli/
therefore (adv) ★★★ /ˈðerfɔr/

COMMUNICATIONS

broadband (n) /ˈbrɔdˌbænd/
broadcasting (n) /ˈbrɔdˌkæstɪŋ/
communications satellite (n) /kəˌmjunɪkeɪʃnz ˈsæt(ə)laɪt/
radar (n) /ˈreɪdɑr/
radio wave (n) /ˈreɪdioʊ ˌweɪv/
signal (n & v) ★★★ /ˈsɪgnəl/
SOS (n) /ˌes oʊ ˈes/
transmission (n) ★★ /trænzˈmɪʃ(ə)n/
transmit (v) ★★ /trænzˈmɪt/
transmitter (n) /trænzˈmɪtər/

EARTH AND SPACE

alien (n) ★★ /ˈeɪliən/
Big Bang (n) /ˌbɪg ˈbæŋ/
Equator (n) /ɪˈkweɪtər/
gravity (n) ★ /ˈgrævəti/
light year (n) /ˈlaɪt ˌjɪr/
longitude (n) /ˈlɑndʒɪˌtud/
meridian (n) /məˈrɪdiən/
moonwalk (n) /ˈmunˌwɔk/
orbit (v) /ˈɔrbɪt/
oxygen (n) ★★ /ˈɑksɪdʒən/
preflight (adj) /ˈpriˌflaɪt/
spacecraft (n) /ˈspeɪsˌkræft/
spaceport (n) /ˈspeɪsˌpɔrt/
spacewalk (n) /ˈspeɪsˌwɔk/
universe (n) ★★ /ˈjunɪvərs/
weightlessness (n) /ˈweɪtləsnəs/

MEDICINE

bacteria (n pl) ★★ /bækˈtɪriə/
cataract (eye) (n) /ˈkætəˌrækt/
disease (n) ★★★ /dɪˈziz/
germ (n) /dʒɜrm/
infectious (adj) ★ /ɪnˈfekʃəs/
inject (v) ★ /ɪnˈdʒekt/
medical (adj) ★★★ /ˈmedɪk(ə)l/
pasteurization (n) /ˌpæstʃərɪˈzeɪʃ(ə)n/
pasteurized (adj) /ˈpæstʃəˌraɪzd/
vaccination (n) /ˌvæksɪˈneɪʃ(ə)n/

NOUN SUFFIXES -SION and -TION

action (n) ★★★ /ˈækʃ(ə)n/
application (= use) (n) ★★★ /ˌæplɪˈkeɪʃ(ə)n/
creation (n) ★★★ /kriˈeɪʃ(ə)n/
decision (n) ★★★ /dɪˈsɪʒ(ə)n/
discussion (n) ★★★ /dɪˈskʌʃ(ə)n/
evolution (n) ★★ /ˌevəˈluʃ(ə)n/
pasteurization (n) /ˌpæstʃərɪˈzeɪʃ(ə)n/
permission (n) ★★ /pərˈmɪʃ(ə)n/
pollution (n) ★★★ /pəˈluʃ(ə)n/
possession (n) ★★ /pəˈzeʃ(ə)n/
production (n) ★★★ /prəˈdʌkʃən/
revision (n) ★★ /rɪˈvɪʒ(ə)n/
solution (n) ★★★ /səˈluʃ(ə)n/
transmission (n) ★★ /trænzˈmɪʃ(ə)n/
vaccination (n) /ˌvæksɪˈneɪʃ(ə)n/

OCCUPATIONS

biologist (n) ★ /baɪˈɑlədʒɪst/
chemist (n) ★ /ˈkemɪst/
engineer (n) ★★★ /ˌendʒɪˈnɪr/
physicist (n) /ˈfɪzɪsɪst/

THE OCEAN

crab (n) /kræb/
depth (n) ★★★ /depθ/
hydrothermal vent (n) /ˌhaɪdrəˌθɜrml ˈvent/
mussel (n) /ˈmʌs(ə)l/
navy (n) ★★ /ˈneɪvi/
ocean floor (n) /ˈoʊʃn ˌflɔr/
salty (adj) /ˈsɔlti/
shrimp (n) /ʃrɪmp/
submersible (n) /səbˈmɜrsəb(ə)l/
underwater (adj) /ˌʌndərˈwɔtər/

VERBS

coat (v) /koʊt/
compare (v) ★★★ /kəmˈper/
contaminate (v) /kənˈtæmɪˌneɪt/
control (v) ★★★ /kənˈtroʊl/
cool (v) ★★ /kul/
depart (v) ★★ /dɪˈpɑrt/
descend (v) /dɪˈsend/
detect (v) ★★ /dɪˈtekt/
disturb (v) ★★ /dɪˈstɜrb/
evaporate (v) /ɪˈvæpəˌreɪt/
evolve (v) ★★ /ɪˈvɑlv/
expand (v) ★★★ /ɪkˈspænd/
focus (v) ★★★ /ˈfoʊkəs/
involve (v) ★★★ /ɪnˈvɑlv/
issue (v) ★★★ /ˈɪʃu/
lead (v) ★★★ /lid/
peer (v) ★★ /pɪr/
prevent (v) ★★★ /prɪˈvent/
rotate (v) ★ /ˈroʊˌteɪt/
submit (v) ★★★ /səbˈmɪt/
transport (v) ★★ /trænsˈpɔrt/

PHRASAL VERBS

come down (v) /ˌkʌm ˈdaʊn/
count down (v) /ˌkaʊnt ˈdaʊn/
hold on (v) /ˌhoʊld ˈɑn/
look down (v) /ˌlʊk ˈdaʊn/
put down (v) /ˌpʊt ˈdaʊn/
take off (flight) (v) /ˌteɪk ˈɔf, ˌteɪk ˈɑf/

EXPRESSIONS

as a result /ˌæz ə rɪˈzʌlt/
Greetings. /ˈgritɪŋz/
set a record /ˌset ə ˈrekərd/
take action /ˌteɪk ˈækʃən/
thanks to … /ˈθæŋks ˌtu/

UNIT 4

advance (n) ★★ /ədˈvæns/
as soon as (conj) /əz ˈsun əz/
big business (n) /ˌbɪg ˈbɪznəs/
cause (n) ★★★ /kɔz/
cruelty (n) ★ /ˈkruəlti/
decrease (n) ★ /ˈdikris/
desert (n) ★★ /ˈdezərt/
executive (n) ★★ /ɪgˈzekjətɪv/
export (n) ★★★ /ˈekˌspɔrt/
fertilizer (n) /ˈfɜrt(ə)lˌaɪzər/
function (n) ★★★ /ˈfʌŋkʃ(ə)n/
gene (n) ★★ /dʒin/
guesthouse (n) /ˈgestˌhaʊs/
hippy (n) /ˈhɪpi/
hoax (n) /hoʊks/
household (n) ★★★ /ˈhaʊsˌhoʊld/
human race (n) /ˌhjumən ˈreɪs/
import (n) ★★ /ˈɪmˌpɔrt/
increase (n) ★★★ /ˈɪnˌkris/
indication (n) ★★ /ˌɪndɪˈkeɪʃ(ə)n/
largely (adv) ★★★ /ˈlɑrdʒli/
life expectancy (n) /ˌlaɪf ɪkˈspektənsi/
microchip (n) /ˈmaɪkroʊˌtʃɪp/
no longer (adv) /ˌnoʊ ˈlɔŋər/
nuclear energy (n) /ˌnukliər ˈenərdʒi/
organization (n) ★★★ /ˌɔrgənɪˈzeɪʃ(ə)n/
overland (adv) /ˈoʊvərˌlænd/
pace (of life) (n) ★★ /peɪs/
paradise (n) ★ /ˈperəˌdaɪs/
partly (adv) ★★★ /ˈpɑrtli/
perfectly (= completely) (adv) ★★★ /ˈpɜrfɪk(t)li/
permit (n) ★ /ˈpɜrmɪt/
point (the whole point) (n) ★★★ /pɔɪnt/
produce (n) ★ /ˈproʊˌdus/
publicity (n) ★★ /pʌbˈlɪsəti/
pulse rate (n) /ˈpʌlsˌreɪt/
researcher (n) /rɪˈsɜrtʃər, ˈriˌsɜrtʃər/
retirement (n) ★ /rɪˈtaɪrmənt/
suspect (n) ★★ /ˈsʌˌspekt/
technology (n) ★★★ /tekˈnɑlədʒi/
threat (n) ★★★ /θret/
unless (conj) ★★★ /ənˈles/
vaccine (n) /ˈvæksin, vækˈsin/
violence (n) ★★★ /ˈvaɪələns/
whale hunting (n) /ˈweɪl ˌhʌntɪŋ/
whaling ship (n) /ˈweɪlɪŋ ˌʃɪp/
whenever (conj) ★★ /wenˈevər, hwenˈevər/

123

WORD LIST

ADJECTIVES
aware (of) (adj) ★★★	/əˈwer/
crazy (adj) ★★	/ˈkreɪzi/
crucial (adj) ★★★	/ˈkruʃ(ə)l/
hand-carved (adj)	/ˈhændˌkɑrvd/
keyless (adj)	/ˈkiləs/
magical (adj) ★	/ˈmædʒɪk(ə)l/
moral (adj) ★★★	/ˈmɔrəl/
obtainable (adj)	/əbˈteɪnəb(ə)l/
sick (adj) ★★★	/sɪk/
slight (adj) ★★★	/slaɪt/
wireless (adj) ★	/ˈwaɪrləs/

CLIMATE CHANGE
atmosphere (n) ★★	/ˈætməˌsfɪr/
carbon dioxide (CO_2) (n) ★	/ˌkɑrbən daɪˈɑkˌsaɪd/
carbon emission (n)	/ˌkɑrbən ɪˈmɪʃn/
carbon-offset project (n)	/ˌkɑrbən ˈɔfset prɑdʒekt/
drought (n)	/draʊt/
energy crisis (n)	/ˈenərdʒi ˌkraɪsɪs/
flood (n) ★★	/flʌd/
global warming (n) ★	/ˌgloʊbl ˈwɔrmɪŋ/
greenhouse gas (n)	/ˈgrinhaʊs ˌgæs/
polar ice cap (n)	/ˌpoʊlər ˈaɪs kæp/
pollution (n) ★★★	/pəˈluʃ(ə)n/

DEBATE
argument (n) ★★★	/ˈɑrgjəmənt/
chair (n & v) ★★★	/tʃer/
debate (n) ★★★	/dɪˈbeɪt/
first (adv) ★★★	/fɜrst/
for and against	/ˌfɔr ən əˈgenst/
in favor (of)	/ˌɪn ˈfeɪvər (əv)/
motion (n) ★★★	/ˈmoʊʃ(ə)n/
propose (v) ★★	/prəˈpoʊz/
pros and cons (n pl)	/ˌproʊz ən ˈkɑnz/
opponent (n) ★★	/əˈpoʊnənt/
oppose (v) ★★★	/əˈpoʊz/
second (adv)	/ˈsekənd/
sum up (v)	/ˌsʌm ˈʌp/
third (adv)	/θɜrd/
vote (n & v) ★★★	/voʊt/

PREFIXES ANTI- and NON-
anti-globalization (adj)	/ˌæntiˌgloʊbəlɪˈzeɪʃn/
anti-GM (genetically modified) food (n)	/ˌæntiˌdʒiem ˈfud/
anti-spam (adj)	/ˌæntiˈspæm/
anti-terrorism (adj)	/ˌæntiˈterərɪzəm/
anti-war (adj)	/ˌæntiˈwɔr/
nonfiction (adj & n)	/nɑnˈfɪkʃ(ə)n/
non-iron (adj)	/ˌnɑnˈaɪrn/
nonviolence (n)	/nɑnˈvaɪ(ə)ləns/
nonviolent (adj)	/nɑnˈvaɪ(ə)lənt/

POLITICS
democracy (n) ★★★	/dɪˈmɑkrəsi/
demonstration (n) ★★	/ˌdemənˈstreɪʃ(ə)n/
direct action (n)	/ˌdɪrekt ˈækʃən, ˌdaɪrekt ˈækʃən/
elect (v) ★★★	/ɪˈlekt/
election (n) ★★★	/ɪˈlekʃ(ə)n/
hunger strike (n)	/ˈhʌŋgər ˌstraɪk/
march (n) ★★	/mɑrtʃ/
political (adj) ★★★	/pəˈlɪtɪk(ə)l/
politician (n) ★★★	/ˌpɑləˈtɪʃ(ə)n/
protest (v) ★★	/prəˈtest, ˈproʊˌtest/
protestor (n)	/prəˈtestər/
racial segregation (n)	/ˌreɪʃl segrəˈgeɪʃn/
representative (n) ★★★	/ˌreprɪˈzentətɪv/
sit-in (n)	/ˈsɪtˌɪn/

VERBS
balance (n & v) ★★★	/ˈbæləns/
clash (v) ★	/klæʃ/
decrease (v) ★★	/dɪˈkris/
desert (v) ★	/dɪˈzɜrt/
estimate (v) ★★★	/ˈestɪˌmeɪt/
export (v) ★★	/ɪkˈspɔrt/
free (v) ★★	/fri/
fund (v) ★★★	/fʌnd/
glow (v) ★	/gloʊ/
halt (v) ★	/hɔlt/
hijack (v)	/ˈhaɪˌdʒæk/
import (v) ★★	/ɪmˈpɔrt/
increase (v) ★★★	/ɪnˈkris/
offset (v)	/ˌɔfˈset, ˈɔfˌset/
permit (v) ★★★	/pərˈmɪt/
plant (v) ★★	/plænt/
produce (v) ★★★	/prəˈdus/
retire (v) ★★	/rɪˈtaɪr/
suspect (v) ★★★	/səˈspekt/

PHRASAL VERBS WITH OUT
carry out (v)	/ˌkæri ˈaʊt/
figure out (v)	/ˌfɪgjər ˈaʊt/
miss out on (v)	/ˌmɪs ˈaʊt ɑn/
point out (v)	/ˌpɔɪnt ˈaʊt/
wipe out (v)	/ˌwaɪp ˈaʊt/

EXPRESSIONS
feel strongly (about)	/ˌfil ˈstrɔŋli/
for instance	/ˌfər ˈɪnstəns/
go trekking	/ˌgoʊ ˈtrekɪŋ/
in addition	/ˌɪn əˈdɪʃn/
in harmony	/ˌɪn ˈhɑrməni/
in theory	/ˌɪn ˈθɪəri/
make a case	/ˌmeɪk ə ˈkeɪs/
make sense	/ˌmeɪk ˈsens/
take a decision	/ˌteɪk ə dɪˈsɪʒ(ə)n/
take notice	/ˌteɪk ˈnoʊtɪs/
What's more …	/ˌwʌts ˈmɔr/

UNIT 5
anti-venom serum (n)	/ˌænti'venəm ˌsɪrəm/
binoculars (n pl) ★	/bɪˈnɑkjələrz/
buck (= dollar slang) (n) ★★	/bʌk/
cannonball (n)	/ˈkænənˌbɔl/
character (= personality) (n) ★★★	/ˈkerəktər/
cover (n) ★★★	/ˈkʌvər/
degree (college) (n) ★★★	/dɪˈgri/
disaster (n) ★★	/dɪˈzæstər/
drill (n) ★	/drɪl/
driver's license (n)	/ˈdraɪvərz ˌlaɪsəns/
fang (n)	/fæŋ/
farmhouse (n) ★	/ˈfɑrmˌhaʊs/
file (n) ★★★	/faɪl/
firmly (adv)	/ˈfɜrmli/
guidelines (n pl) ★★	/ˈgaɪdˌlaɪnz/
hairstyle (n) ★	/ˈherˌstaɪl/
hero (n) ★★	/ˈhɪroʊ/
iceberg (n)	/ˈaɪsˌbɜrg/
jar (n) ★	/dʒɑr/
junior (n) ★	/ˈdʒuniər/
lately (adv) ★	/ˈleɪtli/
lottery (n) ★	/ˈlɑtəri/
male (n) ★★★	/meɪl/
measurement (n) ★★	/ˈmeʒərmənt/
mission (n) ★★	/ˈmɪʃ(ə)n/
neither (pron) ★★★	/ˈniðər, ˈnaɪðər/
pattern (n) ★★★	/ˈpætərn/
physically (adv) ★★	/ˈfɪzɪkli/
pioneer (n) ★	/ˌpaɪəˈnɪr/
possibly (adv) ★★★	/ˈpɑsəbli/
procedure (n) ★★★	/prəˈsidʒər/
qualification (n) ★	/ˌkwɑləfɪˈkeɪʃ(ə)n/
qualify (n) ★★★	/ˈkwɑləˌfaɪ/
reference (n) ★★★	/ˈref(ə)rəns/
search operation (n)	/ˌsɜrtʃ ɑpəˈreɪʃn/
separation (n) ★★	/ˌsepəˈreɪʃ(ə)n/
sink (n) ★★	/sɪŋk/
snowstorm (n)	/ˈsnoʊˌstɔrm/
speculation (n) ★★	/ˌspekjəˈleɪʃ(ə)n/
spy (n) ★	/spaɪ/
surprisingly (adv) ★★	/sərˈpraɪzɪŋli/
survivor (n) ★	/sərˈvaɪvər/
tank (n) ★★★	/tæŋk/
tightly (adv)	/ˈtaɪtli/
trace (n) ★★	/treɪs/
venom (n)	/ˈvenəm/
wasteland (n)	/ˈweɪs(t)ˌlænd/
wax (n)	/wæks/
whereas (conj) ★★★	/werˈæz, hwerˈæz/
while (= whereas) (conj) ★★★	/waɪl, hwaɪl/

ADJECTIVES
daring (adj)	/ˈderɪŋ/
elaborate (adj) ★★	/ɪˈlæb(ə)rət/
fit (adj) ★★	/fɪt/
lime green (adj)	/ˌlaɪm ˈgrin/
pale (adj) ★★★	/peɪl/
record-breaking (adj)	/ˈrekərd ˌbreɪkɪŋ/
short (of) (adj) ★★★	/ʃɔrt/
short-haired (adj)	/ʃɔrtˈherd/
stand-by (adj)	/ˈstændˌbaɪ/
strict (adj) ★★	/strɪkt/
undamaged (adj)	/ʌnˈdæmɪdʒd/
unsinkable (adj)	/ʌnˈsɪŋkəbl/
weird (adj) ★	/wɪrd/
well-fed (adj)	/ˌwel ˈfed/
willing (adj) ★★★	/ˈwɪlɪŋ/

ADJECTIVE SUFFIX -OUS
courageous (adj)	/kəˈreɪdʒəs/
dangerous (adj) ★★★	/ˈdeɪndʒərəs/
infectious (adj) ★	/ɪnˈfekʃəs/
luxurious (adj)	/lʌgˈʒʊriəs/
nervous (adj) ★★	/ˈnɜrvəs/
poisonous (adj) ★	/ˈpɔɪz(ə)nəs/
spacious (adj)	/ˈspeɪʃəs/
superstitious (adj)	/ˌsupərˈstɪʃəs/

BANK
bank clerk (n)	/ˈbæŋk ˌklɜrk/
change (money) (v) ★★★	/tʃeɪndʒ/
exchange (n) ★★★	/ɪksˈtʃeɪndʒ/
receipt (n) ★★	/rɪˈsit/
tens (n pl)	/tenz/
twenties (n pl)	/ˈtwentiz/

FLIGHT
air traffic control (n)	/ˌer træfɪk kənˈtroʊl/
crossing (n) ★	/ˈkrɔsɪŋ/
emergency landing (n)	/ɪˌmɜrdʒənsi ˈlændɪŋ/
flight attendant (n)	/ˈflaɪt əˌtendənt/
fuel (n) ★★★	/ˈfjuəl/
mid-air (n)	/ˌmɪdˈer/
navigator (n)	/ˈnævɪˌgeɪtər/
solo (adj & adv)	/ˈsoʊloʊ/

OCEAN VOYAGES
crew (n) ★★★	/kru/
deck (n) ★★	/dek/
launch (v) ★★★	/lɔntʃ/

WORD LIST

lifeboat (n)	/ˈlaɪfˌboʊt/
lookout (n)	/ˈlʊkˌaʊt/
set sail (v)	/ˌset ˈseɪl/
ship (n) ★★★	/ʃɪp/
voyage (n) ★	/ˈvɔɪɪdʒ/
yacht (n) ★	/jɑt/

SHOPPING

fit (v) ★★★	/fɪt/
match (v) ★★★	/mætʃ/
try on (clothes) (v)	/ˌtraɪ ˈɑn/
tight (adj) ★★	/taɪt/

SPORTS

center forward (n)	/ˌsentər ˈfɔrwərd/
club (sports club) (n) ★★★	/klʌb/
division (second division) (n) ★★★	/dɪˈvɪʒ(ə)n/
goal (n) ★★★	/goʊl/
international (adj & n) ★★★	/ˌɪntərˈnæʃən(ə)l/
professional (adj & n) ★★★	/prəˈfeʃən(ə)l/
quarter-finals (n pl)	/ˌkwɔrtər ˈfaɪnəlz/
round (first round) (n) ★★★	/raʊnd/
score (n & v) ★★★	/skɔr/

TRAIN STATION

change (trains) (v) ★★★	/tʃeɪndʒ/
one-way (ticket) (n)	/ˈwʌnˌweɪ/
platform (n) ★★	/ˈplætˌfɔrm/
round-trip (ticket) (n)	/ˌraʊndˈtrɪp/
ticket agent (n)	/ˈtɪkɪt ˌeɪdʒənt/

YOUTH HOSTEL/HOTEL

double (room) (adj) ★★★	/ˈdʌb(ə)l/
form (fill out a form) (n) ★★★	/fɔrm/
front desk clerk (n)	/ˌfrʌnt ˈdesk klɜrk/
reservation (n) ★★	/ˌrezərˈveɪʃ(ə)n/
single (room) (adj) ★★★	/ˈsɪŋ(ɡ)əl/

VERBS

abduct (v)	/æbˈdʌkt/
announce (v) ★★★	/əˈnaʊns/
arrest (v) ★★	/əˈrest/
attempt (n & v) ★★★	/əˈtempt/
bite (v) ★★	/baɪt/
collect (v) ★★★	/kəˈlekt/
confess (v) ★★	/kənˈfes/
freeze (v) ★★	/friz/
grin (v) ★★	/ɡrɪn/
milk (v)	/mɪlk/
raise (v) ★★★	/reɪz/
supervise (v) ★★	/ˈsupərˌvaɪz/
trick (v) ★	/trɪk/

PHRASAL VERBS

blow up (v)	/ˌbloʊ ˈʌp/
brush up (v)	/ˌbrʌʃ ˈʌp/
fill out (v)	/ˌfɪl ˈaʊt/
knock off (v)	/ˌnɑk ˈɔf, ˌnɑk ˈɑf/
knock out (v)	/ˌnɑk ˈaʊt/
look on (v)	/ˌlʊk ˈɑn/
run out (of) (v)	/ˌrʌn ˈaʊt (əv)/
take up (= start) (v)	/ˌteɪk ˈʌp/
shoot down (v)	/ˌʃut ˈdaʊn/
use up (v)	/ˌjuz ˈʌp/

EXPRESSIONS

beat a record	/ˌbit ə ˈrekərd/
change course	/ˌtʃeɪndʒ ˈkɔrs/
get to know	/ˌɡet tə ˈnoʊ/

Not at all.	/ˌnɑt ət ˈɔl/
Would you mind …?	/ˌwʊd ju ˈmaɪnd/

UNIT 6

aisle (n)	/aɪl/
facilities (n pl)	/fəˈsɪlətiz/
groceries (n pl)	/ˈɡroʊs(ə)riz/
homeland (n)	/ˈhoʊmˌlænd/
mainly (adv) ★★★	/ˈmeɪnli/
originally (adv) ★★★	/əˈrɪdʒən(ə)li/
relative (n) ★★	/ˈrelətɪv/
sarong (n)	/səˈrɑŋ/
sheet (n) ★★★	/ʃit/
side road (n)	/ˈsaɪd ˌroʊd/
slightly (adv) ★★★	/ˈslaɪtli/
snorkeling (n)	/ˈsnɔrklɪŋ/
sweetly (adv)	/ˈswitli/
towel (n) ★★	/ˈtaʊəl/
uncomfortably (adv)	/ʌnˈkʌmfərtəbli/

ADJECTIVES

damp (adj) ★★	/dæmp/
obvious (adj) ★★★	/ˈɑbviəs/
packed (adj) ★	/pækt/
spicy (adj)	/ˈspaɪsi/

ADJECTIVE PREFIX *WELL-*

well-balanced (adj)	/ˌwelˈbælənst/
well-behaved (adj)	/ˌwel bɪˈheɪvd/
well-done (adj)	/ˌwelˈdʌn/
well-dressed (adj)	/ˌwelˈdrest/
well-known (adj) ★★	/ˌwelˈnoʊn/
well-off (adj)	/ˌwelˈɔf, ˌwelˈɑf/
well-paid (adj)	/ˌwelˈpeɪd/

BUILDINGS

exhibition pavilion	/eksɪˈbɪʃn pəˌvɪljən/
hotel ★★★	/hoʊˈtel/
igloo	/ˈɪɡlu/
museum ★★★	/mjuˈziəm/
skyscraper	/ˈskaɪˌskreɪpər/

RESTAURANT

cake (n) ★★★	/keɪk/
cash register (n)	/ˈkæʃ ˌredʒɪstər/
cutlery (Br Eng) (n)	/ˈkʌtləri/
dressing (n) ★	/ˈdresɪŋ/
gravy (n)	/ˈɡreɪvi/
ice water (n)	/ˈaɪs ˌwɔtər/
ketchup (n)	/ˈketʃəp/
menu (n) ★★	/ˈmenju/
napkin (n)	/ˈnæpkɪn/
roll (n) ★★	/roʊl/
special (n)	/ˈspeʃ(ə)l/
tablecloth (n)	/ˈteɪb(ə)lˌklɑθ/
tray (n) ★★	/treɪ/
waitress (n) ★	/ˈweɪtrəs/

VERBS

advise (v) ★★★	/ədˈvaɪz/
date (*relationship*) (v) ★★★	/deɪt/
hesitate (v) ★★	/ˈhezɪˌteɪt/
laze around (v)	/ˌleɪz əˈraʊnd/
rediscover (v)	/ˌridɪˈskʌvər/
remark (v) ★★	/rɪˈmɑrk/
rent (v) ★	/rent/
save up (v)	/ˌseɪv ˈʌp/
sunbathe (v)	/ˈsʌnˌbeɪð/
talk over (v)	/ˌtɔk ˈoʊvər/
turn out (*discovery*) (v)	/ˌtɜrn ˈaʊt/
walk around (v)	/ˌwɔk əˈraʊnd/

wipe (v) ★★	/waɪp/
wrap (v) ★★	/ræp/

EXPRESSIONS

change one's mind	/ˌtʃeɪndʒ wʌnz ˈmaɪnd/
out of the question	/ˌaʊt əv ðə ˈkwestʃən/
take a pill	/ˌteɪk ə ˈpɪl/
You're welcome.	/ˌjʊr ˈwelkəm/

UNIT 7

allowance (*money*) (n) ★★	/əˈlaʊəns/
ankle (n) ★★	/ˈæŋk(ə)l/
appearance (n) ★★★	/əˈpɪrəns/
atom (n) ★★	/ˈætəm/
cancer (n) ★★★	/ˈkænsər/
colleague (n) ★★★	/ˈkɑliɡ/
combination (n) ★★★	/ˌkɑmbɪˈneɪʃ(ə)n/
comet (n)	/ˈkɑmət/
constantly (adv) ★★	/ˈkɑnstəntli/
creativity (n) ★	/ˌkrieɪˈtɪvəti/
criticism (n) ★★★	/ˈkrɪtɪˌsɪzəm/
decade (n) ★★★	/ˈdekeɪd/
dialogue (n) ★★	/ˈdaɪəˌlɔɡ/
DNA (n) ★	/ˌdi en ˈeɪ/
emphasis (n) ★★★	/ˈemfəsɪs/
evaluation (n)	/ɪˌvæljuˈeɪʃn/
explosion (n) ★★	/ɪkˈsploʊʒ(ə)n/
extinction (n) ★	/ɪkˈstɪŋkʃ(ə)n/
failure (n) ★★★	/ˈfeɪljər/
growth (n) ★★★	/ɡroʊθ/
increasingly (adv) ★★★	/ɪnˈkrisɪŋli/
initially (adv) ★★★	/ɪˈnɪʃ(ə)li/
ironically (adv)	/aɪˈrɑnɪkli/
jet (n) ★★	/dʒet/
killer (n) ★★	/ˈkɪlər/
match (= game) (n) ★★★	/mætʃ/
means (= way) (n pl) ★★★	/minz/
message board (n)	/ˈmesɪdʒ ˌbɔrd/
minority (n) ★★★	/maɪˈnɔrəti/
murder (n) ★★★	/ˈmɜrdər/
neighbor (n) ★★★	/ˈneɪbər/
nuclear fission (n)	/ˌnukliər ˈfɪʃn/
option (n) ★★★	/ˈɑpʃ(ə)n/
ownership (n) ★★	/ˈoʊnərˌʃɪp/
personally (adv) ★★	/ˈpɜrsənəli/
policy (n) ★★★	/ˈpɑləsi/
prejudice (n) ★★	/ˈpredʒədɪs/
pulsar (n)	/ˈpʌlsɑr/
recognition (n) ★★★	/ˌrekəɡˈnɪʃ(ə)n/
revolution (n) ★★★	/ˌrevəˈluʃ(ə)n/
shelf (pl shelves) (n) ★★	/ʃelf/
shuttlecock (n)	/ˈʃʌt(ə)lˌkɑk/
status (n) ★★★	/ˈsteɪtəs, ˈstætəs/
subscription (n) ★	/səbˈskrɪpʃ(ə)n/
tool (n) ★★★	/tul/
tower (n) ★★	/ˈtaʊr/
unusually (adv) ★	/ʌnˈjuʒuəli/
user (n) ★★★	/ˈjuzər/
worth (n)	/wɜrθ/

ADJECTIVES

accustomed (adj)	/əˈkʌstəmd/
brilliant (= very intelligent) (adj) ★★★	/ˈbrɪljənt/
creative (adj) ★	/kriˈeɪtɪv/
defensive (adj) ★★	/dɪˈfensɪv/
distinctive (adj) ★★	/dɪˈstɪŋktɪv/
jumbo (-sized) (adj)	/ˈdʒʌmboʊ/
messy (adj) ★	/ˈmesi/
nautical (adj)	/ˈnɔtɪk(ə)l/
neat (adj) ★★	/nit/
social (adj) ★★★	/ˈsoʊʃ(ə)l/

125

WORD LIST

softly lit (adj) /ˌsɑf(t)li ˈlɪt/
stuck (adj) /stʌk/
stylish (adj) ★ /ˈstaɪlɪʃ/
unpleasant (adj) ★★ /ʌnˈplez(ə)nt/
well lit (adj) /ˌwel ˈlɪt/

LANGUAGE
dialect (n) ★ /ˈdaɪəˌlekt/
fluent (adj) ★ /ˈfluənt/
idiom (n) ★ /ˈɪdiəm/
idiomatic (adj) /ˌɪdiəˈmætɪk/
linguist (n) ★ /ˈlɪŋgwɪst/
slang (n) /slæŋ/
term (= word/phrase) (n) ★★★ /tɜrm/

OCCUPATIONS
astronomer (n) /əˈstrɑnəmər/
bus conductor (n) /ˈbʌs kənˌdʌktər/
employer (n) ★★★ /ɪmˈplɔɪər/
entrepreneur (n) /ˌɑntrəprəˈnʊr/
sociologist (n) /ˌsoʊsiəˈlɑdʒɪst, ˌsoʊʃiˈɑlədʒɪst/
street vendor (n) /ˈstrit ˌvendər/

TELEPHONE
engaged (n) ★★ /ɪnˈgeɪdʒd/
landline (n) /ˈlændˌlaɪn/
line (n) ★★★ /laɪn/
subscriber (n) /səbˈskraɪbər/
telecommunications (n pl) ★ /ˌtelɪkəˌmjunɪˈkeɪʃ(ə)nz/

VERBS
acknowledge (v) ★★★ /əkˈnɑlɪdʒ/
award (v) ★★★ /əˈwɔrd/
benefit (v) ★★★ /ˈbenəfɪt/
block (v) ★★ /blɑk/
brainstorm (v) /ˈbreɪnˌstɔrm/
crack (v) ★★ /kræk/
deserve (v) ★★ /dɪˈzɜrv/
fire (from a job) (v) ★★★ /faɪr/
forbid (v) ★★ /fərˈbɪd/
hang (v) ★★★ /hæŋ/
honor (v) ★★ /ˈɑnər/
install (v) ★★ /ɪnˈstɔl/
persuade (v) ★★★ /pərˈsweɪd/
post (on message board) (v) ★ /poʊst/
reflect (v) ★★★ /rɪˈflekt/
repair (v) ★★ /rɪˈper/
transfer (v) ★★★ /trænsˈfɜr, ˈtrænsfər/
transform (v) ★★ /trænsˈfɔrm/
twist (v) ★★ /twɪst/
value (v) ★★ /ˈvælju/

VERB PREFIX RE-
reappear (v) /ˌriəˈpɪr/
rearrange (v) /ˌriəˈreɪndʒ/
rebuild (v) ★★ /ˌriˈbɪld/
recreate (v) /ˌrikriˈeɪt/
rediscover (v) /ˌridɪˈskʌvər/
repaint (v) /ˌriˈpeɪnt/
replace (v) ★★★ /rɪˈpleɪs/
replay (v) /ˌriˈpleɪ/
retell (v) /ˌriˈtel/
rewrite (v) ★ /ˌriˈraɪt/

PHRASAL VERBS
call back (v) /ˌkɔl ˈbæk/
call up (v) /ˌkɔl ˈʌp/
cut off (v) /ˌkʌt ˈɔf, ˌkʌt ˈɑf/
die out (v) /ˌdaɪ ˈaʊt/
find out (v) /ˌfaɪnd ˈaʊt/
go on (= continue) (v) /ˌgoʊ ˈɑn, ˌgoʊ ˈɔn/
go up (= rise) (v) /ˌgoʊ ˈʌp/
hold on (v) /ˌhoʊld ˈɑn, ˌhoʊld ˈɔn/
jot down (v) /ˌdʒɑt ˈdaʊn/
kick off (v) /ˌkɪk ˈɔf, ˌkɪk ˈɑf/
note down (v) /ˌnoʊt ˈdaʊn/
pass on (v) /ˌpæs ˈɑn, ˌpæs ˈɔn/
pick up (v) /ˌpɪk ˈʌp/
put through (v) /ˌpʊt ˈθru/
put up (= build) (v) /ˌpʊt ˈʌp/
put up (on the wall) (v) /ˌpʊt ˈʌp/
speed up (v) /ˌspid ˈʌp/

EXPRESSIONS
be fired /ˌbi ˈfaɪrd/
do well /ˌdu ˈwel/
half a dozen /ˌhæf ə ˈdʌzn/
Keep it up. /ˌkip ɪt ˈʌp/
know the ropes /ˌnoʊ ðə ˈroʊps/
make a deal /ˌmeɪk ə ˈdil/
mix and match /ˌmɪks ən ˈmætʃ/
take care /ˌteɪk ˈker/
take notes /ˌteɪk ˈnoʊts/
under the weather /ˌʌndər ðə ˈweðər/

UNIT 8

aftershave (n) /ˈæftərˌʃeɪv/
airfare (n) /ˈerˌfer/
alarm (n) ★★ /əˈlɑrm/
applicant (n) ★ /ˈæplɪkənt/
application (for a job) (n) ★★★ /ˌæplɪˈkeɪʃ(ə)n/
comfort (n) ★★ /ˈkʌmfərt/
confession (n) ★ /kənˈfeʃ(ə)n/
conservation (n) ★★★ /ˌkɑnsərˈveɪʃ(ə)n/
couple (of) (n) ★★★ /ˈkʌp(ə)l/
crumble (n) /ˈkrʌmb(ə)l/
equation (n) ★★ /ɪˈkweɪʒ(ə)n/
expedition (n) ★★ /ˌekspəˈdɪʃ(ə)n/
fairly (= pretty) (adv) ★★★ /ˈferli/
fan (n) ★★ /fæn/
gimmick (n) /ˈgɪmɪk/
influence (n) ★★★ /ˈɪnfluəns/
living expenses (n pl) /ˈlɪvɪŋ ɪkˌspensəz/
lock (n) ★★ /lɑk/
mentally (adv) /ˈment(ə)li/
native language (n) /ˌneɪtɪv ˈlæŋgwɪdʒ/
nature reserve (n) /ˈneɪtʃər rɪˌzɜrv/
perfume (n) ★ /ˈpɜrfjum/
physics (n) ★★ /ˈfɪzɪks/
poetry (n) ★★ /ˈpoʊətri/
prize-winner (n) /ˈpraɪzˌwɪnər/
quantity (n) ★★ /ˈkwɑntəti/
relativity (n) /ˌreləˈtɪvəti/
solar system (n) ★ /ˈsoʊlər ˌsɪstəm/
spreadsheet (n) ★ /ˈspredˌʃit/
submarine (n) ★ /ˈsʌbməˌrin/
swimmer (n) /ˈswɪmər/
totally (adv) ★★★ /ˈtoʊt(ə)li/
twin (n) ★★ /twɪn/
youth (n) ★★★ /juθ/

ADJECTIVES
best-known (adj) /ˈbestˌnoʊn/
chill-out (adj) /ˈtʃɪlˌaʊt/
endangered (adj) /ɪnˈdeɪndʒərd/
instant (adj) ★★ /ˈɪnstənt/
interactive (adj) ★ /ˌɪntərˈæktɪv/
lazy (adj) ★★ /ˈleɪzi/
short-term (adj) ★★ /ˈʃɔrtˌtɜrm/
single (≠ married) (adj) ★★★ /ˈsɪŋg(ə)l/

EDUCATION
certificate (n) ★★ /sərˈtɪfɪkət/
classroom (n) ★★ /ˈklæsˌrum/
classwork (n) /ˈklæsˌwɜrk/
college (n) ★★★ /ˈkɑlɪdʒ/
curriculum (n) ★★ /kəˈrɪkjələm/
degree (n) ★★★ /dɪˈgri/
educate (v) ★★ /ˈedʒəˌkeɪt/
elementary school (n) ★ /eləˈment(ə)ri skul/
entrance exam (ination) (n) /ˈentrəns ɪgˌzæm(ɪneɪʃn)/
high school (n) ★★ /ˈhaɪ ˌskul/
institute (n) ★★★ /ˈɪnstɪˌtut/
major (v) /ˈmeɪdʒər/
schedule (n) ★★ /ˈskeˌdʒul, ˈskedʒəl/
school rules (n pl) /ˌskul ˈrulz/
subject (n) ★★★ /ˈsʌbˌdʒekt/
tuition costs (n pl) /tuˈɪʃn ˌkɔsts/
uniform (n) ★★ /ˈjunɪˌfɔrm/
whiteboard (n) /ˈwaɪtˌbɔrd, ˈhwaɪtˌbɔrd/

MUSIC AND SONGWRITING
band (n) ★★★ /bænd/
chord (n) ★ /kɔrd/
classical (adj) ★★ /ˈklæsɪk(ə)l/
concert (n) ★★ /ˈkɑnsərt/
concerto (n) /kənˈtʃertoʊ, kənˈtʃɜrtoʊ/
finger pick (v) /ˈfɪŋgər ˌpɪk/
gig (n) ★ /gɪg/
hum (v) /hʌm/
lyrics (n pl) /ˈlɪrɪks/
opera (n) ★★ /ˈɑp(ə)rə/
songwriter (n) /ˈsɔŋˌraɪtər/
symphony (n) ★ /ˈsɪmfəni/
tune (n) ★★ /tun/

NOUN SUFFIX -NESS
carelessness (n) /ˈkerləsnəs/
happiness (n) ★★ /ˈhæpinəs/
illness (n) ★★★ /ˈɪlnəs/
politeness (n) /pəˈlaɪtnəs/
sadness (n) ★ /ˈsædnəs/
thoughtfulness (n) /ˈθɔtfəlnəs/
usefulness (n) /ˈjusfəlnəs/
weightlessness (n) /ˈweɪtləsnəs/

VERBS
admire (v) ★★ /ədˈmaɪr/
allow (v) ★★★ /əˈlaʊ/
behave (v) ★★ /bɪˈheɪv/
drag (v) ★★ /dræg/
explore (v) ★★★ /ɪkˈsplɔr/
fundraise (v) /ˈfʌndˌreɪz/
visualize (v) /ˈvɪʒuəˌlaɪz/
volunteer (n & v) ★★ /ˌvɑlənˈtɪr/

EXPRESSIONS
around the clock /əˌraʊnd ðə ˈklɑk/
as far as I'm concerned /əz ˌfɑr əz aɪm kənˈsɜrnd/
drive someone mad /ˌdraɪv sʌmwʌn ˈmæd/
have children /ˌhæv ˈtʃɪldrən/
It's up to you. /ɪts ˌʌp tə ˈju/
make a contribution /ˌmeɪk ə kɑntrɪˈbjuʃn/
Practice makes perfect. /ˌpræktɪs meɪks ˈpɜrfɪkt/
raise money /ˌreɪz ˈmʌni/
red tape /ˌred ˈteɪp/
take shape /ˌteɪk ˈʃeɪp/

PRONUNCIATION GUIDE

Vowels

/i/	s<u>ee</u>, happ<u>y</u>
/ɪ/	g<u>i</u>ve, d<u>i</u>d
/e/	b<u>e</u>d, h<u>ea</u>d
/æ/	b<u>a</u>d, c<u>a</u>p
/ɑ/	f<u>a</u>ther, h<u>o</u>t
/ɔ/	b<u>ough</u>t, t<u>a</u>lk
/ʌ/	f<u>u</u>n, c<u>o</u>me
/ʊ/	f<u>oo</u>t, c<u>ou</u>ld
/u/	f<u>oo</u>d, tw<u>o</u>
/ə/	<u>a</u>bout, yog<u>a</u>
/ɜr/	b<u>ir</u>d, h<u>ear</u>d
/eɪ/	d<u>ay</u>, r<u>ai</u>n
/aɪ/	r<u>i</u>de, fl<u>y</u>
/ɔɪ/	p<u>oi</u>nt, b<u>oy</u>
/oʊ/	c<u>o</u>ld, b<u>oa</u>t
/aʊ/	h<u>ow</u>, m<u>ou</u>th

Consonants

/b/	<u>b</u>ag, ra<u>bb</u>it
/d/	<u>d</u>esk, col<u>d</u>
/f/	<u>f</u>ill, lau<u>gh</u>
/g/	<u>g</u>irl, bi<u>g</u>
/h/	<u>h</u>and, <u>h</u>ome
/j/	<u>y</u>es, <u>y</u>oung
/k/	<u>c</u>ook, ba<u>ck</u>
/l/	<u>l</u>ike, fi<u>ll</u>
/m/	<u>m</u>ean, cli<u>mb</u>
/n/	<u>n</u>ew, wa<u>n</u>t
/p/	<u>p</u>ark, ha<u>pp</u>y
/r/	<u>r</u>ing, bo<u>rr</u>ow
/s/	<u>s</u>ay, thi<u>s</u>
/t/	<u>t</u>own, ci<u>t</u>y
/v/	<u>v</u>ery, li<u>v</u>e
/w/	<u>w</u>ater, a<u>w</u>ay
/z/	<u>z</u>oo, hi<u>s</u>
/ʃ/	<u>sh</u>op, ma<u>ch</u>ine
/ʒ/	u<u>s</u>ually, televi<u>s</u>ion
/ŋ/	tha<u>n</u>k, doi<u>ng</u>
/tʃ/	<u>ch</u>eese, pi<u>c</u>ture
/θ/	<u>th</u>ing, nor<u>th</u>
/ð/	<u>th</u>at, clo<u>th</u>es
/dʒ/	<u>j</u>eans, bri<u>dg</u>e

IRREGULAR VERBS

Infinitive	Simple past	Past participle
be	was, were	been
beat	beat	beaten
become	became	become
begin	began	begun
bend	bent	bent
bet	bet	bet
bite	bit	bitten
blow	blew	blown
break	broke	broken
bring	brought	brought
broadcast	broadcast	broadcast
build	built	built
burn	burnt/burned	burnt/burned
buy	bought	bought
cast	cast	cast
catch	caught	caught
choose	chose	chosen
come	came	come
cost	cost	cost
cut	cut	cut
dig	dug	dug
dive	dived/dove	dived
do	did	done
draw	drew	drawn
dream	dreamed/dreamt	dreamed/dreamt
drink	drank	drunk
drive	drove	driven
eat	ate	eaten
fall	fell	fallen
feed	fed	fed
feel	felt	felt
fight	fought	fought
find	found	found
fit	fit/fitted	fit/fitted
fly	flew	flown
forbid	forbid/forbad(e)	forbidden
forget	forgot	forgotten
freeze	froze	frozen
get	got	gotten
give	gave	given
go	went	gone/been
grow	grew	grown
hang	hung	hung
have	had	had
hear	heard	heard
hide	hid	hidden
hit	hit	hit
hold	held	held
hurt	hurt	hurt
keep	kept	kept
know	knew	known
lay	laid	laid
lead	led	led
leave	left	left
lend	lent	lent
let	let	let
lie	lay	lain
light	lit/lighted	lit/lighted
lose	lost	lost
make	made	made
mean	meant	meant
meet	met	met
offset	offset	offset
overcome	overcame	overcame
pay	paid	paid
put	put	put
read /rid/	read /red/	read /red/
rebuild	rebuilt	rebuilt
retell	retold	retold
rewrite	rewrote	rewritten
ride	rode	ridden
ring	rang	rung
rise	rose	risen
run	ran	run
say	said	said
see	saw	seen
sell	sold	sold
send	sent	sent
set	set	set
shake	shook	shaken
shine	shone	shone
shoot	shot	shot
show	showed	shown
shut	shut	shut
sing	sang	sung
sink	sank/sunk	sunk
sit	sat	sat
sleep	slept	slept
slide	slid	slid
speak	spoke	spoken
speed	sped/speeded	sped/speeded
spend	spent	spent
spread	spread	spread
stand	stood	stood
steal	stole	stolen
stick	stuck	stuck
strike	struck	struck
swim	swam	swum
take	took	taken
teach	taught	taught
tell	told	told
think	thought	thought
throw	threw	thrown
understand	understood	understood
wake	woke	woken
wear	wore	worn
win	won	won
write	wrote	written

Macmillan Education
Between Towns Road, Oxford OX4 3PP
A division of Macmillan Publishers Limited
Companies and representatives throughout the world

ISBN 978-0-230-41523-2

Text © Judy Garton-Sprenger and Philip Prowse 2012
Design and illustration © Macmillan Publishers Limited 2012

This edition published 2012
First edition published 2008

All rights reserved; no part of this publication may be reproduced, stored in a retrieval system, transmitted in any form, or by any means, electronic, mechanical, photocopying, recording, or otherwise, without the prior written permission of the publishers.

Original design by Giles Davies Design Ltd
Page make-up by eMC Design Ltd
Illustrated by Jamel Akib pp28-29; Kathy Baxendale pp65, 89; Graham Bury (Apple Agency) pp27, 76; Paul Daviz p63; Vince Fraser p48; Clive Goodyer pp 56, 67, 78; Javier Joaquin (The Organisation) pp88, 108 and Kate Sheppard pp18, 44, 70, 96.
Cover design by Studio Montage
Cover images courtesy of Corbis (skiers, plane) and Getty (Himalaya).

The authors would like to thank all the team at Macmillan for everything they have done to create *Inspired 4*. We are most grateful to Catherine Smith for her sterling work on the whole series, along with Janet Battiste for her work on the Student's Book, Shira Evans for revising the Workbook, and to Elise Pritchard for revising the Teacher's Book. We would also like to thank John Marshall Media for producing the recorded material, and the actors who bring the book to life.

We owe an enormous debt of gratitude to teenage students and their teachers in many different countries who welcomed us into their classrooms and contributed so much to the formation of *Inspired*. In particular we would like to thank teachers and classes in Argentina, Greece, Italy, Poland, Spain, Switzerland, Turkey and Uruguay. We are equally indebted to all those participants on teacher training courses in Europe, South America and elsewhere from whom we have learnt so much, in particular British Council courses in the UK and overseas, and courses at the University of Durham and NILE in Norwich.

The author and publishers would like to thank the following for permission to reproduce their photographs:
AFP pp56, 68; **AFPP** p30(cr); **Alamy**/J.Arnold Images p24(c), Alamy/K. Bain p13(7), Alamy/Blend Images p63(t), Alamy/Brownstock p105, Alamy/Bubbles p35(br), Alamy/Custom Medical Stock Photo p24(bc), Alamy/R. Daly p107(cl), Alamy/D.Dennis p73(B), Alamy/D.Hurst p13(4), Alamy/G. Balfour Evans p73(A), Alamy/G.Du Feu pp81(cr), 107(tl), Alamy/Form Advertising p80, Alamy/ImageSource p52, Alamy/isifa Image Service s.r.o/ © DACS 2011 p78(a),Alamy/Kolvenbach p24(tc), Alamy/KPZ Photo p98(t), Alamy/D.MacDonald p50(b), Alamy/Mary Evans Picture Library p100(b), Alamy/MBI p107, 20(bl), Alamy/Mouse in the House p44, Alamy/A.Nettle p16(B), Alamy/A. Pharyos pp52-53, Alamy/A.Rodriguez pp24(tc), 24(b), Alamy/First Shot p98(bl), Alamy/R.Stamforth p73(C), Alamy/Studiomode p16(E), Alamy/M.Uemura p94(br), Alamy/H Weidman Photography p41, Alamy/World History Archive p42(b); **Bananastock** p21(tl); **Blend Images** p9(cr); **BrandX Pictures** pp34(B), 36(l); **Bridgeman Art Library**/J.Opie p26; **Comstock** pp13(5), 86(A), 104; **Corbis** pp35(cr), 70, Corbis/D.Azubel p78(e), Corbis/Bettmann pp54(c), 54(cr), 54(m), 61(D), 62(cr), Corbis/Hulton Deutsch pp61(E), 66(t), Corbis/N.Kaszerman pp87(D), 100(cr), Corbis/R.Morsch pp6-7, Corbis/M.Powell p62, Corbis/L.Williams/NG Society p102(cl), Corbis/J.Warga p78(C); **Cultura** p108; **European Union 1995-2011** pp46,47; **Frank Lane Picture Agency**/F. Nicklin p81(cl); **Gagosin Gallery London** p22(A); **Gallo Images** p84; **Getty RF** p13(2), Getty/N.Emmerson p74(tr), Getty Images Entertainment pp72, 98(r), Getty Images Sport p69; **Grand Resort Lagonissi** pp60(B), 78(b); **Greenpeace**/J.Sutton-Hibbert p54(tr); **Guardian News and Media Ltd**/D. Levene/The Horizon Field by Antony Gormley pp8(A), 22(D); **Hulton Archive** p102(t); **Image Source** pp21(cl), 82(t); **Iwantoneofthose.com** pp9(C), 12(A),12(B),12(C); **Kobal Collection**/20th Century Fox/Paramount p24(t); **Mary Evans Picture Library** p38(br); **NASA** p37; **Press Association Photos**/Y.Mok p86(B), Press Association Photos/P.Noble p22(C); **Photodisc** pp36(cr), 49, 103(bl),107(cr); **Photographers Choice** pp20-21(b), 90(tr); **Photolibrary** pp64(tr), 79(c), 79(t), 79(cr), Photolibrary/W.Faidley p16(D), Photolibrary/MB.Madhaven pp61(c), 74-75(b), Photolibrary/K. Mellenthin p103(t); **Radius Images** p110; **Rex Features**/Everettt Collection p16(A), Rex Features/S.Cook p23, Rex Features/I.McCarney p32(cr); **Science & Society Photo Library** p43; **Science Photo Library** p42(t), Science Photo Library/P.Rona/OAE/National Undersea Research Program/ Dr Ken MacDonald pp 35(bl), 38(cr), Science Photo Library/Science Source pp87(C), 90(cr); **sOccket** © p12(D); **Still Pictures** p58; **Stockbyte** pp9(E), 10; **Stone** p32(tl); **Superstock**/Bluegreen images p82(c), Superstock/ Glow Images Cuisine p13(8), Superstock/Marka p13(1), Superstock/Pixtal pp14(2), 8(B), Superstock/Photolibrary p13(3); **Tate Gallery**/Courtesy Chris Ofili - Afroco and Victoria Miro Gallery, No Woman No Cry p22(C); **Taxi** pp50(tr),20(tl); **The Agency Collection** p20(ml); **The Image Bank** p77; **Time & Life Pictures** pp42(cr), 100(tr); **Vetta** p21(bl); **Virgin Galatica** pp35(D), 40; **Richard Waite** pp60(A), 64(cl), 64(cr); **Zero Creatives** p16(F).

The authors and publishers are grateful for permission to reprint the following copyright material:
Page 48: Extract from '2020 Vision: Live to 120' taken from www.smh.com.au copyright © Australian Associated Press 2004 reprinted by permission of the publisher;
Page 102: Extract from 'The School We'd Like' by Dea Birkett, copyright © Dea Birkett 2001, first published in the *Guardian* 05.06.01, reprinted by permission of the author;
Page 92: Extract from 'How mobile phones are transforming Africa' by Fred Bridgland, copyright © Fred Bridgland 2005, first published in *Sunday Herald* 13.03.05, reprinted by permission of the author;
Page 94: Extract from 'This man is worth £100,000 a year' by David Crystal, copyright © David Crystal 2000, first published in High Life Magazine June 2000, reprinted by permission of the author;
Pages 28 and 33: Extracts from 'The Professor and the Ferryman' and 'The Two Painters' both taken from *Stories For Thinking* by Robert Fisher (Nash Pollock, 1996), copyright © Robert Fisher 1996, reprinted by permission of the author;
Page 64: Extract from 'Fun is my Business' by Laura Barton, Susie Steiner, Dominic Murphy, Simon Hattenstone, Kirsty Scott, Caroline Roux and Gareth McClean, copyright © Guardian News and Media Limited 2003, first published in the *Guardian* 09.08.03, reprinted by permission of the publisher;
Page 101: 'Confessions of a Runner' from *Wicked World* by Benjamin Zephaniah (Puffin, 2000), text copyright © Benjamin Zephaniah 2000, reprinted by permission of the publisher;
Page 76: Extract from *The Lost Continent* by Bill Bryson (Black Swan, a division of Transworld, 1989) copyright © Bill Bryson 1989, reprinted by permission of Random House Group Ltd. and Greene & Heaton. All rights reserved;
Page 68: Extract from 'It's a Man's Game' by Jo Tuckman copyright © Jo Tuckman 2005, first published in the *Guardian* 05.01.05, reprinted by permission of the author;
Page 84: Extract from interview with Piers Vitebsky 'Day in the Life' by Sarah Woodward, taken from *CAM* magazine no. 47, reprinted by permission of Piers Vitebsky.

Definitions adapted from the *Macmillan English Dictionary for Learners of American English* copyright © Macmillan Publishers Limited 2002. www.macmillandictionary.com

These materials may contain links for third-party websites. We have no control over, and are not responsible for, the contents of such third-party websites. Please use care when accessing them.

Although we have tried to trace and contact copyright holders before publication, in some cases this has not been possible. If contacted we will be pleased to rectify any errors or omissions at the earliest opportunity.

Printed and bound in Thailand

2016 2015 2014 2013 2012
10 9 8 7 6 5 4 3 2 1